The Enlightened Society

The Enlightened Society

The Economy with a Human Face

by
Kurt F. Flexner
Memphis State University

Lexington Books

D.C. Heath and Company/Lexington, Massachusetts/Toronto

LIBRARY OF CONGRESS
Library of Congress Cataloging-in-Publication Data

Flexner, Kurt F.
The enlightened society : the economy with a human face / Kurt F.
Flexner.
p.   cm.
Includes index.
ISBN 0-669-19930-3 (alk. paper)
1. Economic policy.   2. Economics—History.   3. Income
distribution.   I. Title.
HD82.F585   1989
330.9—dc19   88-23285
                                                                        CIP

Published simultaneously in Canada
Printed in the United States of America
International Standard Book Number: 0-669-19930-3
Library of Congress Catalog Card Number: 88-23285

The paper used in this publication meets the minimum requirements of
American National Standard for Information Sciences—Permanence
of Paper for Printed Library Materials, ANSI Z39.48-1984.

ISBN 0-669-19930-3

89 90 91 92 8 7 6 5 4 3 2 1

Contents

Figures and Table

Figures

Table

Foreword

Economics can be very cold and calculating. We need to think hard about intricate issues, but there should be a heavy dose of humanism behind the cool analysis. Kurt Flexner has provided a book about economics that has a real heart and soul. At the same time, it is insightful about where the overall economy now stands, where it is moving, and how it treats the diverse groups in our society. His analysis is based on an attractive blend of economics, as such, together with history, social psychology, sociology, and political science. From a historical point of view, Dr. Flexner's analysis shows an excellent grasp of both economic history and the history of economic thought.

This book is written in an easy-to-read, lucid style of prose. Politically, it steers a sound middle course between right and left extremes. Most of all, it is realistic. Kurt Flexner is no slave to aesthetics or highly formal statements of economic propositions; he avoids the making of unreal assumptions in deriving economic conclusions. In fact, he tears restrictive assumptions apart. In the end, we get a lively interpretation of economics of our times, derived from a firm historical base. It is anything but a rendition in the spirit of "the dismal science."

I would classify this book as a study in *political economy,* with good values that the author can skillfully defend. The historical analysis extends from medieval times through nineteenth-century scholar-philosophers and the Industrial Revolution up to the present. He translates history for the reader into an analogue for the present.

A feature of this book is that Kurt Flexner can build his story in an economical way on just three "great books": *The Wealth of*

Nations by Adam Smith, *Das Kapital* by Karl Marx, and *The General Theory of Employment, Interest and Money* by John Maynard Keynes. He could have cluttered the presentation by being overly detailed, with more extensive references, but by concentrating as he does on the truly great works in our subject, which he perceptively chooses, he is able to make a more focused set of arguments based on his grasp of all the social sciences together.

Since Dr. Flexner is not timid about making value judgments, thus making his book much livelier, he is able to take up the important issues concerned with the distribution of wealth and income. In doing this, he shows the limitations of pure theoretical economics. He recognizes that markets are far from perfect; that consumers lack full sovereignty, being under the strong influence of the corporate sector; and that market dynamics do not always serve society well.

I find it refreshing to have an economics book that shows appropriate concern about the quality of life amid cool economic calculus and that takes a strong position on moral and ethical values in our socioeconomic setting.

Lawrence R. Klein
Benjamin Franklin Professor of Economics and Finance
University of Pennsylvania

Acknowledgments

I cannot submit this book for publication without expressing my heartfelt thanks to friends and fellow economists who have taken the time to read all or part of the manuscript over the years during which it was in preparation. Their thoughts and criticisms have been invaluable.

Among those who have given me the benefit of their wise counsel are Lawrence Klein (Benjamin Franklin Professor of Economics and Finance, University of Pennsylvania), to whom I am especially indebted for reading the entire manuscript and consenting to write the foreword; Robert Solow (professor of economics, Massachusetts Institute of Technology); the late Gunnar Myrdal (Wicksell Professor of Economics, University of Stockholm); Robert Lekachman (professor of economics, Herbert H. Lehman College, City University of New York); Daniel Fusfeld (professor of economics, University of Michigan); the late Arthur Burns (one-time professor of economics, Columbia University); the late Walter Heller (former professor of economics, University of Minnesota, Minneapolis); James Crown (professor of political science, New York University); and Dr. Taylor Sims, dean, Fogelman College of Business, Memphis State University.

I owe a special debt of gratitude to my longtime friends Maynard Gertler (economist and publisher of Harvest House, Montreal), and Joseph MacMurray (former chairman of the Federal Home Loan Bank Board), and Donald Schaffer (associate professor of psychiatry, University of Tennessee, Memphis), for their encouragements and insights.

I also want to thank my friends in the business world who read parts of the manuscript and have allowed me to profit from their extensive experience through numerous discussions. These include P.K. Seidman (former chairman of Seidman and Seidman), Allan R. Bennett (chairman of Helena Chemical Corporation), and Robert P. Bryant (former vice chairman of Carson, Pirie, Scott and Company). Although I have greatly benefitted from their constructive criticism, I alone must take the final responsibility for the ideas expressed and the conclusions drawn in this book.

The thoughts set forward in these pages have been taking shape in my mind for many years. In putting them on paper and preparing the manuscript for publication, I have received invaluable assistance from my wife, Josephine, who proofread the entire manuscript and made many excellent suggestions. She also made herself indispensable in typing and suffered patiently until the job was completed. I am greatly indebted as well to my secretary, Donetta Minderman, and to my former secretary, Rene Nivens, and offer them my sincere thanks for their hard work in preparing the manuscript.

Finally, I cannot close without expressing appreciation to my son Peter, who read this manuscript and made valuable observations and criticisms, and to my son Thomas, with whom I have had many discussions concerning the numerous issues that make up the content of this bok. His frank commentaries have been most helpful.

Introduction

Modern historians have been fascinated with what they regard as the inevitable rise and fall of empires since Gibbon wrote the *Decline and Fall of the Roman Empire.* Arnold Toynbee, in his twelve-volume history of the world, traced the rise and fall of twenty-six civilizations. More recently, Professor Paul Kennedy's book, *The Rise and Fall of the Great Powers,* made the bestseller list.

It is the objective of this book to challenge these theories. Scholars are often too anxious to use the past as an omen for the future. They set a trap for themselves by basing their predictions upon a static model of human and social evolution.

Two ideas make up the central theme of this book. First, when humanity begins to recognize the value of *timely* and *rational* adjustments to rapidly changing conditions produced by the advancing frontiers of knowledge, we will be able to escape the otherwise inevitable decline and fall of great nations and civilizations. Second, by making humanity the *nucleus* of the social sciences, including economics, the chief goal of the really great economists (to improve the human condition) will become a realistic alternative to the present sterile emphasis on measuring economic progress solely by statistical gains in the Gross National Product and its components.

The conventional wisdom of such nineteenth-century theories as laissez-faire and Marxist communism has become obsolete on the eve of the twenty-first century. The U.S. and Soviet economies are in such shambles that it is no longer considered heresy to criticize formerly sacred ideologies.

We are already suffering the labor pains of a new era soon to be born. Will it be a more enlightened age?

We are moving from the industrial period to a new high technology, service-oriented consumer age. This is producing radical changes in our culture and in our human and social relations. Traditional economic policies are proving unrealistic in dealing with the complex problems produced by the changes. By ignoring the vital forces of history, the United States is condemning itself to a repetition of the errors of the past and therefore inviting its own decline as a great power. It is not yet too late to reverse this trend if we are willing to cut the umbilical cord that ties us to static and outworn nineteenth-century utopian ideas.

This book challenges a number of sacred traditional theories that have been made obsolete by time. It introduces new ideas that I hope will arouse readers' curiosity and help them to understand a more realistic approach to those problems that threaten our existence.

People should not be reluctant to read this book because they regard economics as dull or beyond the comprehension of the layperson. That is indeed the case with too many books on the subject. It is not, I think, true of this book—although it was written to inform readers, not to amuse them.

Every effort has been made to make the book understandable and interesting. It is aimed at the informed public as well as the student of economics and the professional economist. It should answer many questions for those who are perplexed about the radical changes that have alienated many people and left them without values and with little hope.

Finally, from this book the reader will perhaps acquire a sense of optimism about the future and understand that the dire predictions of historians are inconsistent with a *positive approach* to the years that lie ahead.

Part I
Humankind in the
Industrial Age

———————

1
In Search of
Peaceful Coexistence

At the Crossroads

Science and technology have enabled us to fight successful battles against hunger and disease, raising the life expectancy of a newborn child from thirty years five hundred years ago to nearly eighty years in the developed world today. Science and technology, however, have also enabled us to wage increasingly more destructive wars. Our achievements in the pursuit of knowledge have not been matched by our efforts to become civilized. We have not yet succeeded in building political relationships between nations and regions that are capable of producing peaceful coexistence. History has thus become a race between science and technology, which enable us to produce material wealth and to wage increasingly destructive wars, and efforts to live in peace and to improve the human condition.

If such efforts to build successful political relationships continue to lag behind scientific progress the future of the human race is dim. The ability of nations to destroy each other *must* be kept in check until new methods of cooperation can be developed. If we are able to do that, the human race may yet produce a world more civilized and humane than we are now able to imagine.

Were we to paint a canvas depicting the highlights of human history, much of the canvas would be assigned to wars and other forms of violence. A good deal of space would be devoted to the great advances in science, technology, and discovery. Much less space would be required to depict the successful attempts to live in peace and harmony. Most of these would fade into short distances between wars and revolutions. With what are these political relationships on which so much depends concerned? Essentially the control and allocation of the world's resources, without which we cannot satisfy some of the most important human needs, wants, and ambitions. Most changes in the social structure have come about as a result of force and violence rather than through voluntary accommodation. The meaning of war and revolution cannot be grasped without an understanding of this.

The concepts of "private rights" and "social rights" play an important role in the efforts to achieve peaceful coexistence and to improve the human condition. All our material requirements involve either private or public rights. The right to own a home is an example of the first. The right to enjoy the pleasures of a public park is an example of the second. On the international level, sovereignty over the natural resources and markets within certain geographic boundaries may be considered the private right of a country. The use of the oceans beyond the so-called national limits would be considered a public right as applied to nations.

Most resources are subject to the private rights of individuals and nations. The world's resources are far from evenly divided or prorated among all nations. The political relationships that have been established in regard to them, therefore, have a significant bearing on war and peace.

Our perception of private and public rights is the basis for our laws and customs, which greatly influence individual and national behavior. Individuals, though part of a community and a nation, must rely on themselves for acquiring enough of the world's resources to provide a livelihood for their families. To assure success in this enterprise, they are motivated to accumulate and possess. A sense of security becomes the primary drive in most people. The greater the insecurity, the greater the need to accumulate. Insecurity in the individual as well as collective insecurity in a nation are the characteristics that greed and war feed upon.

A person depends upon a job or accumulated wealth for satisfying needs and wants. A nation depends on resources and markets for the satisfaction of its collective needs. Most nations acquire the resources they need through trade with other nations. This often leads to uncertainties because international relations (unlike the internal affairs of a nation governed by laws) are based on power rather than on an established legal structure. Countries are, therefore, tempted to acquire control over resources and markets through military might or political pressure and intrigue. This is the essence of imperialism, colonialism, and neocolonialism. At this stage of human development, we depend for our security primarily on power rather than on cooperation.

Humankind has the capacity for creating a more humane world, but we have proved beyond a doubt that we are willing to destroy what we cannot have if our sense of insecurity is strong enough. This is not difficult to understand. We generate a love for the things we need, but because of inherent insecurity, we must *possess* the things we love. We are willing to destroy those who threaten our possessions. That is the psychological basis of war and conflict.

In recent decades, we have reached a point, for the first time in human history, in which we are fully capable of destroying humanity and civilization. We are at the same time moving toward a political maturity that will enable us to establish political relationships conducive to peaceful coexistence.

We must fully appreciate the fact that until now, war did not have the potential for destroying humankind. Suddenly the danger is real. We will lose the race between war and peace, annihilation and survival, unless we succeed in staving off disaster until we, our children, or their children are capable of establishing techniques for organizing the world in a way that makes peaceful coexistence a realistic alternative to war.

The Critical Problems

By advancing the frontiers of knowledge through science and technology, we continue to remake the world. We have irreversibly transcended the state of nature, often without understanding adequately the consequences of our actions. The things we are creating, a whole new material world, are threatening to take control of our culture, our values, and—if we allow them—our future.

Advancing the frontiers of knowledge has not enabled us to become the masters of our own fate. At this state of evolution, we have exchanged the restrictions imposed by nature with new restrictions imposed by the things we create. Advances in science and technology bring about changes to which we must conform. The Industrial Revolution, for example, made specialization and trade inevitable. People could not remain aloof to the conditions this created; they had to conform to survive. Craftspeople and small landholders gave way to the large masses of workers needed by the ever-growing factories.

Does the advancement of knowledge condemn us to a future in which we are mere pawns to be manipulated by the products of our creations? If our judgment matched our scientific ability, we would have much better control of our destiny. We would be able to avoid some problems altogether, learn to solve other problems without creating friction and confrontation, and manage to tolerate problems beyond our control. In other words, knowledge does not automatically lead to understanding, and knowledge without understanding is potentially dangerous.

One of the most urgent tasks facing this generation is to develop theories and policies that are consistent with the dynamics of the world in which we live. It is possible, even likely, that when we see the world as it really is, we shall begin to acquire the understanding necessary to control the things we create. To gain such understanding, however, a sense of history is required.

As we develop more knowledge of the real world we must reexamine such concepts as democracy, freedom, equality, and wealth. Defining these concepts in utopian terms, as we have done in the past, has exposed us to the dangers of self-delusion. This has prevented us from judging the consequences of our actions realistically and wisely.

Traditional economic theory is concerned with the creation of wealth based on a complex network of price relationships. This has all but divorced it from the human relationships that are actually involved in the creation of wealth, and from people for whom wealth is created. As a result, traditional economic theory has become excessively abstract, and, what is worse, neutral in regard to the extreme materialism characterizing today's technocratic societies.

Unless the delicate balance between materialism and idealism is fully appreciated, the advancement of knowledge could become an instrument of self-destruction. Science and technology are neutral; we cannot afford the luxury of neutrality in the production, distribution, and consumption of wealth. The concept of wealth has to be built on a foundation of moral values or value judgments if the objective of wealth is to abolish poverty and to improve the quality of life, which is the meaning attached to wealth by the great classical economist, Adam Smith, whose *Wealth of Nations* (1776) revolutionized economic thinking. It was also expressed in the writings of the great neoclassical economist, Alfred Marshall, more than a hundred years later and by the critic of capitalism, Karl Marx.

One of the profound problems in economic theory today is the absurd assumption that value judgments have no place in it. This has all but eliminated economics as a social science and has made it excessively abstract and often irrelevant in moral terms. While economists have taken refuge from the complexities of modern life in an ivory tower of abstract mathematical relationships, the real world has not stood still. Value judgments have indeed found their way into economic activity.

Most of the great economists of the past believed it was obvious that consumption was the end of production, that production was merely the *means* to an end. They knew that when the materialistic aspects of consumption are combined with idealistic goals, consumption becomes the road to survival and the vehicle for a better life. Stripped of its idealism, consumption becomes an aimless, impulsive, and often ill-conceived attempt to satisfy human wants.

One of the most dangerous developments in the U.S. economy is the use of sophisticated psychological techniques employed in mass-media advertising for the purpose of creating a demand for the products and services of our corporate economy. The danger lies in the manipulation of human values for the purpose of creating a reliable and profitable market.

A successful and profitable economy is indeed desirable and in the public interest. It would be tragic, however, if this were only possible by making consumption a means to this end. In a healthy economy, as the great economists have well understood, it has to be the other way. The reason is obvious. Human beings are part of nature and their needs are deeply rooted in their evolution. For individuals to be sane and healthy, their physical, psychological, and social needs must be satisfied. The same is true of a society as a whole.

This does not mean that we must forever increase production. It means that we must make sure that what we consume in the broad sense is consistent with our needs. Production must be subordinated to consumption and consumption must be based on a dual foundation of both materialism and idealism. Today's highly materialistic technocratic society is an obstacle to such an aim.

Exactly what is the technocratic society? The technocratic society is primarily managed by technical experts, and two of its goals overshadow all others: economic growth and military power to facilitate economic growth. Although the individual and democracy are often eulogized, both are subordinated to the needs of the economy and the security of the nation.

In a more humane society, the physical and psychological needs of the individual and the quality of the environment become important social goals. This does not mean that either economic development or national security is inconsistent with the goals of such a society. It means that new approaches to economic development and to national security have to be adopted. These should be based on values and goals that help to satisfy the real requirements of human beings.

Values and goals were at one time established by religious teaching. Some religions still play an important role in our culture. Values and goals today, however, are largely determined by mass-media advertising and editorial policy, which reflect to a considerable extent the requirements of our corporate economy.

The Industrial Revolution made the values and goals of the feudal agrarian society obsolete. It generated new goals and values that were reflected in the teachings of the Protestant Reformation. These were again changed by the requirements of the Managerial Revolution, which transformed entrepreneurial capitalism into the technocratic society.

As we search for ways to transcend the technocratic society, we must seek new values and goals consistent with a humane society.

The sources of values and goals in the Western World have been the Roman Catholic Church, the Reformation, and mass media. How will priorities be determined in the next stage of evolution? That is one of the vital questions of our day.

Before we can deal with the problems involved in transcending the technocratic society, we have to identify the great controversies and issues of today that must be resolved. Among these are:

- The schizophrenic behavior of governments, which practice an extreme form of political and economic nationalism, while championing such causes as free trade and international cooperation.

- The illusion in capitalist countries that power must be controlled in the public sector but not in the private sector, coupled with illusion in the socialist countries that power must be controlled in the private sector but not in the public sector. The former fallacy helped bring Adolf Hitler to power in Germany, after which the privately owned cartels were given a free hand. The latter fallacy gave rise to Stalinism in the Soviet Union, when the power of the state could not be questioned.

- The failure to distinguish between rational and irrational behavior in such relationships as competition, freedom, liberty, and democracy. This has turned great ideals into dangerous antisocial behavior.

- An armaments race between superpowers that seems to be intended as a weapon of mutual destabilization. This is likely to lead to economic disaster in both countries.

- A population explosion in the Third World that is a major obstacle to economic development and the abolition of poverty.

If the social sciences are to be of any use in dealing effectively with such problems, they should develop rational approaches consistent with the dynamics of the world in which we live. To see the world as it really is, we must replace the arbitrary segmentation of knowledge with a new approach. We must also rely more on realistic observations of the world and less on assumptions that promise automatic solutions or even utopias.

An Economic Foundation for a More Enlightened and Humane Society

The Industrial Revolution gave birth to the conditions that created the technocratic society. At the same time, the Age of Enlightenment in the eighteenth century—which produced such giants as Rousseau, Voltaire, and Hume—spawned the philosophical idealism that gave birth to the utopian visions of freedom, liberty, and democracy. This became the essence of nineteenth-century liberalism. The incompatibility between the technocratic society and nineteenth-century liberalism deprived much of the modern world of an essential link between materialism and idealism.

It is unfortunate that the social sciences, including traditional economics, have not dealt realistically with this problem. As a result, we live in a world torn apart by a schism between idealistic philosophy and an extremely materialistic way of life.

We are extolling the virtues of liberty, equality, and democracy without adequate regard for the conditions and limitations of the real world. As a result, these great ideals are abused and manipulated by people in power. They pay homage to the ideals while using entirely different, often contradictory, methods to contend with the real world of the Industrial Revolution and Technological Revolution. Traditional economists who base their theories on this nineteenth-century liberalism are praised and honored, while their recommendations are virtually ignored.

The classical economic system of the nineteenth century (entrepreneurial capitalism) is based on the concepts of liberty and equality. The classical economists assumed that if the private sector operated the economy, even without accountability to the government, all people would enjoy the fruits of liberty. They also assumed that buyers and sellers would be equal in a free-market system through the natural law of supply and demand.

They made another assumption that completed the philosophical trilogy of classical capitalism. The free market would allocate resources and distribute income in such a way that it would produce "the greatest good for the greatest number." In brief, classical capitalism was built on a philosophy of freedom, equality, and liberty—freedom from the power of the state, equality for all buyers and sellers, and liberty to pursue one's own interests.

Unfortunately, this idealistic concept could not stand up under the materialistic pressures of the nineteenth century. We should not blame the idealism built into the foundation of the system. Neither should we fault the materialism built into the system that evolved. The fault is that nineteenth-century idealism (which served to redefine such concepts as democracy, liberty, equality, and freedom) could not predict our twentieth-century world! Incompatibility between the idealistic foundation and the materialistic superstructure was inevitable.

Ideas that influence human behavior must be carefully developed so that they reflect the conditions of the real world in which they serve as a foundation for human activity. This means that the idealism that produces such ideas as democracy, liberty, and justice must be based on actual conditions and on what is realistically possible. It should not be based on the utopian fantasies, which describe much of the idealism of the past three centuries.

The trouble with traditional economics is not that it seeks the greatest good for the greatest number. Rather, the problem lies in the method developed for reaching this goal. We must learn to combine realistic aims with practical and effective means in order to build a more humane society. The task before us is difficult but not impossible.

First, we must agree on goals and values. Then, we must develop a new foundation on which to base our theories and policies. A better way must be found for individuals and organizations to participate meaningfully in the decisions that determine their destiny and the quality of their lives. Is our definition of democracy confined to the rights to vote and to speak out? Some form of participation in the actual decision-making process in order to avoid alienation and to motivate people in the workplace and in the community is also necessary.

Constructing economic theories with the conditions existing in the world today requires abandoning our reliance on utopian assumptions. The market-price mechanism—even if it were pure and perfect, which, of course, it cannot be in our modern economy—is only one of the important elements involved in the allocation of resources and in the process of solving problems of an economic nature. Some economists have recognized this, but they have failed to integrate into the main body of their theories the other elements involved. Unless these other elements are specifically identified and made an integral part of economic theory and policy, economists will be unable to deal realistically with most problems. Although a free market is an essential part of a democratic society, the tendency to rely *solely* on the market mechanism for satisfying the physical and psychological needs of humankind is an anachronism in today's highly complex society. Nor can the market mechanism be relied on to make the necessary adjustments to the continuous radical changes initiated by technological progress. The market, for example, cannot make the necessary adjustments in time to prepare the worker for the changes in demand for labor brought about by radical changes in technology. This is a long-range educational problem.

When economic theories begin to reflect the conditions of the real world and take into account the significant differences existing at different times and places in the evolution of a modern economy, such ideas as freedom, liberty, and democracy will be seen as dynamically evolving social goals, indispensable in paving the way to survival and a more humane economy. Used as they are today, such terms often become mere slogans reflecting hypocrisy rather than idealism.

The task before us is very challenging. We are losing control over the world we have created. Our attachment to utopian theories that came into existence two or three centuries ago has closed our minds to an objective examination of the world as it really is.

Having been unable to deal realistically with the problems that confront us, we have become frustrated. This creates adversary relationships between people and between nations. Adversary relationships lead to confrontation and disaster. In the past and still today, we try to reduce our insecurity by using power and pressure. This is always counterproductive because in an adversary relationship, when one side gains strength, the other side becomes more

insecure. A competitive effort to increase power and pressure, therefore, leads to greater insecurity on both sides, which is the reason
why it is counterproductive.

To sum up, a more humane society requires that we learn to
solve our problems through accurate appraisals of the conditions
that exist. If this is possible, we shall succeed in reducing insecurity.
This is the first step necessary for creating the conditions for survival and for an enlightened and more humane economy.

2
Capitalism—The Ideal and the Reality

The Classical Economists—The Creators of the Ideal

It often happens that the universal belief of one age of mankind becomes to a subsequent age such an absurdity, that the only difficulty there is, is to imagine how such a thing could ever have appeared credible.
—John Stuart Mill

John Stuart Mill, one of the founders of classical capitalism, might have modified his prophetic expression of wisdom by acknowledging that it does not necessarily apply to the most zealous believers. He also could have added that many universal beliefs are not absurd at the time of their conception. They become absurd when they are adhered to after the conditions that gave them birth have changed enough to make them obsolete.

Mill's words apply to the beliefs that the classical economists had to condemn if their own beliefs were to take their place. His comments are a fit beginning for this book, which is written in the hope that the absurdity of some obsolete beliefs can be demonstrated so that new beliefs, better attuned to the Nuclear Age and Space Age, can then take their place.

As "the child is father of the man" in the fertile poetic mind of William Wordsworth, the great nineteenth-century English poet laureate, so the past is father of the present, which in turn is father of the future. To ignore history is to misjudge the present and to miscalculate the future. An acquaintance with the beliefs of classical economists and the circumstances that gave birth to capitalism is necessary for understanding the problems of today and the challenges of tomorrow.

The evolution of industrial capitalism led to many new ideas and beliefs that were articulated by such social and economic philosophers as Adam Smith, Thomas Malthus, David Ricardo, and John Stuart Mill. They provided the intellectual framework for classical capitalism, beginning with Adam Smith's *The Wealth of Nations* in 1776.

John Maynard Keynes, the most influential economist of this century, observed in his most widely read book that, apart from contemporary moods, "the ideas of economists and political philosophers, both when they are right and when they are wrong, are more powerful than is commonly understood. . . . Practical men, who believe themselves to be quite exempt from any intellectual influences, are usually the slaves of some defunct economist."[1]

John Kenneth Galbraith, perhaps the best-known North American economist in the public mind, enlarges upon Keynes' statement by pointing out: "For in economic affairs decisions are influenced not only by ideas and vested economic interests. They are also subject to the tyranny of circumstance."[2] Galbraith, however, goes on to explain how the racial doctrines of Hitler and others of his party caught on in Germany: "the power of vested interests is vastly exaggerated compared to the gradual encroachment of ideas."[3]

A study of economic history reveals that the influences having the biggest impact on what people believe and act upon are, in fact, all three: ideas, vested interests, and the tyranny of circumstances.

Adam Smith, whose ideas gave birth to classical capitalism, was educated at Oxford University after he completed his secondary schooling in his native Scotland. Born in 1723, the son of a customs official, he was greatly influenced by the ideas of David Hume and other philosophers of the Age of Enlightenment. Hume, a fellow Scotsman twelve years older than Smith, wrote passionately about freedom as a means of improving the human condition.

At the age of thirty-five, Smith was made a professor of logic at the University of Glasgow. A few years later, he became professor of moral philosophy. As a philosopher, Smith was a man of reason.

He had become familiar with the writings of Voltaire, who at the time was generally regarded as "the man of reason," and visited him at his chateau on the French border near Geneva.

To both Smith and Voltaire, reason reigned supreme. They considered it superior to religious or secular authoritarian doctrine. Smith saw the "economic man" as one who made rational decisions that enriched him and increased the wealth of nations. This led to the central theme in classical economics—humankind's pursuit of self-interest would result in the greatest good for the greatest number.

Smith's writings reveal his concern with the poverty of the masses and his belief that such poverty can only be alleviated if a nation's resources are wisely used and not wasted on wars. He observed that a nation's wealth could be greatly enlarged with specialization and trade in a free market.

By making the pursuit of self-interest and specialization in a free market the essence of the new system, his work won immediate popularity with the merchant class. By basing the new economics on the natural laws of the market, he endowed classical capitalism with the dignity and halo of a secular religion.

The beliefs that Adam Smith wanted to replace with new ideas were embodied in the doctrine of mercantilism. He saw in mercantilism the glorification of the state. This was inconsistent with his search for freedom as a basis for increasing the *real* wealth of a nation, for abolishing poverty, and for improving the human condition.

To understand the evolution of mercantilism as it emerged after the Reformation, it is important to realize that nationalism was an integral part of its birth and development. Mercantilism is the economics of nationalism. Its aim is to enable a nation to fight successful wars and dominate world markets. Many of its critics ridicule it and belittle its significance. They judge it by the standards of the classical market, which developed later, rather than by the requirements of the new nationalism, which fostered it. Compared with the benefits to be derived from specialization and trade in a free market, mercantilism rates a low grade. Their theoretical models, however, often conceal more than they reveal. England and France, for example, were engaged in lengthy colonial wars—

by-products of the new nationalism, which depended on mercantilism to provide resources and markets. Neither country possessed all
the resources necessary for fighting and winning its colonial wars.
Even mercenary soldiers were brought in from abroad. Imports and
mercenary soldiers had to be paid for—not in local currency, but in
gold and silver. The economy had to be regulated so as to earn the
gold or silver needed by the state to finance its national ambitions.
The needs of the masses were subordinated. National expansion
and the mercantilism that served it became the main concern of the
nations that came to the fore after the collapse of the Holy Roman
Empire. It was the expansion of nationalism by military means and
mercantilism (the economic doctrine that made this possible) that
Adam Smith set out to replace with his doctrine of capitalism.

To get at the essence of classical economics, a question fundamental to all forms of political economy has to be raised. Who shall
make the decisions regarding (1) what is to be produced, (2) how
shall it be distributed, and (3) under what conditions are production
and consumption to take place?

Before the rise of commerce and industry, Europe was largely
agrarian, and the political system that governed it is referred to as
feudalism. Under feudalism, the word of God as conveyed by the
church answered these questions. After the decline of feudalism, the
state made these decisions in countries in which nationalism had
reached maturity. To Adam Smith and the other classical economists, it seemed inappropriate for the church and the state to make
these decisions.

Classical economics, as it developed during the nineteenth century, involved everyone who could find a job and had an income.
The assumption was that if all people entered the market, either as
producers or consumers, and no one had any arbitrary power, the
natural laws of the market would work through the tiny voices of
each buyer and seller. (It was assumed that all sellers and buyers
were a very small part of the market.) The free choices of the buyers
would determine demand and the free choices of the sellers would
determine supply. The interaction of supply and demand would
generate answers to economic questions such as prices, wages, and
output. Free choice and the natural laws of the market would allo-

cate resources efficiently, thereby creating the wealth with which to abolish poverty.

Churchmen such as St. Thomas Aquinas looked to God for a guide to the good life. Classical economists sought the answer to their economic questions in the laws of nature and rational people rather than in the word of God. Their preference for the laws of nature over the laws of the church and the state was largely due to their contempt for the conditions under which the masses had lived under feudalism and mercantilism. It was also partly due to their lack of confidence in the discretionary decisions of other people in regard to economic matters. They preferred the "unseen hand" of the free market, guided by the economic laws of nature.

In their view, the free market could solve all economic problems without the aid of the state. It did this through its magic wand, the price mechanism, which was assumed to allocate most efficiently all resources in their model of the economy. If anything went wrong— too much of one thing or too little of another—whether labor or the final product, the price mechanism was expected to correct the error automatically.

Perhaps the most beautiful part of the system that Adam Smith built is that he conceived it to be just. His emphasis was on the creation of wealth—not wealth for its own sake, but to improve the life of consumers and to put an end to poverty and the misery it created. "Consumption is the sole end and purpose of all production; and the interest of the producer ought to be attended to, only so far as it may be necessary for promoting that of the consumer. The maxim is so perfectly self-evident that it would be absurd to attempt to prove it."[4]

So great was the faith of the classical economists in the natural laws of economics that government intervention was to be avoided whenever possible. It should be noted, however, that the private sector the classical economists preferred to the public sector was one in which private power could not be abused. They assumed that the private sector was subject to the laws of the pure market.

The struggle for the market, which was finally won by the merchant class in England at the beginning of the nineteenth century, laid the foundation for great economic progress through the abundant flow of goods and services. Free trade was a prerequisite if benefits were to be derived from specialization. The classical system was based on the assumption that the flow of labor, capital, goods, and services would be free and unimpeded. Upon this its success depended.

Adam Smith and the other classical economists perceived in the main body of their theory a world that was free from arbitrary power, giving their system the mobility it required. It is logical that they should have done so, since they assumed an orderly world governed by natural laws. It was a utopian philosophy and its benefits were conceived to be worldwide, through free trade among nations.

Smith saw the natural laws operate in the economic relationships between nations in the same way they did within the boundaries of a single nation. He thought all nations would benefit from subordinating their narrow national interests to the greater benefits that could be derived from the free flow of goods and resources among the nations. He saw free trade as a superior alternative to mercantilism and nations at war.

There is no question that this classical model had much appeal. It offered freedom, efficiency, and economic growth with which to combat poverty plus the potential of peace through free trade. Most of its concepts were new and radical as well as utopian, appealing to the bourgeoisie because of its stand against any form of government control.

Smith's popularity stemmed from his belief that employers should not be restricted or regulated in their use of labor. The manufacturers and merchants found this very appealing. Regulations that applied to labor and production were considered harmful so far as economic activity was concerned, regardless of what other merits they might possess. In his view, economic efficiency would lead to an increase in national wealth and to the abolition of poverty.

A man of peace, Adam Smith understood why nations fought wars. He believed that the same ends could be accomplished in a more civilized way through free trade and lamented the obstacles nations put into its path at the request of industries that wanted to keep foreign trade out in order to obtain a monopoly in the domestic market. He blamed governments for such practices, but was fully aware that their policies reflected pressure from private industry.

It is doubtful that trade among nations ever really followed the pattern of the classical model. Perhaps the reality of international economic relations came closer to the observation of Thucydides, the ancient Greek historian, who believed that in international relations only one thing is certain: the strong take from the weak what they can, and the weak grant to the strong what they must.

The classical economists were faced with a challenging problem. They had created an economic theory built around a utopian view of the free market, but although the division of labor and free trade in classical economics was established as a basis for efficiency and growth, economic development or growth was not inevitable—it had to be encouraged. The state could not openly be used for this because it would conflict with their theory of the pure market.

The real problem in regard to economic development was how to acquire the capital necessary for growth. David Ricardo, who should quite properly be called the cofounder of classical capitalism, answered this question with his "iron law of wages." Unlike Smith, Ricardo was not an academician. He was a wealthy stockbroker and a member of Parliament. Born in 1772, four years before Adam Smith published *The Wealth of Nations*, he was the son of a Jewish family that had come to England from Holland only a few years before his birth. Being of Orthodox faith, they would not allow him to marry a gentile. He was thus forced to choose between a Quaker English physician's daughter, for whom he openly professed his love, and his family, synagogue, and place in the family business. He chose his lady love and with relatively little capital, embarked upon a career. He became a wealthy stockbroker.

His iron law of wages was based on the two simple concepts invented by him and his friend Thomas Malthus, an English clergyman who had changed his profession to become one of England's leading economists. Ricardo believed that the cost of producing an item would tend to be equal to the cost of labor. Malthus believed that population increases geometrically—2, 4, 8, 16, and so on—while the food supply increases only arithmetically—2, 3, 4, 5, and so on. To Malthus, this meant that in the absence of birth control, nations are doomed to periodic famine, wars, or other catastrophes, which serve as a check on population expansion.

To Ricardo, Malthus's theory of population meant that wages could never rise above the subsistence level—the bare necessities of life. If they were to rise above that level, a population explosion would lower them again. Hence the iron law of wages.

In Ricardo's view, the workers created the total value of the product they produced (Ricardo's Theory of Value). But a worker could not be paid the total value, or saving and investment for economic growth would be zero. However, in the early stages of economic development wages were very low even when workers received the total value of their output. Workers certainly could not be expected to save. Yet some of the output *had* to be saved and kept from being currently consumed.

Since Ricardo believed that labor was the source of all value, he had to find a way to justify paying workers less than the value of their output. Ricardo defined capital as that part of the product of labor that was not paid to the worker. The employer retained a "profit" by paying labor less than its full share because he or she was in a position to do so. The employer invested this profit in the business for growth and more profits. To Ricardo, the problem of saving and investment and economic growth was solved.[5]

Thomas Malthus, the Anglican clergyman who preferred debates on the political economy with David Ricardo to sermons on theology, was a realist (empiricist). Ricardo, like Adam Smith, was a rationalist or a man of reason. To Smith and Ricardo, facts were principles rightly conceived by an orderly mind. To Malthus, facts were observations made in the real world of human activity. Principles of the kind that Smith and Ricardo used as a basis for classical economics were in Malthus's view a proper basis for theology.

To David Ricardo, the rationalist, supply and demand through the natural laws of the market and the iron laws of wages would keep the economy operating efficiently. To Malthus, the realist, low wages would lead to underconsumption and a glut on the market or what modern economists call a recession. It is interesting to observe how a rationalist and an empiricist looked at the same human activity and perceived conflicting results. As Aristotle knew, the method we employ in our perceptions determines what we perceive.

The emphasis on individual liberty became a major element in the growing popularity of classical economics, called laissez-faire capitalism by the early nineteenth-century French economist Jean Baptiste Say. To the British manufacturer, liberty meant that the state must not interfere in the relationship between the employer and the employee, except to prohibit employees from forming unions. This was accomplished through the anticombination acts, which derived their moral justification from the writings of the utilitarians. They believed that the greatest happiness for the greatest number results when all economic decisions are based on the principle that a free market allows individuals to pursue their own interests and thereby to maximize pleasure and to minimize pain.

The utilitarians had an oversimplified vision of humankind and society. They were not concerned with social dynamics (the concept of society as a social organism that changes and evolves over time). Nor did they seem to be aware of humankind's complicated nature, which psychologists since Freud have believed to be motivated by complex and conflicting drives.

John Stuart Mill had a more sophisticated version of utilitarian philosophy. Born in London in 1806, eleven years before Ricardo's *Principles of Economics* appeared, he was the son of James Mill, the ablest disciple of Jeremy Bentham, leader of the eighteenth-century school of philosophical radicals. This group of brilliant intellectuals was dedicated to considering the serious social problems of their day and introducing practical reforms designed to deal with these problems. Their writings were greatly influenced by John Locke, the seventeenth-century Whig philosopher, and by Rousseau and Voltaire, the leaders of the French Enlightenment, who also influenced such intellectuals of the American Revolution as Jefferson and Paine (and, later, Thoreau).[6] John Stuart Mill held that all individuals should pursue their own interests consistent with the prevailing social ideals. For that to happen, however, the state would have to play an active role as the guardian of the public interest. This was, however, inconsistent with his (the utilitarian) doctrine.

It is not surprising that the utilitarian and the classical economists based their assumptions on inadequate evidence, for the social and psychological sciences were still primitive and often leaned on arbitrary dogma. The collection of data and facts from the other social and psychological sciences, as we know them today, was not available to the classical economists.

Not all English philosophers of the period were utilitarians. Thomas Macaulay (1800–59), a statesman, historian, and essayist, attacked Mill's utilitarianism as unsound.

> Our objection to the Essay of Mr. Mill is fundamental. We believe that it is utterly impossible to deduce the science of government from human nature. How then are we to arrive at just conclusions on a subject so important to the happiness of mankind? Surely by the method which, in every experimental science to which it has been applied, has significantly increased the power and knowl- edge of our species. By the method of induction, by observing the present state of the world, by assiduously studying the history of past ages, by sifting the evidence of facts . . . . by perpetually bringing the theory which we have constructed to the test of new facts.[7]

The utilitarian philosophy served as a rationalization for noninterference in economic affairs during the developing stages of the Industrial Revolution. This noninterference on the part of government in the relations between employers and employees has been interpreted by social critics as a green light for the exploiters of labor. There is no doubt that the government in the name of liberty closed its eyes to the exploitation—often brutal and harmful—of workers. In the end, the utilitarian philosophy did not lead to the greatest good for the greatest number in the nineteenth century. Instead, economic development made the industrial capitalists rich and powerful, while the vast majority of workers lived in or on the edge of poverty and had little or no voice in the events that shaped their destiny. The pleasure–pain principle was not relevant to the great masses, because conditions created by the Industrial Revolution were highly unfavorable to most workers, who were considered expendable. Their wages were barely enough to pay for a drab existence—if they had jobs at all.

In spite of its lack of realism and its utopian embellishments, the classical system should not be underestimated. It set in motion the ideas that inspired practical people with business instincts to create wealth—albeit for selfish reasons—which eventually helped to abolish poverty for the majority of the people in countries where capitalism became the basis for economic development.

The Struggle for Freedom of the Market

Radical social reforms have been extremely rare in human history until the past hundred years. Prince Otto von Bismarck, who united the separate German states into a unified Germany in 1871, after his victory over France in the Franco-Prussian War, was known as Germany's conservative Iron Chancellor. Before his retirement in 1881, he introduced such great social reforms as social security and free public education for the masses. Roosevelt's New Deal was another example of radical reform or accommodation to social pressures without violent revolution. The radical reforms initiated in England after World War II are other examples of change without violence.

The struggle for freedom of the market, which transferred economic power from the church and sovereign to the merchant and industrial capitalists, did not meet the requirements of nonviolent revolution by accommodation. This struggle could not have been resolved by radical reforms because it challenged the very foundation of the Roman Catholic church, the Holy Roman Empire, and later the power of the monarchs who ruled by "divine right." Oliver Cromwell and George Washington were revolutionaries of the violent kind, not reformers by accommodation.

The deep-seated grievances that gave rise to violent revolutions also tend to inspire philosophers and poets with a passion for liberty and justice. It was quite natural, therefore, that the great struggle for freedom gave rise to such powerful and eloquent voices of liberty as Locke, Rousseau, Voltaire, Bentham, and Mill, the radical philosophers and the philosophers of the Age of Enlightenment whom we have already met.

Since the arbitrary power of the church and sovereign had stood in the way of justice, justice was conceived to be the child of liberty. The tyranny of the divine-right rulers (and before them the medieval Roman Catholic church) had generated strong passions against any form of state or church power, so that a weak government was regarded by the new bourgeoisie as the best guarantee for individual liberty.

A major part of the struggle for freedom in western civilization since the end of the feudal period (the sixteenth century in England) centered around the effort to establish a market free of the shackles of church and state. The freedom for which a Puritan Parliament and Oliver Cromwell beheaded Charles I and briefly ousted the ruling Stuart family, and for which George Washington defeated the British army, was to a large extent the freedom to buy and sell. This meant that money could buy what it liked, and the entrepreneur or trader made the rules rather than the sovereign or the church.

The struggle for a market in which the rules were to be made by the new entrepreneurial bourgeoisie was a rebellion against feudalism and divine-right monarchy. The Holy Roman Empire and its spiritual partner, the Roman Catholic church, had created a powerful form of social organization in the beginning of the ninth century that retained its sweeping control until the Reformation over seven hundred years later. Feudalism was an elaborate system that evolved quite naturally from the environment in which it was conceived and that nourished its growth and development. The lack of technology, specialization, and trade determined the character of economic opportunity. Transportation was extremely primitive, which made trade impractical. Without trade, specialization could not develop, and money as we know it today played almost no role in the feudal economy. The vast majority of the people were serfs who possessed and enjoyed few worldly goods; they were compensated for this with the promise of salvation and eternal life in what was conceived to be the "hereafter."

The political system was fundamentally simple. At the top of the feudal domain was the feudal lord, whose word was the law so long as he was loyal to the Roman Catholic church. The church, with its monopoly on salvation, had enormous power and exacted the best land in the form of the sale of indulgences. If a feudal lord did not prove loyal, he could be excommunicated—which meant the loss of salvation not only for himself but for all the nobles, knights, and serfs in his domain. This usually kept him loyal until the Reformation.

Slowly technology did advance. Transportation grew in importance, and the stage was set for specialization and trade. Manufacture and commerce, though comparatively primitive for several centuries until the Industrial Revolution, led to the formation of towns and cities. The economic foundation of feudalism gave way to the new economics based on specialization and trade.

As was to be expected, there still remained a major obstacle to the development of the bourgeoisie's market. The church still made the rules by which people were expected to live and work. The struggle for freedom during this period centered around the desire to get the church to change some of its rules that conflicted with the interests of the rapidly growing merchant class. A seemingly hopeless conflict developed between salvation and the freedom to buy and to sell.

The Reformation offered an ingenious solution. The merchant class could have both salvation and the freedom to buy and to sell at the same time. The monopoly of the Roman Catholic church came to an end. Henry VIII became the Defender of the Faith in England by establishing the Anglican church. Martin Luther allowed the Germans and others to seek salvation through a new church, free from the shackles of Rome, bearing his name. Others, such as John Knox and John Wesley, created churches that supported the special interests of their followers. The power of Rome was broken and the stage for nationalism was set.

Although in the new Protestant states, the old church had been replaced by the new churches, these did not inherit the power of the Roman Catholic church. This power was transferred to the sovereign through a concept called divine-right monarchy. The ruler had power under this theory not only over the nation but over the national churches as well. Thus, the merchants had won the struggle against the church, but the freedom to buy and to sell was not yet won. The divine-right kings and queens now made the rules, and this brought on new conflicts of interest.

The wealth of the new merchant class and the new commercial squires and landowners depended on the expansion of the market, but their political power was inadequate. The arbitrary power of the monarch stood in the way. The royal monopolies and the royal power to tax were conceived as threats to the development of the market and the great riches it promised. The struggle for the free-. dom to buy and sell and the profits this promised now had to overcome the threat the monarch represented, as long as the merchant class could not control the crown. The history of England from 1649 to 1688 portrays this struggle. The divine-right rule of the Stuarts was replaced with a constitutional monarchy giving the merchant capitalists and the gentry a check on royal power.

The merchant class, in its fight for the market, solicited the aid of the masses (that is, the people without property). The masses believed that the struggle for freedom should be based on the principle of liberty and justice for all. Nowhere, however, did the revolutions of the seventeenth and eighteenth centuries lead to this.

The French Revolution became a major battle for the control of the market by the French bourgeoisie or merchant class ("the Third Estate"). The French masses who stormed the Bastille undoubtedly thought that the struggle for freedom from the Bourbon king would result in liberty and justice for them. Danton, the bourgeois revolutionary, knew better when he exclaimed "all ownership, whether individual, or industrial, or territorial shall be maintained forever." The day for liberty for all had certainly not yet come. Revolutions should not be judged by the dreams of the philosophers who influence them, nor the poets who embellish them, nor the chantings of the masses who hope for a better life. Will Durant, in his masterful ten-volume history of civilization, expressed the essence of the struggle for freedom at the time of the French Revolution: "The middle classes did not wish to overthrow the monarchy, but they aspired to control it; they were far from desiring democracy, but they wanted a constitutional government."[8] Such a government could protect their property and their right to buy and to sell in a market in which *they* made the rules. The French monarchy was overthrown and the masses tasted for one brief moment in history the power and the glory that are the fruits of victory.

The demands of the common people, often excessive, threatened the security of the crusaders for the market, which made them anxious to return to what they thought was the original purpose of the French Revolution—to free the market from the powers of the king and the church. Napoleon accomplished this by putting everything in its proper place, including the masses, who had mistaken the revolution as their own. He did this with the Code Napoleon after declaring "The Revolution has returned to the principles with which it began; it is at an end."

Napoleon in his quest for empire used his armies to unify Europe under his control. He found that his ambitions clashed with the ambitions of the British. The dream of empire soon kindled the passions of all those nations who saw the market as a source of great wealth, and Napoleon had stepped on their toes. His struggle with the British and his defeat at Waterloo can be better appreciated if it is realized that the man who defeated Napoleon, Arthur Wellesley, played a prominent role in the East India Company, which helped Britain attain the wealth that served the nation well in building an empire. The British were delighted when Napoleon waged his counterrevolution, putting an end to the threat the masses posed. Republicanism and democracy were not the aspirations of the Whigs and the Tories, and they were not to be confused with the struggle for the market. It is natural that Napoleon was welcomed by the British when he brought the French Revolution to an end, but opposed by them when he took the struggle for the market to all parts of Europe. It was to be expected that the two prime champions of the market—each competing for its rich fruits—should clash. Arthur Wellesley, the Duke of Wellington and head of England's East India Company, was, if anything, the logical conqueror of the French emperor.

The leaders of the American Revolution and those who nursed the former British colony into a full-fledged nation were greatly influenced by the French Enlightenment writings of Voltaire, Rousseau, Diderot, and others. They were also influenced by the writings of John Locke, the great Whig philosopher. Their passion for freedom was nursed by the romantic and humanitarian outcries of these philosophers. It was also nursed by the more practical considerations of the freedom to buy and to sell without the interference of a British king (George III) who resided three thousand miles away from their shores.

The king did not interfere with the more personal freedoms of the American colonies, such as religion and social behavior. His interest was for Britain to benefit from what the colonies bought and sold. Through such devices as taxes and regulation of imports and exports, the British monarch interfered with the colonists' dream of a market free from the control of rulers and popes.

It is doubtful that most American colonists saw the revolution only as a struggle for the freedom of the market. The passions that came into play when local patriots dumped a shipload of tea into the Boston harbor were not kindled by the freedom of which Rousseau or Voltaire wrote, but rather by a desire to keep the British from interfering with their freedom to buy and to sell without being taxed.

The struggle for the market, which had put an end to feudalism and had given rise to nationalism, had replaced the absolute power of church and monarch with a constitutional form of government, and it had transferred much of that power to the merchant class.

The right to buy and sell without church or state interference was by no means the only factor in the social revolution leading from agrarian feudalism to commercial capitalism and, later, industrial capitalism. Freedom from the tyranny imposed by an authoritarian church and state was an important factor in kindling the passions of those who fought the revolutions. It was, however, the very practical consideration of gaining for the bourgeoisie the right to buy and sell under rules established by them that provided the money, willpower, and organization necessary for the ultimate success in this struggle.

The Monopolists—The Creators of the Reality

The best laid schemes of men and mice oft gang agley.
                                                            —Robert Burns

Humanity in its struggle for freedom has not yet learned how to balance the interests of the individual with the interests of society (the common good).

Utilitarianism and laissez-faire capitalism provided the idealistic philosophical foundation for the nineteenth-century economic development in Britain and the United States. In a few centuries, the pendulum had swung from one extreme to another. At one extreme the individual was subordinated to the state and church, which ruled with absolute power for the "common good." At the other extreme the state and society were subordinated to the private interest of the individual. As it turned out, the masses were again exploited—this time by a new power structure generated by laissez-faire.

The history of the struggle for the market had resulted in the dissolution of most social and legal relationships developed during seven centuries of feudalism. The victory of laissez-faire and utilitarianism was interpreted by nineteenth-century economists to mean that all people were free and equal in the newly created heaven on earth—the free market.

The new era of the free market turned out to be more complicated than the utilitarian philosophers and classical economists had anticipated. The Industrial Revolution produced a series of new inventions that revolutionized the methods of production. These new methods required a high degree of human cooperation in contrast to the preindustrial era, in which specialization was very limited and people were, in the economic sense, more isolated from one another.

The capitalist system was the social organization on which the Industrial Revolution thrived. It created new relationships built on cooperation to a much larger degree than the feudal system that it had replaced. The people of the market had effectively destroyed the system that bound peasant to landlord, landlord to feudal lord, feudal lord to sovereign, and sovereign to Holy Roman Emperor and Pope. It became necessary not only to replace this system but to improve it. The classical market and utilitarian philosophy did not lend themselves very well to that task because they emphasized the pursuit of self-interest rather than cooperation.

Under the free-market doctrine, social cooperation was masked by the "unseen hand." The price of labor and the price of every commodity and service were assumed to be determined by the law of supply and demand in a free market. What was in reality a relationship between people appears to have been in classical economic theory only a relationship between prices. The unseen hand (which was assumed to have its origin in natural law) served to conceal the actual relationship between worker and employer, between competing employers, and between the leaders of finance and the leaders of the industrial market. It preserved the illusion of individual liberty in a world rapidly becoming more and more dependent on human and social cooperation. No wonder the price mechanism was held in such high esteem by the people who thrived in the free market!

The social relationships that of necessity became an integral part of industrial capitalism emerged as gigantic cooperative efforts in spite of their utilitarian origin. The Industrial Revolution could not have succeeded if the capitalists who furnished its drive had not had access to a large supply of workers. But if all people were free and equal, how could one person compel other free people to work for him and to abide by his rules? In primitive agricultural societies, before the advent of capitalism, this was accomplished through slavery or some other form of compulsory relationship. The Industrial Revolution made slavery unnecessary for the creation of a labor market. The industrial process required capital, without which a worker was unable to produce. If the capitalist-employer owned the capital, the workers *had* to work for him if they wanted to work at all. Their labor now became a commodity to be bought and sold on the market. This was a far cry from Locke's concept of property, which he perceived to be the product of labor, used and owned *by those who produced it*. It was also quite different from the utilitarian doctrine, which perceived all people to be equally free in pursuit of their own interests. The owners of capital, as it turned out, had a decided advantage.

How did the capitalists acquire the means of production that enabled them to buy not the worker as in slavery, but the worker's labor? The Industrial Revolution showed the way. In the early days of capitalism, the workers owned their simple tools with which they produced handcrafted commodities such as shoes, clothing, and furniture. They did this in small shops, which were often a part of their homes. The merchant capitalist bought their products and traded them in markets often quite distant from their places of origin. In time, merchants' profits accumulated sufficiently to enable them to establish "factories." The steady stream of new inventions enabled them to buy more sophisticated equipment and tools. This made it possible for them to offer workers wages that exceeded their earnings in their own primitive shops. As the factory grew in size and efficiency, it was able to compete more aggressively with the workers who still maintained their own shops. Eventually, the system of independent workers gave way to the factory system. The factory owners owned the means of production, and the formerly independent worker became an input in the advancing industrial processes.

Karl Marx and other nineteenth-century socialists saw in this transition the exploitation of the worker, and they blamed private ownership of the means of production under capitalism for the growing misery of the masses. There is no question that the workers were exploited and that equality in the pursuit of self-interest was a myth. The exploitation of the worker was, however, typical of economic development in general rather than of capitalism as such. During the early stages of economic development in any system, past or present, the worker seems to get exploited.

As factories grew in size and economic importance, their owners developed relationships with bankers, financiers, and the rentiers who owned the natural resources. New social relationships evolved that determined the structure of capitalism during the Industrial Revolution. These accommodations between worker, employer, banker, rentier, and government replaced the unseen hand. Such historical and institutional economists as Marx and Thorstein Veblen recognized this, but the mainstream of conventional economists failed to consider these relationships in the development of theory and policy.

Industrial capitalism raised the standard of living significantly for perhaps 25 percent of the world's population. But so far it has not been able to spread prosperity throughout the world as Adam Smith had predicted. In fact, capitalism has developed three characteristics alien to the doctrine of laissez-faire: monopoly, economic nationalism, and economic crisis.

The growth of monopoly is perceived to be the natural outcome of technology, fostered by the Industrial Revolution, rather than a product of greed and lawlessness. The people who presided over the process that led to monopoly were often greedy, but, without great technological advances, monopoly would not have developed.

Small shopkeepers could not have become giant firms without great changes in science and technology.

Laissez-faire was based on a system of competition between all buyers and sellers in free markets. This type of competition could not be harmful because all "units" in the market were assumed to be small and unable to exert arbitrary power over their competitors. In fact, it was the free play of competition in the free market that was expected to bring justice and happiness to all.

The Industrial Revolution changed all this. The laissez-faire system of pure competition was based on the free entry and exit of firms in every industry. Less efficient or submarginal firms would be forced to leave the industry and be replaced by new and more efficient firms under the laws of the free market. What looked in theory like a perfectly balanced and just system kept businesspeople in genuinely competitive industries in a constant fear of bankruptcy. The fear was real enough because bankruptcies were common.

As firms grew in size, the problem of economic insecurity became increasingly painful and created serious difficulties. Large firms required ever larger outlays of capital investments. This could not be justified if competition by other firms generated market insecurity leading to total ruin.

The tendency toward monopoly is not, as Milton Friedman seems to think, something imposed on the free market by the state.[9] It is inherent in the nature of economic development under both capitalism and socialism that insecurity in intranational and international markets is an obstacle to further growth and development. The protection the state granted to the leaders of the market in the form of tariffs, patents, and so on was a response to their pleas that without such protection, they could not survive. The original laissez-faire states could have ignored such pleas, but the states that have witnessed the structural changes brought on by the Industrial Revolution could not be so aloof.

The same insecurity that has led to the monopolization of major industries has led to the emergence of a nationalism that has replaced free trade with new and more effective versions of economic mercantilism. For a brief period, the real international division of labor created a genuine system of free trade among the major nations that had experienced economic development. This period, which came to an end at the start of World War I, was not the result of the natural laws of the market extending beyond national boundaries. It was produced by a brief peace during which British statesmanship managed international trade in line with the principles of a free market, as detailed in chapter 3.

Economic development, aided by the Industrial Revolution, gave rise to a few powerful nations whose economies relied on the resources and markets of other regions. Their own industries could not grow and prosper without these. The insecurity that led to the rise of monopolies within a country was again rekindled by an even more threatening competition from abroad. Adam Smith's dream of free trade and the free division of labor was shattered by the rise of a nationalism which found foreign competition as undesirable as the monopolists found domestic competition.

Monopoly and nationalism became more and more the trend in nations experiencing economic development. This system was still called capitalism, but it was a world apart from the utopian doctrines of utilitarianism and laissez-faire.

The classical economists saw in the natural laws of the market, guided by the unseen hand, a beautiful system of economic growth and justice. But the utopian dreams of the classical economists did not come true. Instead, the system that evolved was guided not by the unseen hand but by the requirements of monopolistic industries and their political counterparts—nations.

The price mechanism could not make the automatic adjustments envisaged by the classical economists, and the system became plagued by a series of recurrent crises. It was a different world in essence and in structure, and the promise of stability could no more come true than the utilitarian belief that all people should be free and equal.

Markets and resources are important to *all* industrial nations, and free trade requires the subordination of purely national interests to the interests of the world economy. This is a very idealistic way of looking at the world, and powerful nations have not been willing to subordinate their own interests, regardless of the ideology of their system. Nations competing for raw materials and markets for their finished products do not feel secure competing with one another. This is not surprising when one considers the history of competition and monopoly even within a nation.

Although the colonial wars played a prominent role in the history of Europe during the eighteenth century, and British imperialism reached its height by the end of the nineteenth century, the principles of free trade were praised by most British politicians in their public speeches. Notwithstanding British policy in India, China, Africa, and elsewhere around the globe, British economists continued to teach international economics in terms of free trade and pure market theory. The real economic relations between nations and regions never entered into the development of orthodox international-trade theory.

Imperialism was adopted as a national policy long before nations officially abandoned the policy of laissez-faire. The same factors that caused monopolistic concentration within a country led to a preference of imperialism over a reliance on free trade. While monopoly reduces the risk of failure in the domestic market, imperialism reduces it in the international market. This has created conflicts and problems, the outcome of which will shape our destiny for a long time to come. It has also given birth to much hypocrisy, preventing people from practicing what they preach.

In retrospect, the utilitarian laissez-faire doctrine missed its utopian mark. The liberty enjoyed by the capitalists in the pursuit of their own interests, however, enabled them to acquire the capital that served as a basis for economic growth. The utilitarian doctrine disguised the greed or ambition of the few as the pursuit of happiness for the many. Greed and ambition led to profits, and profits fed the Industrial Revolution. Could it have been done in some other way? Probably not in the past; perhaps in the future.

3
The Decline and Fall of Laissez-Faire Capitalism

Laissez-Faire Produces Problems and Critics

The Industrial Revolution created many problems, of which unemployment and miserable working conditions were the two most visible. Unemployment and human misery became the lot of the masses throughout most of the nineteenth-century in the developing countries.

The invisible hand was challenged almost from the beginning. Economic development created many problems, as is natural when human and social relationships change. The utilitarians promised the greatest good for the greatest number, yet the masses lived in poverty. The classical economists promised the optimization of economic goals through the free market, but unemployment was common. The actual relationship between employer and worker challenged Mill's theory that in a free market all people are free to pursue their own interest for the greatest good.

Robert Owen was convinced that the environment in which people live determines their character as individuals and social beings.[1] He did not agree with the classical economists that the natural laws of the market, as reflected in the price mechanism—guided by the unseen hand—would lead to the greatest good for the greatest number.

A great deal of pressure was brought to bear on the government by the Owenites and other groups for reform. Not only the radicals turned against the utilitarians, whose philosophy was held responsible for the economic and social misery of early-nineteenth-century Britain. Macaulay wrote in the *Edinburgh Review*:

> We entertain no apprehension of danger to the institutions of this country from the utilitarians. Our fears are of a different kind. We dread the odium and discredit of their alliance. . . . There is not and we firmly believe there never was in this country a party so unpopular. They have already made the science of political economy—a science of vast importance to the welfare of nations—an object of disgust to the majority of the community.[2]

After the Napoleonic wars, unemployment was a major problem in Britain. The discontent of the worker grew as unemployment increased, without relief in sight. Parliament, made up of employers and landowners, felt threatened, and in 1817 much repressive legislation was passed. The right of habeas corpus was suspended. Public meetings of any kind without the express permission of the authorities were forbidden. Several acts were passed that restricted the freedom of the press and provided for punishment of those who were found guilty of "blasphemous and seditious" libel. There were many other repressive acts. Laissez-faire and utilitarianism certainly had not led to the greatest good for the greatest number, and the free market had not, as it turned out, encouraged political freedom for all.

In the light of this, it is difficult to understand the views held by some current disciples of utilitarianism and laissez-faire. Professor Milton Friedman erroneously believes that "historical evidence speaks with a single voice on the relation between political freedom and a free market. I know of no example in time or place of a society that has been marked by a large measure of political freedom and that has not also used something comparable to a free market to organize the bulk of economic activity."[3] Professor Friedman may be surprised to learn that the only time in history when the free market really did exist, before monopolies put an end to it in the late nineteenth century, it did not lead to political freedom for the majority of people.

There was much criticism and opposition to the utilitarian doctrine and laissez-faire because the human relationships it produced and the problems it created differed considerably from the utopian model. The weakness of the laissez-faire doctrine, as of all other utopian models, was that it was static and did not allow for technological advances and for the dynamic character of human and social relationships. It was Marx who overshadowed all other nineteenth-century critics of capitalism, precisely because his criticism was built on a dynamic and historical analysis. He too, however, eventually succumbed to the temptation of building a utopia.

Marx was born on May 5, 1818, in Trier, Germany, only one year after Ricardo's *Principles* was published in Britain. Born of Jewish parents who before his birth converted to Christianity, Marx became an atheist. He regarded religion as "an opiate of the people" and believed that it taught them to acquiesce when they should resist the oppression keeping them poor and miserable.

Marx spent much of his life in Britain, where he met Friedrich Engels, son of a wealthy German family engaged in the manufacture of textiles in Germany and Britain. Marx and Engels were both upper-middle–class intellectuals whose contact with the masses was chiefly in their writings.

Marx was extremely well read in philosophy and economics and had a brilliant grasp of history. He was thoroughly versed in classical economics and saw it as a theory of exploitation. Although he was never recognized by the mainstream of his fellow economists because of his radical views, he became the London correspondent of the *New York Herald,* a very conservative newspaper. He served in that capacity for many years and became that publication's highest-paid journalist. He died in 1883, probably not suspecting the impact his writings would have on human history.

Marx's criticism of capitalism was quite different from that of the other well-known critics, who appraised its structure and its consequences as if it existed in a historical vacuum. Marx was the first economist to analyze an economic system from a historical and dynamic point of view. He perceived capitalism as a necessary step in the process of economic development. He also understood its political and social framework. Unlike modern economists, he did not put his main effort into analyzing abstractly what determines the price of a cup of tea; he concentrated rather on the various social relationships that produce a cup of tea.

Marx saw the fight for freedom of the market as only one step in the fight for freedom for all people. He disagreed with critics who believed that the free market could continue to exist if abuses were corrected through reforms. To Marx, socialism was the logical result of capitalism. Socialism had to wait, however, for its time in history, after capitalism had created necessary "preconditions." These were, in Marx's view, the socialization of labor and a mass movement of workers seeking freedom through cooperation. Marx pointed out that most workers are already "socialized" during the advanced stages of capitalism.

In Marx's view, there was a very good reason why capitalism had to precede socialism. If the necessary preconditions for socialism did not exist, if productivity and production did not make sufficient progress, socialism would merely generalize poverty. His criticism of capitalism, therefore, did not prevent his praising its role in history.

> The bourgeoisie has been the first to show what human activity is capable of achieving. It has executed works more marvelous than the building of Egyptian pyramids, Roman aqueducts and Gothic cathedrals; it has carried out expeditions surpassing by far the tribal migrations and the crusades.[4]

To Marx, the class concept of capitalism was of primary importance. The two classes were made up of those who owned property and those who were propertyless. Property referred to the means of production: factories, machinery, tools, and so on. The propertyless workers depended for their livelihood on those who owned the means of production—the capitalists. Without them, they could not work. The capitalists, therefore, had great power over the worker. They made the rules of production; the workers were transformed into the economic input and their values as human beings were sacrificed. The capitalists, in Marx's view, alienated the workers from their values as human beings.

Marx's theory of economic crises under capitalism is much too limited when judged by today's problems. Profit played an important role in his theory of crises. He was critical of the capitalist drive for greater and greater profits, because the new technology should be used to make the life of the worker more tolerable, more creative. Marx found a contradiction in the drive for profits. The drive for profits led producers to produce more than the workers were able to purchase with their low wages. The economic crisis was, therefore, a matter of underconsumption.

His theory of the worsening crises of capitalism, which he thought would ultimately lead to its decay, has produced much controversy. The theory was based on his prediction of a falling rate of profit. Technology would be responsible for that. As more and more capital would be used to increase efficiency, the rate of return on capital would decline. The owners of capital would try to offset this by increasing production, which would glut the market and lead to crises that would continue to worsen. In Marx's view, it was ironic that improved technology should contribute to the decline of capitalism.

Marx, who criticized his fellow economists for building static models, did in this instance, I think, the same thing. He built a static model in which profit had to decline. Yet the rate of profit has not declined as he predicted. Why not? Because great technological innovations have counterbalanced the tendency for profits to decline as capital increases. This may indeed be one reason why the capitalist system has thrived rather than decayed, as predicted by Marx.

Although Marx's analysis was dynamic insofar as he regarded economic systems as evolving social institutions, he failed to predict adequately the dynamic character of the enormous technological advances since the midnineteenth century. This played havoc with some of Marx's predictions as well as with the static theories of the traditional economists.

Marx was a brilliant analyst of the capitalist system. His knowledge of history, sociology, and politics made him the outstanding social scientist of his time. There was much truth, as well as some error, in his theories of exploitation, surplus value, worker alienation, crises, and imperialism. No one is safe in making predictions for the distant future. Change is unpredictable.

If Marx were alive today, he would probably alter his economic analysis, because the facts have changed. If he had been less certain of his facts and more pragmatic he would not have become the founder of one of the most powerful secular religions of all time.

The End of the Gold Standard

Laissez-faire was challenged, as we have seen, by the Industrial Revolution, which encouraged the birth of giant companies and colonial expansion. Free trade and the monetary system (the international gold standard) going hand in hand with it survived without serious problems until World War I. After that, both were in distress until the early 1930s, when they gave way to economic nationalism.

The theory of the gold standard is an important part of the classical model, which relies on the free market for the efficient allocation of resources. Many people view the gold standard as proof that economic laws will work if they are not tampered with. Let us examine the facts and the fancies associated with the gold standard.

Two factors played a major role in the relatively free flow of world trade marking the last quarter of the nineteenth century and the early years of the twentieth century: the enormous economic expansion and the comparatively stable conditions in the British Empire and in the heart of that empire—England. These factors were largely responsible for the emergence of an international currency (the pound sterling) and the availability of long- and short-term capital where it was needed. Without this flow of capital, world trade would have run into serious difficulties and the gold standard could not have functioned, as indeed was the case after World War I.

To understand what has been called the Golden Age of International Economic Relations, it is necessary to take a look at, first, the actual relationship between Britain and the rest of the world and, second, the gold standard in principle and practice.

Great Britain, a nation only one-twentieth as large as the United States, dominated world trade for more than a third of a century prior to the first world war. It is the popular view that Britain's success in world trade and finance was due to its adherence to an international gold standard. Britain did indeed adhere in principle to the gold standard, which served as the international monetary system during that period. The view, however, that the gold standard was responsible for the uninterrupted flow of trade leaves much of the real story untold.

What differentiates foreign trade from domestic trade is that foreign trade involves many national currencies that must be converted into one another if trade is to flow freely. In domestic trade, the buyer and the seller use the same currency, so convertibility is not an issue. In foreign trade, the *buyer's* (importer's) currency has to be converted into the currency of the *seller* (exporter) or into a currency acceptable to the seller.

For currencies to be convertible into one another, a rate of exchange has to be established. Under a gold standard, the value of each currency is established in terms of gold, which makes it possible to express the value of each currency in terms of the value of every other currency. If, for example, an ounce of gold costs twice as many U.S. dollars as British pounds, the rate of exchange between the pound and the dollar is 1:2.

The international gold standard is based on a rather simple concept that coincides with the doctrine of free trade as envisaged by Adam Smith. The essence of this system is the subordination of national economic stability to the free flow of world trade. This means that nations have to be willing to tolerate domestic economic disturbances, such as inflations and recessions, in order to enjoy peaceful international economic relations.

The requirements are as follows. All nations on this standard correlate their supply of money with their stock of gold. This means that the supply of money has to be increased if the supply of gold rises, and decreased if the supply of gold shrinks. The ratio between gold and the monetary unit (the dollar, for example) remains constant and holders of money (paper currency) have the right to convert this currency into gold without restriction.

How does such a system encourage a free and constant flow of trade? World trade can be carried on without interruption only if nations have the ability to pay for their imports in gold or in currencies acceptable to the exporters of other nations. They acquire such currencies or gold through their exports, from capital investments by investors from other nations, and from bank deposits belonging to foreign nationals. These and the mining of gold were the methods of obtaining it prior to World War I.

A simple example will illustrate how the gold standard is supposed to function. If France continues to import more than it exports and if foreign capital investments are not enough to make up the difference, France's gold reserve and other currencies available to foreign exporters will soon be depleted. Under the gold standard theory, this will be avoided thus: As France ships gold to pay for the trade deficit, the French money supply will shrink, causing interest rates to rise. This will result in an economic contraction in France. At the same time, France's higher bank rates, resulting from a contraction in the money supply, will attract foreign deposits. The economic contraction will reduce French imports, while the increased bank deposits from foreign nationals will increase France's holding of foreign exchange. This will continue until France's exports and imports are in balance, at which time its economy will return to normal conditions.

If the opposite had been the case and France had a chronic export surplus, the problem would be solved through the opposite process. France would receive gold from the deficit countries, and its money supply would increase, resulting in higher prices and lower interest rates. The higher prices would reduce France's exports, and its lower interest rates would cause French nationals to transfer some of their deposits to the importing countries. Presto, the problem would be solved.

In general, the theory of the gold standard suffers from the same inadequacies as the classical theory. It is based on abstract logic instead of the conditions of the real world. What made the gold standard perform adequately prior to World War I was not its inherent logic but the conditions existing in the British Empire.

What were these conditions? Britain had become the center of the world trade partly because of its successful management of the Industrial Revolution—which stands as a tribute to British capitalism—and partly because of its success in building an empire. The British made up for what they lacked in size by acquiring foreign regions that, with the help of the British navy, were colonized. As a result, they organized a large part of the globe into a world market for resources and finished products—a market that they dominated.

It was quite natural, therefore, that the British pound should have become the key international currency desired by everyone in the execution of foreign trade. Since Britain held the leading position as the world's importer, exporter, and banker, who could challenge the pound's supremacy? The pound sterling could be used almost anywhere in the world, because there was nothing better at that time as a currency for world trade. What made this system work so well was Britain's ability to export an enormous volume of capital that it had accumulated in its role as the financial center of the world's dominant empire. During the four decades prior to World War I, about 40 percent of Britain's savings were invested overseas; by 1914, about 25 percent of its national income came from these investments. By comparison, the United States, which replaced Britain as the dominant economic power, invests a much smaller proportion of its savings and wealth overseas.

Britain was able to make such large overseas investments because it was small and had much surplus capital to spare. The opposite was true of the United States. The Marxist view that a capitalist country must export capital if its investments are to bear fruit was especially true of Britain, but not so true of the United States, at least in the past. The vast undeveloped U.S. frontier offered profitable investment opportunities to the more developed eastern United States.

By now it should be clear why the British experience lent itself so well to the maintenance of a gold standard and why, after World War I, when the British Empire began to decline and the United States began to dominate world trade, the gold standard did not fare so well.

The abundant availability of British long- and short-term capital prevented severe deficits and surpluses in national foreign trade balances. This, in turn, took the pressure off gold. Britain kept the world well supplied with pounds, and gold was called upon to play only a relatively minor role. As a result, the supply of gold was adequate for its role in world trade. Before World War I, the Bank of England had a gold reserve of between 30 and 40 million pounds. After World War II, its gold reserves were twenty to thirty times as large, but inadequate because of the decline of the pound sterling in world trade.

It is true that the volume of trade has considerably increased, which some economists have taken as an explanation of why the gold standard declined. In their view, the supply of gold became inadequate. A look at the facts does not support this. In the immediate postwar years and afterward until the early 1930s, foreign trade did not increase sufficiently in relation to the world supply of gold to endanger the gold standard. It was the enormous cost of World War I that all but bankrupted Britain, which greatly reduced the effectiveness of the pound sterling as a key currency. The U.S. dollar, which replaced it in terms of international demand, did not take over the role of the pound as the key international currency.

Why did London's policies encourage the free flow of world trade while U.S. policies discouraged it? A world depression and the rise of economic nationalism provide a large part of the explanation.

The Great Depression of the 1930s and the Rise of Economic Nationalism

At the end of the nineteenth century, two formidable new industrial nations, the United States and Germany, appeared on the world market and began to challenge Britain's supremacy in world trade. This took the form of aggressive trade and currency competition, the first altering the pattern of trade and the second leading to the new industrial powers' creation of separate gold reserves in competition with the pound sterling. This resulted in a gold shortage that threatened a serious shrinkage in the world money supply. Some economists who perceive economic problems as vagaries of monetary policy explain the depression of the 1890s as a result of a world gold shortage. The fact is that competitive nationalism and not monetary policy created the shortage. This is a vital factor in the understanding of economic behavior.

If a newly emerging nationalism was the cause of the depression of the 1890s, then what was the cause of economic revival during the decade and a half before World War I? Would it not be logical to assume that the competitive rivalries of the great powers should have led to steadily worsening economic conditions until their battle field confrontation in 1914?

Economists usually explain this phenomenon by pointing out the opening up of the South African gold mines, which led to an increase in the world money supply. Yet, the increase in the gold supply could not, by itself, have led to economic revival and comparatively peaceful political relations *if it had not been possible for the rival powers to engage in colonial expansion without colliding with one another!* Africa was partitioned, India was extensively exploited, Burma was annexed, and South Africa and China were opened up for trade. The new economic opportunities fed the economic revival of the early 1900s. The increase in the gold supply and the lower cost of gold production, resulting from the newly discovered cyanide process, facilitated recovery but did not cause it.

The rise of the United States and Germany as major economic powers unbalanced the British network of international trade and finance. World War I, fathered by a new nationalism, put the finishing touches on the golden age of the British Empire. The era of free trade, made possible by the supremacy of the pound sterling, gave way to new forms of unmasked nationalism and severe convertibility problems. The freedom of the market, which the classical economists had envisaged as extending across national boundaries, once more gave way to mercantilism. The free market was unable to cope with the complex realities of the Industrial Revolution in a world divided into nations competing bitterly for resources and markets.

After World War I, international trade was so disturbed by the emergence of rival currencies that huge surpluses and deficits began to pile up. In the prewar years, the British, as the world bankers, were able to prevent such aberrations, and the gold standard performed well. After the war, the gold standard could not cope with the huge settlements imposed on it by the chronic deficits of a number of nations.

What caused these excessive deficits and surpluses? The obvious answer, of course, is that the pound sterling had been the foundation of a de facto international monetary system and gold had been its de jure counterpart. The golden age of the British Empire was as close as the world has ever come to an international monetary policy. When this empire began to disintegrate, conflicting national policies created huge gaps in the balance of payments and there simply wasn't enough gold to fill them.

The gold-standard concept, as we have seen, requires that each nation subordinate its national economic policies to the requirements of international economic stability. The new nationalism reversed this and created the stresses that led to the collapse of the gold standard and the deterioration of trade in the 1930s. It is understandable that the industrial nations, concerned more with internal price stability and full employment than with stable exchange rates, pursued policies that were inconsistent with the international gold standard, which required adjustments in national price and production levels for the maintenance of a free flow of trade among nations.

Many attempts were made during the 1920s to save the gold standard, but the huge deficit balances accumulated by several important nations, notably Britain, led to an unprecedented drain on gold. This drain forced Britain off the gold standard in 1931, an example the rest of the world followed during the next few years.

The collapse of the gold standard was a major blow to classical economic theory and faith in the free-market concept. But it was the world depression of the 1930s that led to the Keynesian revolution and government intervention in the execution of economic policy.

The Great Depression of the 1930s, which spread throughout most of the industrialized world, cannot be explained by orthodox economic theory. There is, in fact, no simple explanation, but several factors stand out as major causes overshadowing all others.

The fear of inflation with its political repercussions, as experienced by European countries after World War I, virtually paralyzed the economic intelligence of central bankers in the 1920s. Germany, Austria, and several Eastern European countries experienced runaway inflation. Josef Schumpeter (the noted Harvard economist who had come to the United States from Austria, where he had been finance minister during that country's postwar inflation) warned his fellow economists of the dangers of inflation. He argued that the postwar boom of the 1920s had to be "cured" with a tight money policy. The fear of inflation also seems to have been the key factor in the U.S. Federal Reserve policy in the late 1920s and early 1930s. The tight money policy of the 1920s for curing inflationary booms was consistent with traditional economic theory. The fear of inflation on the part of central bankers was quite natural, considering the runaway inflations after the war, which caused the collapse of several governments.

Professor Friedman blames the antiinflationary monetary policies for the Great Depression. President Hoover and Professor Schumpeter were more realistic in their appraisals. Herbert Hoover asserted after he left the presidency that a major factor behind the Great Depression was the War of 1914–1918. Professor Schumpeter agreed with this and pointed out that the great costs of the war caused the Great Depression.

It is the inevitable reversal of a credit explosion that initiates the downturn, which in the past has usually resulted in a depression. Wars or rearmament programs usually set a credit cycle in motion, and the effort to maintain prosperity afterwards causes the cycle to explode with the inevitable downturn.

At least that has generally been the case in the past. World War II proved an exception because the United States enjoyed the benefits of economic supremacy and the simultaneous occurrence of a technological revolution. As a result, the rate of growth in the United States was great enough to absorb the shocks of the credit cycle, producing a series of minor recessions instead. The credit explosions of the 1980s contain the roots of another depression. Whether these roots will bear fruit will depend on the success of the policies adopted to prevent depression. This is unpredictable.

Another factor in the Great Depression of the 1930s was the lack of accommodation to the structural changes occurring after World War I, partly as a result of the war itself. Europe's dependence on U.S. agriculture during the war greatly increased the production of food in the United States. The rapid recovery in European agriculture after the war was not offset by a cutback in U.S. production. As a result, the prices of foodstuffs and fibers came under a severe downward pressure. In addition, agricultural technology improved so much that considerable farm labor was replaced by machines. About 25 million people left farms to take up life in towns and cities during the 1920s.

The advances in agricultural technology, the decline in world demand for U.S. agricultural products, the fall in agricultural prices, and the relocation of labor from farms to cities were symptoms of an agricultural revolution. The free market was unable to accommodate these changes. Consequently, the process of production suffered serious distortions reflected in a severe deflation.

Income distribution and the stock market crash also played a role in the economic decline. Income distribution was strongly skewed to favor the middle- and upper-income classes. As a result, prosperity depended on business investments and consumer expenditures of the higher-income groups, who also owned most of the corporate stocks.

The stock market crash of October 1929 was a traumatic experience for business and higher-income consumers. As stock prices came tumbling down, firms became increasingly cautious about their investment decisions. Consumers too, whose expenditures had reflected a previously bullish market, were forced to cut back. A wave of caution and pessimism blanketed the nation. Aggregate demand fell, and this (combined with the fear of inflation on the part of the Federal Reserve plus the distortions caused by the agricultural revolution) provided the conditions for the severe depression that followed.

World War I and the Great Depression were manifestations of the lack of intelligent accommodation to changes generated by an industrial and agrarian revolution. Neither the national nor the international market mechanisms could cope with them. It was clear that the utopian dream had turned into a nightmare.

In England, John Maynard Keynes (who became the most influential economist of this century) was beginning to stir strong passions with his criticism of traditional economics. Born in 1883, the year Marx died, he was educated at Eton and Cambridge, the son of highly respected parents. His mother was the mayor of Cambridge and his father was the chief administrative officer of Cambridge University. In addition to becoming Britain's most famous economist since Alfred Marshall, he was also bursar of Cambridge University, where he held the chair of economics.

The Great Depression gave Keynes, later to become Lord Keynes, the evidence he needed to discredit laissez-faire as a viable economic doctrine. This antagonized many of his fellow economists, but he was too important to be ignored. The neoclassical economics of Alfred Marshall (which superseded the earlier classical economics of Adam Smith, David Ricardo and John Stuart Mill) was now superseded by the economics of John Maynard Keynes.

The Keynesian Revolution—The End of Laissez-Faire

It is astonishing what foolish things one can temporarily believe . . . .
particularly in economics where it is often impossible to bring one's
ideas to a conclusive test.

—John Maynard Keynes

The whole classical economic system depends on the logic of the
market mechanism. In the capitalism that developed during the
nineteenth century, much economic activity—for instance, wars and
preparation for war—was not subject to the laws of the market.
Nor were rapid technological changes (induced by the Industrial
Revolution), which altered political and social relationships. Nor
were disturbances in the economic process that did not respond to
price changes, such as severe depressions.

In the 1930s, the longest, deepest, and most widespread depression of the industrial world convinced some of the most eminent
economists that the laws of the market could not be depended upon
for solving certain economic problems. The most famous of these
was John Maynard Keynes. If one were to select the three books in
economics that have had the greatest impact on economic policy in
the various regions of the world, one would have to include Adam
Smith's *Wealth of Nations,* Karl Marx's *Das Kapital,* and John
Maynard Keynes' *The General Theory of Employment, Income and
Money.*

Unlike the works of Smith and Marx, Keynes' *General Theory*
is not a model for a new utopia. In fact, it challenges only one
of the major tenets in the classical doctrine: full-employment equilibrium. The concept of full-employment equilibrium is an important factor in laissez-faire. Equilibrium means that there is no tendency to move away from that position. The neoclassical
economists of the late nineteenth and early twentieth centuries held
that the laws of the free market would make full employment and
equilibrium occur at the same time.

The assumption of full-employment equilibrium is vital to the classical doctrine because it makes government intervention unnecessary when the economy experiences inflation or unemployment. In the classical model, the laws of the market (supply and demand) automatically restore full-employment equilibrium when the economy deviates from a position of full employment and stable prices. If stability in every market and in the economy as a whole is automatically achieved, government intervention in the economy is assumed unnecessary.

The Keynesian model too is built on the concept of equilibrium. But in his model of the economy, equilibrium can occur at *any level of unemployment*. Hence, unemployment can exist when the economy is in equilibrium. By rejecting the classical assumption of automatic full-employment equilibrium, Keynes opened the door to government intervention.

The *General Theory* leaves the basic principles of classical economics untouched. It neither questions nor challenges such fundamental concepts as private ownership and control of the economy, let alone the allocation of resources and income distribution through competition in the market. It is revolutionary in only one respect: its discovery of unemployment equilibrium. This is indeed a break from classical economics because it makes government intervention necessary for economic recovery and full employment.

By the time of the Great Depression of the 1930s, laissez-faire had been discredited as a workable system everywhere except by the main body of the economic profession. It was considered daring to cast doubt upon theories that had become sacrosanct, and Keynes' *General Theory* was regarded by the faithful as a radical departure.

Keynes' theory of unemployment was based on his belief that private investment determined the performance of the economy. The volume of private investment was based on profit expectations and the cost of borrowing the funds for the investment (the interest paid for such funds). Keynes called this the marginal efficiency of capital, which is British financial jargon for net profit expectations.

The simplest way to explain the difference between pre-Keynesian neoclassical economic theory and Keynesian theory is to compare the two during a recession. In the neoclassical theory, the price system of a free market solves the problem. If unemployment exists, a fall in wages helps to restore full employment. If the fault lies in commodity prices being too high, a fall in these brings the economy back to normal. If interest rates are too high, discouraging investment, lower interest rates solve the problem. The return to full employment is automatic and centers around an adjustment in the various prices involved. In a free market, this is assumed to be merely a matter of supply and demand doing their work.

In the Keynesian model of the economy, a recession is caused by a low level of investment resulting from poor profit expectations. If the recession is severe enough, a fall in interest rates is inadequate for offsetting low or negative profit expectations. In financial jargon, the marginal efficiency of capital would be too low to generate an upturn. Lower wages would not help, because that would merely lower the demand for goods and services even more. Keynes came to the conclusion that the marginal efficiency of capital does not respond to market forces (prices) and requires something outside the market (fiscal policy) to generate full employment when the economy is in a serious recession. (Fiscal policy is defined as the strategic use of the federal budget—taxes and government spending—to influence demand in the economy.)

The acceptance of fiscal policy put an end to the doctrine of laissez-faire because the balanced budget is a necessary part of that doctrine. If all economic matters could be left to the private sector, and if the market mechanism could be depended on to restore full employment, there would be no reason for the government budget ever to be unbalanced. An unbalanced budget was regarded as undesirable by the classical economists because they believed it would prevent the invisible hand from doing its job. A government deficit in the classical model would prevent the laws of the market from functioning properly.

Keynes was not discouraged by the discovery that the classical model erred in regard to full employment. He believed that the capitalist system could be saved with fiscal policy. This was tantamount to saying that sometimes an unbalanced budget is better than a balanced one.

Keynes reasoned that a depression represented idle resources, both human and physical. This he attributed to inadequate demand resulting from declining profit expectations. He pointed out that those causes were outside the market mechanism and, hence, the market was helpless in dealing with the problem. He was nevertheless optimistic, because he believed that public investment was a good enough substitute for private investment when the latter was inadequate for full employment.

A tolerance for federal deficits did not originate with the *General Theory*. The Civil War and World War I were partly financed with debt, and by the time Herbert Hoover left the presidency in 1933, the U.S. public debt was about $20 billion, nearly 40 percent of the Gross National Product.

Although the idea of government borrowing is probably as old as government, the concept of using the public debt as an instrument of economic policy was popularized by Keynes. He recommended that the government use fiscal policy (that is, its budget) to help stabilize income and employment. If the economy suffers from unemployment, a tax cut might stimulate the economy by inducing more spending. Since the income tax was almost negligible in the early 1930s when Keynes wrote his *General Theory*, he relied more heavily upon changes in government spending to stimulate the economy. An increase in such expenditures financed by a deficit has an expansionary effect (since by increasing the public's ability to buy goods and services, demand is raised). In any case, the more serious the depression, the stronger the fiscal measures have to be. Increased public investment was, in his view, more potent than a tax cut.

Keynes did not regard a federal deficit as undesirable as long as its function was to put idle resources back to work. He believed that the income generated from public investment would be several times as large as the initial deficit and that the latter would more than justify itself as the increase in income resulting from it would generate enough new tax receipts to retire the debt.

As it turned out, it was war and armament expenditures, and not Keynesian full-employment fiscal policy, that was ultimately responsible for the largest part of this debt. President Franklin D. Roosevelt's fiscal policies, designed to combat unemployment, added $20 billion to the national debt between 1933 and 1941. These policies helped to reduce unemployment from over 25 percent in 1933 to a little over 10 percent in 1941. World War II was so expensive that it was politically impossible to finance it with tax revenues alone. As a result, the national debt rose from $40 billion in 1941 to over $200 billion by the end of the war, four years later.

Like the invisible hand, the unbalanced budget came to be relied upon as an economic wonder drug. Unlike the invisible hand, however, the unbalanced budget was not managed by the laws of nature, but by the discretionary policies of mere mortals. This reflected an important philosophical transition from a reliance on sacred economic "laws" to a reliance on a far less sacred body of men and women who made and executed economic policy. To the faithful followers of Adam Smith, this was, secularly speaking, the ultimate blasphemy.

The belief of Keynes and some prominent Keynesians that a deficit created by fiscal policy during a recession can be repaid by additional taxes generated by a full-employment economy was never actually tested. World War II, the Korean War, the Vietnam War and a prolonged Cold War have made it impossible to apply a fiscal policy in which recession deficits are neutralized by full-employment surpluses.

The *General Theory* suffers from some of the same oversimplifications that have made classical economics all but obsolete. The structure of the economy and the market, as well as all other human factors and social relationships, are exempt from the analysis, which is supposed to identify the causes of such economic maladies as inflation and unemployment. As a result, the policies that traditional and Keynesian economists have produced to deal with these maladies suffer from serious shortcomings.

Keynes saw the flaws in the classical doctrine, but he was a faithful believer in the capitalist system. He did not question the utopian dream, but he was convinced that it could not survive without the help of government. How much of the utopian dream of the classical economists and the utilitarian philosophers survived the two-hundredth anniversary of *The Wealth of Nations* (1976)? One-third of the population of the world is attempting economic development via an entirely different route. Russia and China have chosen the communist path, bypassing the capitalist stage that was a necessary prerequisite to communism according to the Marxian explanation of history. (Actually, neither the Soviet Union nor China has communism as defined by Marx. They have forms of socialism they refer to as communism.) Many of the Third World Nations, constituting about half of the world's population, are taking a hard look at both the socialist and the capitalist countries. The course they will ultimately choose is not yet predictable.

How has the utopian dream fared in the capitalist nations experiencing considerable economic development? In the previous pages, we have seen that corporate concentration and powerful labor unions have radically changed the blueprint for laissez-faire. Economic unilateralism, imperialism, and war have altered the course of free trade that the classical economists regarded as a prerequisite for peace and prosperity. Was the utopian dream pushed off course by evil and greedy people and nations, or is there another explanation? To the faithful, change is always regarded as a sign of weakness and an unwillingness to make the necessary sacrifices for the dream that gave life to the past. The answer to this question is important because without it, the past does not throw light upon the future.

Greed was indeed a factor in the transition from laissez-faire to big corporate capitalism. It was science and technology, however, aided by greed, that made possible the leap from the capitalism of Adam Smith to the capitalism of John D. Rockefeller.

4

The Reign of
Corporate Capitalism

The Industrial Revolution Outgrows the House
That Adam Smith Built

Faith can have awesome consequences. The true believers in the classical free market regard the changes, which have all but eliminated it, as "deviations" that are not critical enough to require basic alterations in assumptions and conclusions. As a result, economic policies designed to correct economic problems frequently have little or no effect and sometimes they make the problems worse.

The classical market is more than a place where buyers and sellers or borrowers and lenders meet and transact their business. Its unique quality is its assumed ability to make automatic adjustments. This rests on two assumptions. First, no component of the market, such as a buyer or a seller or a combination of buyers and sellers, is big enough or powerful enough to exert any arbitrary influence on the market. If such influences are present, the market cannot make the automatic adjustments necessary for preventing economic breakdowns. The second assumption is that all the factors that create such problems as unemployment and inflation respond to the corrective mechanism of the market. If either of these conditions is not met, the market mechanism cannot automatically restore "normal" conditions where problems exist.

One of Keynes' important contributions in his *General Theory of Employment, Income and Money* is his discovery that the marginal efficiency of capital (profit expectations) does not respond to the corrective forces of the market. This challenged the necessary conditions for laissez-faire.

In the house that Adam Smith built—the free-market economy—price is relied on to allocate and distribute resources efficiently. Everything that matters in an economic sense is subject to market prices. Labor, which is regarded as an input, responds to its price, called wages. Credit responds to a price called interest, and entrepreneurship responds to profit, which is its special price. Land also has its own price, called economic rent. These prices are established by the laws of supply and demand. The market price is the only price at which the quantity that is offered for sale is equal to the quantity that buyers are willing to purchase. At this equilibrium price, buyers and sellers are satisfied. (In other words, when supply equals demand so that the market is stable, the point of equilibrium has been reached.)

If all economic factors are functions of the market as Adam Smith believed, then it follows that all disturbances can be corrected by the price mechanism. Markets must not be "planned" by people; they must be left to the laws of nature or the unseen hand. If markets are planned or controlled to any significant extent, then the so-called corrective forces of the market cannot work. The difference between the free market and planned market is not one of degree; it is a matter of two distinctly different entities. The free market, as envisaged by the classical economists, possesses a self-corrective mechanism, but the planned market does not.

Few economists, if any, would define the market in the United States (or any other major industrial nation) as a free market in the sense that it actually performs automatically the corrective adjustments expected of it in the classical doctrine. The major part of a modern economy consists of planned markets. The word *planning* is not limited to socialist economics, nor does it simply mean to set goals for the future. Planning in the large corporations has a significant impact on the structure and functions of the market economy.

The bulk of economic activity in the United States is controlled by the so-called Fortune 500 corporations. These corporations account for more than two-thirds of the final goods and services sold in U.S. markets. Most of the basic industries are composed of just a few firms. Steel has six corporate producers; aluminum, three;

copper, three; automobiles, four; and nickel, one. Five major oil companies control the bulk of the processes in oil production and distribution. This type of concentration has existed for some time. Today's conglomerate corporation has extended its control into food, the mass media, and so on.

Advancements in science and technology have made planning a condition of corporate success. Corporate planning out of necessity has to include some control over supply and demand. The modern government, even in a capitalistic private-enterprise economy, is called upon to help insure the conditions of supply and demand that help corporate plans to grow into profitable ventures.

Science and technology have radically altered the process of production in large corporations. Highly specialized managers and technically sophisticated experts have replaced the entrepreneur who once made all the decisions. The time involved from the idea to the blueprint to the sale of a product has been lengthened from a few weeks or months to several years, sometimes ten years or more. The capital required for a sophisticated enterprise has increased from a few thousand or million dollars to billions of dollars. The materials required for many modern products have become far more sophisticated and are often located in other countries. The supply of labor for many products can no longer be drawn mainly from semiskilled workers. It must come from specially trained people, whose training must keep pace with changes in technology, which advances at an ever-increasing pace.

The time and capital requirements of a modern high technology enterprise make the free-market mechanism unreliable as a source of supply and demand. With an abundant supply of unskilled or semiskilled labor and conventional raw materials, the price mechanism could be counted on to accommodate the supply requirements of an earlier and simpler economy. This same price mechanism cannot insure the availability of high technology skills and esoteric materials and processes when they are needed. These must be planned for ahead of time, often years in advance. Otherwise, the high technology timetable becomes jammed, which increases the risk of failure.

In many industries, new products and innovative changes require very large capital expenditures, often billions of dollars over a five- or ten-year period. The capital market, which has provided the capital for our industries, has paved the way for corporate expansion. It was a necessary adjustment of the Industrial and Technological Revolutions.

Another unrealistic aspect of the classical free market is almost complete reliance on natural law as the force behind all economic decisions. So far as the economy is concerned, the state is given a neutral role. Power is of no significance in the laissez-faire model because it is assumed to be controlled by the unseen hand. In spite of all the historical evidence to the contrary, the classical economists assumed that wealth could be created without the emergence of power. They regarded people as economic beings and not as political ones; hence the term *economic man*.

The classical economists were not naive. They recognized the existence of such human drives as power, fame, wealth, and security. In their system, however, these drives were controlled by the natural laws of the market. Adam Smith believed, for example, that although each producer might like to charge as high a price as possible, competition of the pure market would prevent people from charging more than the market price, and self-interest would prevent them from charging less. This reflected the intellectualization of an ideology rather than an observation of the real world.

In such an economy, all decisions are left to the market: what should be produced, how much should be produced by each firm and industry, and the pricing of all outputs and inputs. All decisions are assumed to be arrived at democratically by a large number of buyers and sellers who make up supply and demand. Profit, too, is arrived at in this way and could, therefore, never be excessive except in the short run.[1]

Since social justice, according to the classical economists, is achieved automatically by the natural laws of the market, the government has no place in the economy. Its functions are limited largely to national security, both internal and external, and to the protection of life and property.

The free market, unimpeded by public authority, as well as by private concentration of power, is regarded as a natural condition best suited to maximizing the use of scarce resources. The concentration of economic power is viewed as economic lawlessness rather than the result of technological and social evolution. This belief is reflected in the antitrust laws enacted to protect the free market from the consequences of economic concentration. Since 1890, when the first antitrust law (the Sherman Antitrust Act) was enacted in the United States, economic concentration has greatly increased. In most of the major industries, competition has resulted in an attrition of firms until the number left was small enough for survival. The antitrust laws, being designed to deal with lawlessness rather than technological evolution, could not prevent this.

The Supreme Court of the United States has not yet discovered how to prevent the development and growth of monopoly. This is demonstrated in a 1920 decision involving the United States Steel Corporation. In its decision, the Court laid down the opinion that "size alone is no sin." Actually the Court came to grips with reality, namely that law cannot be used to control size, which is a matter of technology and economics. Unfortunately, size is also a major factor in economic power. The classical economists abstracted from power by assuming smallness of the economic unit. When firms became big, the court was forced to assume that bigness does not necessarily lead to economic power. This is quite an assumption, but the Court saw no other alternative. Although the AT&T decision appears to contradict this, the fact is that economic concentration is greater than ever, aided as it is by the merger and acquisition movement.

The philosophers of laissez-faire, who saw in their doctrine the cradle of freedom, looked upon the state as a threat to their system. This is understandable, since in the eighteenth and early nineteenth centuries, the firm was still relatively small and powerless compared to its later versions spawned by the Industrial Revolution. The state, and before that the church, had been wielders of arbitrary and ruthless power, which had finally been tamed by the people who fought to free the market.

The Industrial Revolution and now the Technological Revolution have changed all that. The global corporation bears little resemblance to the mill or the butcher shop that served as the production model for laissez-faire. Today's corporation is still privately owned, but there the resemblance ends. Its source of economic power is accumulated in part from tax write-offs, direct subsidies, and grants for research and development, which represent social (not private) capital. The state has once more become an important part of the economy! It has done this in two ways: through the creation of social capital and through its fiscal policies designed to stabilize demand. Since both functions are vital to the success of the U.S. economy, it is highly unlikely that they will be abandoned in the interest of laissez-faire.

It is important to understand that laissez-faire came to an end not as a result of government intervention but rather as a result of changes that ultimately created global corporations and privately planned markets. Even if the government abandoned its economic responsibilities, laissez-faire would not come back, and the U.S. sector of the global corporate economy would be greatly weakened.

Even the most ardent supporters of laissez-faire cannot escape the fact that the classical model bears little resemblance to actual experience. It was the emergence of power that made the difference between fact and fancy—power embodied in the firm, in labor unions, and in government. The problems that arose with economic development encouraged the rise of power. Technology, which gave rise to bigness, made competition an obstacle to growth and security. Firms that were able to used power to tame competition.

Individual workers saw themselves at a great disadvantage vis-à-vis the comparatively powerful employer. This gave rise to labor unions, which in turn became powerful. War, poverty, unemployment, and the need to protect the environment enlarged the scope and power of the government.

Political and economic organizations cannot be properly perceived unless the concept of power in its various forms is given its rightful place in social dynamics. Power is not an externality to be dismantled at will; it is inherent in the human character and reflected in all social institutions. It cannot be eliminated; it can only be replaced or altered. It can, however, be organized to serve a socially desirable purpose or a socially destructive one. Laissez-faire, by ignoring the role of power in social dynamics, has left this outcome to chance.

The failure to recognize the inevitable development of uncontrolled and unaccountable power in the economic decision-making process is only one of the major shortcomings of the traditional theory of capitalism. Another is the unsupported assumption that all economic variables or elements are responsive to the laws of the market.

Much of what constitutes today's economy is not responsive to the corrective features of the market mechanism. One example, profit expectations, is beyond the control of any market. It is subject to the uncertainties of the world in which we live as well as to the arbitrary decision of powerful firms. Other examples are the result of corporate planning. Corporations, with the help of government, attempt to reduce the insecurity of supply and demand as a condition of investing the enormous amounts of money required by modern high technology enterprise. The government attempts to stabilize conditions of supply through diplomatic and military strategy. It attempts to stabilize conditions of demand through fiscal policy.

Not least of the deficiencies of the traditional market system is its failure to build into economic theory and policy human needs of a noneconomic nature. Such needs as self-esteem, income security, and work satisfaction are given no place in the process of economic optimization. As a result, traditional economic theories and policies do not begin to play a useful role in the solution of painful economic and social problems.

The Rise of the Global Corporation—The Firm Outgrows the Nation

> The mere spot that merchants stand on does not constitute so strong an attachment as that from which they draw their gain.
> —Thomas Jefferson

The modern corporation has not only outgrown the free-market mechanism; it has also outgrown its political counterpart, the national government. The failure to create an international organization built on a foundation of law—and capable of enforcing its laws—reflects on our inability to match the great advances in science and technology with necessary changes in the political and social structures. As a result, the Nuclear Age and Space Age have become a threat instead of a blessing.

During the nineteenth century, U.S. political development was closely linked to industrial development. As the markets and operations of the new corporations extended beyond state boundaries across the nation, some of the powers of the states were transferred to the national government. During the Civil War a national banking system was created. As the railroads covered the nation, domestic trade became a matter of national concern and the Interstate Commerce Act was passed. The growth of corporate enterprise also became a matter of national concern and the Sherman Antitrust Act was passed. In 1913, the Federal Reserve System, which laid the foundation for a national monetary policy, was created. The evolution of national government reflects the political accommodation of economic change.

Just as the latter half of the nineteenth century saw the development of the national corporation, so the latter half of the twentieth century is witnessing the rapid evolution of the global corporation. This type of corporation is spreading all over the world through subsidiaries; it is not totally bound by the laws of the countries in which it is domiciled because it can escape them by moving part or all of its operations elsewhere. Its chief objectives are profits and greater control over its markets. It does not regard national boundaries as significant to its operations and investments.

A global corporation locates its operations in places convenient to resources and markets. It pays special attention, however, to wage rates, labor laws, tax laws, environmental laws, safety laws, and so forth. As a result, the laws a nation enacts may cause it to lose investment and employment, because domestic companies may prefer to operate or invest elsewhere. In the global economy, the corporation chooses the country where it wants to locate and produce. This may create serious dislocations in the country in which the headquarters are situated, but as Professor Charles Kindleberger (a leading U.S. authority on the international economy) states: "The international corporation has no country to which it owes more loyalty than to any other."[2]

The development of the oligopolistic market[3] and, more recently, the emergence of global enterprises have profoundly changed the anatomy of capitalism. Oligopoly was the natural result of entrepreneurs' efforts to shield their enterprises from the threat price competition posed to growth and survival. The crusaders for the free market eventually realized the dangers of a market that was "too" free. The Rockefellers, Carnegies, and Vanderbilts and their investment bankers soon realized the great benefit of a market dominated by them. As corporations grew in size, they found that they could increase their profits by ignoring national boundaries and by producing wherever it was cheapest to do so. This one fact alone profoundly changed the conditions on which the capitalist system was built.

It is not at all surprising, of course, that the national corporation is giving way to the global corporation in much the same way that the entrepreneurial enterprises gave way to the national corporation, and for the same reasons: profits and market shares subject to an ever-advancing technology. For many corporations, the rate of profit is higher from foreign operations—in some instances, two to three times as much—as from domestic operations.

As the poet Shelley wrote: "Nought may endure but mutability." The whole structure of international trade has been profoundly altered by the rise of the global corporation. An increasing volume of U.S. exports and imports are bought and sold by foreign subsidiaries of U.S. global corporations. It is likely that this figure will become even larger as technology spreads. Economists and politicians have barely begun to examine the impact this development will have on the future of the U.S. economy. Certainly nothing is being planned to cope with such changes.

Why has the global corporation made the economic significance of national boundaries obsolete? It looks at the entire world, without boundaries, in its effort to optimize resources and profits. Being mobile, it is not restricted by the laws of any nation. It can escape unfavorable laws by locating its operations in a nation where laws are more favorable to its objective. Consequently, no nation can afford to plan its future without regard to the decisions of the global corporation, and this is likely to influence profoundly the laws and economic conditions of all nations.

U.S. companies that have shifted large parts of their operations to other parts of the world are too numerous to mention. In all cases, the effect has been a reduction in the number of U.S. employees in these firms. General Instruments, for example, cut its U.S. payroll by thousands of employees and increased the number of its Taiwanese employees by an even larger number. This makes economic sense, but it creates serious problems for the internal conditions of a nation.[4]

A world without borders, which was part of the utopian dream, is not as popular with some groups as it is with global corporations. Labor unions obviously see the global corporation as a threat to their bargaining power. They regard global policies as unfair because the American worker is at a disadvantage competing with cheap foreign labor. The global corporation has increased its mobility by duplicating processes in different countries so that operations can be shifted with ease.

Many underdeveloped countries regard the coming of the global corporations with skepticism because they know they cannot control it. The most notorious example of global power was the part ITT played in overthrowing the government of Salvador Allende Gossens in Chile. Even in the most industrialized nations of the world the global corporation exerts great power on the body politic, and this is frequently reflected in the foreign policies of such nations. U.S. policy in regard to Central America and the Middle East reflects the interests of U.S. global corporations.

Although nationalism may make little economic sense, the global corporation as it exists today is not a substitute for government, because it is accountable to no one except itself. What is challenged by the global corporation in its present form is not merely nationalism, but the whole concept of democratic government.

Exit: The Heroic Age of Capitalism
Enter: The Age of the Corporate Society

The crusaders for a market free from the church and the state—people who laid the foundation for capitalism—dramatized and glorified the economic freedom of the individual. Those whose genius harnessed the Industrial Revolution under the banner of capitalism included such men as John D. Rockefeller, Cornelius Vanderbilt, Andrew Carnegie, J.P. Morgan, Andrew Mellon, Thomas Hill, Henry Ford, and a few dozen others. They were the heroes of the Industrial Revolution.

Work, duty, and acquisition were given the status and the dignity of a religious faith. Max Weber called this new "morality" the spirit of capitalism.[5] It provided the spark that led the inventions of the Industrial Revolution to become the foundations of the great industries of modern times.

Capitalism, as it advanced through the nineteenth century, did not reflect the kind of freedom envisaged by the early economic philosophers because most workers toiled under miserable conditions and were exploited by their employers. Yet the freedom that did exist was essential to economic growth. The relatively few who possessed the drive, the energy, the intellectual requirements, and Weber's spirit of capitalism could generally become entrepreneurs. The ablest or the most determined of these became the leaders of the newly emerging enterprises. The moral value system given birth by the rapidly growing Protestantism was a vital ally of the Industrial Revolution. Hard work and thrift became the road to salvation, and the successful entrepreneur challenged the saints as a role model.

The economic freedom enjoyed by the entrepreneurs, and essential to their success, was academic for the vast majority of workers, who had as much chance of becoming entrepreneurs as they did concert pianists. Freedom is like a flower. It does not thrive equally well under all conditions. The economic freedom of the classical economists favored those who possessed the special attributes of the successful entrepreneur in much the same way that honor and glory in the Colosseum of ancient Rome came to those who possessed the special skills of the gladiator.

The economic freedom that helped to create powerful entrepreneurs spilled over into the political arena. The British Parliament and the U.S. Congress during the nineteenth century and the first third of the twentieth century were largely made up of men who were put into positions of power by the leaders of business and finance. The exceptions were few during this period in which laissez-faire dominated the U.S. and British economy. Women, workers, and certain ethnic minorities exercised neither political nor economic power and had no direct representation in the halls of Parliament or Congress.

In the light of the British and U.S. experience of the nineteenth century (during which time laissez-faire enjoyed its greatest triumph), it is less than clear how one prominent student of economic freedom, Professor Milton Friedman, reached some of his conclusions. He asserts: "The kind of economic organization that provides economic freedom directly, namely competitive capitalism, also promotes political freedom because it separates economic power from political power and in this way enables one to offset the other."[6] The facts were exactly the opposite. Those who possessed economic power were heard loud and clear in the political sector; those who lacked it remained voiceless.

The freedom that enabled the entrepreneurs to advance their own interests did, in the end, lead to considerable economic growth. It can be praised for that, but it cannot be claimed that it enabled people to find the greatest good through the pursuit of their own interests. The entrepreneurs used their political power to make sure that the workers could not pursue their interests if they conflicted with the profitability of the firm. It can be argued that such a policy was necessary for economic growth, but it cannot be argued that economic freedom gave all people a reasonable chance in their pursuit of happiness during the age of laissez-faire.

In spite of the injustices and human misery produced by nineteenth-century economic development, the successful entrepreneurs emerged as its heroes. They were often feared and frequently condemned, but they became the role models of American youth and the reality of the American dream.

Just as the Industrial Revolution created the entrepreneurs the Technological Revolution gave rise to a new type of business leader—the manager of large enterprises. Many small, new, technologically oriented firms, however, continue to perform vitally important entrepreneurial functions in the modern global economy. They are frequently the innovators and creators of new ideas. The original type of entrepreneur still functions there. They are able to assume risks far costlier for the large corporation with an enormous overhead and a complex organization than for the small firm with less overhead and a simpler organization. If the small, innovative firm succeeds, it sometimes grows into a large corporation. More often, however, it merges with existing firms in what has become a conglomerate merger movement. Entrepreneurial capitalism today, therefore, operates chiefly on the *frontier* of economic activity and in industries where the small firm is still economically feasible.

Although the global corporation bears no resemblance to the "pin factory" of Adam Smith or the "representative firm" of the later neoclassical economists, global corporate managers resemble the nineteenth-century entrepreneurs in that they possess drive, energy, intelligence, and determination; they see salvation in the spirit of capitalism. At that point the similarities end.

The great entrepreneurs were, on the whole, nationalist in their outlook. The global managers have a distinct international outlook and regard national sovereignty, where it affects their operations, as an undesirable interference. As a matter of fact, much of the opposition to government is initiated or supported by the global corporation, which regards all forms of national regulation as an obstacle to its development. Like the entrepreneurs, the global managers do not hesitate to solicit national military power when foreign nations threaten their interests.

Whereas the willingness to take financial risk is an absolute requirement for the entrepreneur, what is required of the global corporate manager is highly developed organizational skills. The financial risks are taken by the corporation, as the corporate managers usually own a negligible part of the corporate equity.

The entrepreneurs of old sank or swam with their "ships." The corporate managers can sink while the ship is still very much afloat. By the same token, they can survive a sinking ship by taking command of a new one. How is it possible for the corporate manager to take control without the benefit of majority ownership?

The answer lies partly in the fact that ownership is widely dispersed and partly in the fact that the knowledge and information required to operate a large corporation, especially a global one, are concentrated in relatively few individuals. As John Kenneth Galbraith states: "The one thing worse than the loss of power by the small or passive stockholders would be its uninformed exercise."[7]

In the management of a large corporation, the significant factor is not ownership but control. Perhaps the most interesting example of this fact is found in the economy of the Soviet Union. The Soviet constitution explicitly refers to the means of production as being *owned* by all the people. It is obvious that very few Soviet citizens have a voice in the actual control. Scholars will undoubtedly maintain that capitalist concepts of ownership differ from the Soviets. It should be obvious, however, that millions of small U.S. stockholders have no more control in the affairs of large corporations through their ownership functions than the average Soviet citizen has in the Soviet economy.

Control of the large U.S. corporation or large Soviet enterprise is generally in the hands of a small group. This group may change from time to time, but the change is not initiated by the average Soviet citizen or the average American stockholder. This does not mean there is no difference between the U.S. and the Soviet systems. There are important differences. The argument here is simply that control no longer necessarily originates from ownership in the United States, and it never has originated from ownership in the Soviet Union.

The great entrepreneur who dominated the heroic age of capitalism can be compared to the male *Apis mellifera* (the mythological bull) who "accomplishes his act of conception at the price of his own extinction. . . . The vital requirement is that both technology and planning remain relatively simple—or limited."[8]

Why has the Technological Revolution replaced the great entrepreneurs with corporate managers? The complexities of a modern enterprise depend on highly organized cooperation. The rugged individualism of a Henry Ford, which was eminently suitable when technology and materials were far more simple, is an obstacle in the global corporation.

The change that has replaced the great entrepreneurs with the powerful corporate managers is a change from the power of capital (ownership) to the power of organized knowledge and judgment. In the modern business enterprise, cooperation is not only desirable—it is essential. The same thing is true of society in general and of government in particular.

There is much confusion about the transition from the classical utopia to the modern global economy. There are still important debates carried on in defense of the individual, who is portrayed as a victim of collectivization. It is important that the essence of this transition be clearly understood. The utilitarians and the classical economists saw their utopia as a system in which power had no place. In regard to power, all individuals were conceived to be somehow equal. This utopian system was quickly transformed into the heroic age of capitalism in which the rugged individualism of the great entrepreneurs dominated. This in turn gave way to the global economy in which organized cooperation is essential for economic success.

The Changing Character of the Class Struggle

During the heroic age of capitalism, when the ownership of capital formed the basis for economic control, the capitalist had power over the worker, because without capital the worker could not work. The owners of capital somehow felt that the worker owed them allegiance, because, after all, it was their capital that enabled the worker to work and to eat. The necessity for eating and other human needs thus became the basis for the class struggle. The owners of capital and the workers had different ideas about what the workers needed in order to survive. In the early period of capitalism, the class struggle was romanticized by the fact that those who owned and controlled the capital were, like the workers, real people. They could see each other and hate each other, if they were so inclined. When the capitalist had been replaced by the impersonal corporation, whom could the worker blame?

Has the class struggle become an antiquity that belongs to the heroic age of capitalism? Probably, because the type of exploitation that Marx regarded as the heart of the class struggle is characteristic of the early stages of economic development. It is not limited to capitalism, although the form this exploitation took in Britain during the nineteenth century was undoubtedly greatly influenced by the structure of British capitalism. In the United States, the form and consequences of that exploitation were different. The Western American frontier gave the worker an alternative, and American society was much less rigidly structured than British society.

Out of the class struggle of the nineteenth century, which produced violent clashes between the worker and the capitalist employer, grew the labor-union movement. Its philosophy and structure had their origins in the class struggle. The labor union, as it gained strength, gave the worker a more equal voice with the employer. Actually, until the 1930s, only the craft union had any influence on employer–labor relations in the United States.[9] Even this influence was fought by the employers, who in the nineteenth century managed to get anticombination acts passed, greatly limiting the power and influence of the craft union.

The Great Depression of the 1930s brought the class struggle to a head in the United States with the creation of unions that organized the industrial worker.[10] The union movement gained strength for several decades and reached its peak during the Kennedy and Johnson administrations. Since then, both union membership and power have been on the decline.

The labor unions were to fight for a larger share of the pie and to improve the conditions under which the worker labored. The more ruthless the employer, the more important unions became.

In the past few decades, the makeup of the labor force has changed as a result of technological progress and the desire of management to reduce its dependence on labor. The percentage of white-collar workers has steadily increased since the postwar period, while the percentage of blue-collar workers has significantly decreased. A few decades ago, the blue-collar worker dominated the labor scene. Today, the white-collar worker makes up the largest share of the labor market.

The evolution of industrial and technological development was quite naturally accompanied by the evolution of the individual and the individual's social relationships and organization. The impact of such changes is very great. They affect values, attitudes, motivation, and goals—a fact that economists have failed adequately to take into consideration. As a result, conventional economic theory is still based on the oversimplified model of the "economic man" of the utopian dreams of the eighteenth and nineteenth centuries.

Several major changes in the U.S. economy have radically altered the so-called class struggle and are forcing labor unions to play a new role. Since the Great Depression, the government has been brought into the economy to help stabilize aggregate demand as a means of controlling unemployment. As the government began to regard itself responsible in the fight against unemployment, unions lost some of their importance as the guardian angels of jobs.

One of the functions of unions is to force employers to increase the wages of the workers periodically. The labor union provides workers with a countervailing power in their battle for higher wages. The workers believing that they and their employers have opposite interests is part of the class struggle.

The modern corporation is anxious to live in peace with labor as part of its search for security. It does not want to be party to a class struggle that would undermine its security. It tries to meet reasonable demands of labor even where this may lead to somewhat lower profits or higher prices. The ability to raise prices by means of monopolistic practices has had a dampening effect on the class struggle, because workers are usually more sensitive to the wages they receive than the prices they pay to sustain themselves—unless inflation becomes excessive. The corporations' desire for a peaceful relationship with labor has reduced the role of the union as a countervailing power. The United States' loss of economic supremacy has also had a dampening effect on union power.

Although loyalty to the union is still a factor in organized labor, the mature corporation also expects its employees to be loyal, and it uses the corporate technostructure and the reward system to encourage loyalty. The worker in a mature corporation becomes part of the technostructure and receives identity from it. This is the case in such countries as Japan, but is only the beginning of a trend in the United States.

Participatory management, which identifies the worker as an active part of the decision-making process is beginning to be more seriously considered, and this is likely to become a major factor in the elimination of the class struggle. The class struggle was correctly perceived by Marx in the context of his time. Workers today face a new kind of struggle—their role and identity in an increasingly impersonal technostructure. Their enemy in the future will not be the capitalist, but such alien concepts as working robots at least in the short run.

5
The Creation of Poverty through the Wasteful Use of Human Wealth

Inflation—A Triumph of Folly and Conflict

We have seen that capitalism, like all living things and institutions, has evolved to such an extent in the past two hundred years that it resembles its classical models no more than a moth does a butterfly. Unfortunately, today's economic theories do not yet reflect these structural changes, so that most economists still prescribe the same remedies as in the past—except in larger doses or in the form of a new drug, such as Keynesian fiscal policy. Inflation, unemployment, and underemployment in their modern forms are three economic illnesses that are used to demonstrate how problems remain unsolved because they are treated with obsolete remedies.

Milton Friedman, one of today's heirs apparent of the classical economists, believes that all inflation is caused by too much money chasing too few goods.[1] He blames inflation on a discretionary monetary policy that allows the money supply to fluctuate with changes in the demand for credit.

The demand for credit originates in the various sectors of the economy. Consumers purchase homes, cars, furniture, and countless other items for which they cannot or choose not to pay out of current income. The business sector, which borrows for operating and expansion purposes and more recently for a wave of takeover schemes and speculative investments, is a large user of credit.

Other major users of credit are the public sector and the foreign sector. All levels of government—local, state, and federal—are substantial users of credit. They borrow to finance schools, hospitals, roads, transfer payments, rearmament, wars, and numerous other useful or useless projects. The foreign sector borrows to finance all or part of its excess imports, if any, over its exports. In recent years, the unprecedented U.S. foreign trade deficits were financed with loans and investments from abroad.

The demand for credit has deep roots in the history and culture of a nation and the value system these produce. It is not merely a matter of whims that can be turned on and off.

In the light of this, it is strange that Professor Friedman and other modern classical economists have made the money supply the primary cause of inflation. They attempt to support their claims by pointing out that there is a high degree of correlation between increases in the money supply and increases in the price level. The monetarists do not seem to distinguish between a high degree of correlation and a causal relationship. Professor Friedman must believe that if the money supply had been held to a constant rate, the abnormal demand for credit on the part of the federal government would have disappeared.

It is doubtful that President Reagan's inflexible commitment to tax cuts and a military buildup would have been abandoned even if the Federal Reserve had attempted to hold the money supply to a constant rate of growth. Increases in the supply *shrank* while the federal demand for credit and the resultant budget deficits soared to record heights in 1981 and 1982. This kept interest rates extremely high and led to the worst recession since the Great Depression of the 1930s. The huge and unprecedented federal-budget deficits would have led to a serious inflation after 1982 if it had not been for a number of timely and fortuitous circumstances.

What happened had little to do with Federal Reserve or White House policy in regard to the money supply. The OPEC price structure collapsed, the agricultural sector experienced a serious depression, and an overvalued dollar led to artificially low import prices. The huge inflow of foreign savings, together with these other developments, permitted the government to finance deficits without an inflation. In fact, the antiinflationary influences of these four occurrences allowed inflation to decline in spite of the record-break-ing deficits and a significant step-up in the money supply after 1982, which reached an annual growth rate of 16 percent in 1986.

Some of the most serious and devastating inflations in history have resulted from armaments races, wars, and other forms of violent conflicts between nations or empires. The armaments race between the United States and the Soviet Union of the 1980s has increased the national debt by 150 percent, or from $1,000 billion to $2,500 billion from 1980 to 1988. The international oil crisis of the 1970s and the armaments race of the 1980s together have increased the world money supply sixfold between 1970 and 1987. At the same time, the supply of Eurodollars has increased from $90 billion in 1970 to over $2,000 billion in 1987. This reflects a worldwide money or liquidity explosion, resulting in large part from the armaments race, the oil crisis, and the merger and acquisition movement.

Although wars and international conflicts have produced serious inflations, there are other structural causes of inflation. It is not merely a matter of too much money chasing too few goods, which is usually a symptom rather than a cause of inflation.

The founders of the utopian free-market system did not foresee in the late eighteenth and early nineteenth centuries the changes in technology that would someday replace this free-market system in a dominant part of the economy with a system in which large firms take control over the market mechanism. This shift began in the last part of the nineteenth century; since then, corporate concentration has taken place at a steadily increasing pace. The difference between an industry in which the firm has no control over prices and one in which the firm administers prices is one of the factors that can produce inflation.

The big corporations bought labor peace with their ability to shift higher labor costs to the consumer through the price mechanism. In the free-market economy, this cannot be done. The higher labor costs have to be paid for through lower profits. If wage demands exceed increases in productivity some firms will be forced to leave the industry.

Shifting the increased labor costs to the consumer via the price mechanism is one more factor that creates inflation. Another cost that can be passed on to the consumer by oligopolistic firms is a higher cost of borrowing resulting from a tight money policy designed to combat inflation. It is ironic that the process designed by the neoclassical economists to combat inflation (i.e., stringent monetary policy and high interest rates) should result in higher interest costs to be passed on to the consumer through the price mechanism, thus adding to the inflation.

Monetary policy designed to combat inflation has other interesting results. The smaller sector of the economy in which the free market is working, and which is not dominated by large oligopolistic firms, is adversely affected by high interest rates because such firms cannot shift higher interest costs to the consumer via the price mechanism. This sector takes the brunt of the effects of an antiinflationary monetary policy, and many smaller firms are lost during periods of tight money. This increases industrial concentration, which further reduces the effectiveness of monetary policy.

Other developments have made the economy inherently inflationary. The treatment of environmental protection as a private cost instead of a social good gives a new twist to inflation. In this case, prices are rising, but only because we are adding a new product—environmental protection—to an existing product (a car, for example). Suppose we add a $1,000 gadget to a car in order to protect the environment from pollution; as it now stands, this raises the price of the car by $1,000. Actually, the gadget is another commodity vital to the interest of the public. Strictly speaking, it is not a matter of inflation, although the cost of living is increased. To keep such social benefits as environmental protection from raising prices, one must treat them either as separate commodities purchased directly by the consumer or as social goods paid for out of taxes. In either case, the consumer pays directly or indirectly.

The private sector saves both voluntarily and involuntarily. About 20 percent of such savings comes from the household sector, and this is in every sense voluntary saving. The remainder comes from the business sector or from abroad. Corporations like to have control over as much of their investment funds as possible rather than depend on the uncertainties of the capital markets. They accomplish this by pursuing a price policy that enables them to accumulate internal cash flow. How do they get these funds? Through the price mechanism. Such corporations could probably sell their products at lower prices if they financed all their capital expenditures through the sale of stocks, because their expansion would be more closely correlated to the actual demand for their product as judged by the capital markets.

Although consumers provide the funds that make up the internal cash flow for corporate investment, they do not do so voluntarily. In fact, consumers are not even conscious of the fact that they are doing so. The corporation that has control over its prices can in this way force the buyer to supply its capital requirements in the form of retained earnings.

The global corporate economy, which neither the classical economists nor Karl Marx foresaw clearly in the development of their theories, has produced a structural mobility of money that can be very inflationary. Eurodollars and petrodollars are owned or held by large global banks and corporations outside the United States. They are also owned by the foreign branches or subsidiaries of large U.S. corporations. They may be dollar deposits in foreign branches of U.S. banks attracted by relatively high interest rates. They may be OPEC dollar deposits in banks outside the United States. In whatever way they are accumulated, they represent a large pool of international liquidity owned by the global corporation or global bank that can be moved easily from nation to nation and currency to currency.

Although international liquidity is desirable and necessary in international trade, it can be and has been inflationary when the private interests of the global owners and holders of Eurodollars and petrodollars clash with the public policies of national governments. This happened most visibly in 1968–69 in the United States when the inflow of Eurodollars neutralized antiinflationary policies of the Federal Reserve. It also happened about the same time in Germany when higher interest rates resulting from German monetary policy designed to *combat* inflation caused an inflow of Eurodollars that *added* to the inflation.

Another example of market control and one more factor in inflation is the global corporation's use of "transfer pricing" (the location of corporate operations in various parts of the world so that profits can be maximized by taking advantage of tax differentials). The purpose of transfer pricing is to maximize profits and to minimize tax liabilities. A global corporation with a subsidiary located in one country that exports manufactured products and another subsidiary located in another country that imports these products can reduce its tax liabilities if it overprices the products in the country with a relatively high tax rate to reduce its taxable profits, and underprices the products in the country with lower tax rates to increase its taxable profits. This practice contributes to inflation in the country in which the products are overpriced.

The complex and diverse nature of inflation is being recognized by a growing number of economists. However, neither the economics profession nor the U.S. government have been successful in abandoning old solutions that were rarely adequate even when the problem of inflation was much less a structural one than it is today. Inflation today is inherent in the structural complexities of our economic system; it is not merely the result of too much money chasing too few goods. It is, in fact, inherent in all economic systems at the present time.

Inflation affects some sectors of an economy much more than others. It makes the poor even poorer, and it redistributes income unfairly in other ways as well, which makes it a serious political problem. It is not likely that much will be done so long as inflation is not perceived as what it really is—a serious weakness in the structure and behavior within a nation and between nations.

Unemployment—The Treatment of People as an Impersonal Resource

The classical system did not work as smoothly as envisaged by the champions of the pure market. Periodic disturbances came to be expected and this led to the development of a variety of business-cycle theories. They all had one thing in common—the assumption that disturbances are caused by wrong expectations and decisions or by unavoidable bottlenecks. It was thought that the free-market mechanism would make the necessary adjustments. This is philosophically similar to the belief that human illness is caused by excesses and will be cured by the self-correcting abilities of the body and the mind. There is some truth in this belief but the problem lies in what is left unsaid. Bacteria, genetic problems, viruses, and so on are causes of disease that are frequently too powerful for the body to correct automatically. At such times, external remedies must be applied to control the disease.

The same logic applies to business-cycle theories. If it is assumed that all causes of recessions and inflation are "economic excesses" or bottlenecks that the market mechanism can automatically adjust, then no external measures need to be taken. This is the position of the traditional business-cycle theorists. Keynes challenged their views by introducing the concept of inadequate demand caused by something *outside* the self-adjusting market—the marginal efficiency of capital, which, translated, means net profit expectations.[2]

So far as unemployment and recessions are concerned, Keynes' theory is not as revolutionary as it might appear. He saw only one threat to full employment—a declining marginal efficiency of capital. He was not concerned about structural obstacles that deprive the market of its self-equilibrating capacity. As a result, his solutions do not apply to many of the conditions that produce unemployment and recessions.

What are the structural causes of unemployment that make the market ineffective as an adjustment mechanism? In other words, what factors are responsible for the inherent instability of the market?

We should recall that the classical market is described as inherently stable. That is, if aggregate demand declines, the classical market will experience a fall in prices, wages, and interest rates, which will serve to restore demand to a normal level or full-employment equilibrium.

One type of unemployment results from markets in which prices and wages are administered by oligopolistic firms[3] and organized labor unions. The automatic adjustment that governs the classical utopia does not exist in the privately "planned" sector of the economy.

Saving and investment, whose inequality is a factor in both recession and inflation, are subject to different conditions in the free-market economy and the privately planned oligopolistic economy. The classical economists saw a simple relationship between saving and investment that they believed would assure their equality and economic stability. A fall in total demand, they reasoned, leads

to a fall in prices, wages, and interest rates, but does not cause unemployment to any significant extent. As a result of lower incomes,
people save less. Savings are further reduced by falling interest rates,
which stimulate investment. At the same time, falling prices and
interest rates motivate people to consume more.

The classical market as it was conceived by its utopian archi-
tects and as it is still conceived by their modern disciples will, as a
result of all the automatic adjustments in prices, wages, interest
rates, saving, and investment, have no difficulty in making the necessary corrections when aggregate demand is either too high or too
low in relation to aggregate supply. But in today's economy, there
are no automatic adjustments in any of the economic variables such
as wages, prices, interest rates, saving, and investment because of
monopolistic conditions in the private sector and discretionary policies in the public sector. As a result, there are no automatic market
adjustments when aggregate demand is inadequate in relation to
aggregate supply. This is one of the causes of unemployment.

Contrary to both the classical and the Keynesian theories, saving (for the most part) is no longer a function of income and interest
rates. As noted earlier in this chapter, the bulk of saving comes from
the business, not the household, sector. The choice today is to a
much lesser extent a decision between saving and consumption than
it was fifty or a hundred years ago. That choice is relevant only for
the household sector, which produces about 20 percent of saving.
The business sector generates about 80 percent of total saving in
the economy. Most of the saving is generated by large corporations
that have control over their prices.

The question now arises how these corporate savings will be
invested. There are no automatic market adjustments because the
choice is not between consumption and saving in this sector, and
the free price mechanism does not come into play. The relationship
between saving and investment is an entirely different one than in
the free market. In the privately planned market, investment decisions are unrelated to saving decisions, which makes equality between saving and investment coincidental rather than a matter of
market adjustments. This is Keynes' explanation of unemployment.

What determines investment in the privately planned sector?
Profit expectations. A decline in aggregate demand is not met with

a fall in prices and wages, as in the classical market system. Instead, employment falls and this leads to a further decline in demand and profit expectations. As Keynes explained, unemployment can be offset by an increase in public spending, which should bring about a return to normalcy. This approach is a significant departure from the classical utopia in which government action is not required because the market system makes all the necessary adjustments.

There is another problem causing unemployment that has assumed significant proportions. The global corporation can place its investments and operations almost anywhere in the world. As we have seen, wage levels, fringe benefits, labor laws, tax laws, environmental laws, and other regulations are among the chief determinants of a global corporation's decisions concerning where to invest and where to operate. As a result, the volume of investment within U.S. boundaries may be considerably less than the volume of saving, which is a cause of recessions and unemployment.

The most serious threat to full employment at the present time is the growing structural discrepancies between the supply of labor and the demand for labor. In this connection there are at least three factors responsible for unemployment: rapid technological progress, management's desire to depend less on union labor, and a lagging educational system.

People and nations have committed themselves to economic development because their material needs depend upon it. Economic development relies upon technology. In the stage it has now reached in the United States, the proper handling of technology makes the difference between profit and growth on the one hand, and failure on the other. Technology has become the pied piper to whose music we dance. People have become an economic input in the evolution of economic development that exists today.

To management, technology has more than the one function of profit maximization. It also serves through automation to reduce the need for blue-collar labor, which, in the major industries, is unionized. Since the 1960s, blue-collar labor has steadily decreased in importance until today it is less than one-half of the total labor force. Although labor peace has been bought with inflation, management prefers to substitute machines and automated equipment for labor.

Another reason for replacing people with machines is the firm's desire for security. We have already seen that corporations have spent the past hundred years trying to tame competition in order to reduce insecurity.

The replacement of workers with machines and automated equipment has changed the makeup of the labor force. White-collar workers trained in technology, computer programming, marketing and sales, operations management and research, human resources management, and so on have gradually replaced the blue-collar worker until today they have become the dominant part of the labor supply.

There is another factor in the decline of demand for the blue-collar worker: the increase in service industries. These industries rely chiefly on white-collar labor. Although the increase in service industries was a normal part of economic development, it coincided with the technological replacement of blue-collar labor. To the extent that blue-collar labor does not readily convert to white-collar labor, structural unemployment becomes a serious problem. At the same time, there are shortages in the highly educated and trained labor force required for the new jobs created by the Technological Revolution.

The classical economist did not foresee this problem because of their reliance on the market mechanism. In the construction of their utopian model, they conceived of humanity as the imaginary "economic man." The Industrial Revolution was still on the horizon, and technology (as we know it) had not yet begun to make its impact felt.

Unemployment today has become a problem deeply rooted in technology and the cultural, social, and psychological character of labor. As we have seen, it is also rooted in the oligopolistic structure of markets and the globalization of the economy.[4] Business-cycle theory, which had its origins in the free-market model of the classical economists of another era, cannot explain it.

Only when we understand how the oligopolistic world economy really works is it possible to comprehend the unrealistic and oversimplistic solutions of many modern classical economists. It is hopelessly misguided of them to assume that by holding the money supply to a constant rate of growth and by allowing interest rates to fluctuate with changes in aggregate demand, a satisfactory level of employment in an oligopolistic global world economy will result.

Political policies in regard to the international competition for resources and markets are a major cause of economic instability, producing both inflation and unemployment, sometimes simultaneously in the form of stagflation. The geopolitical ambitions and plans of nations periodically result in rearmaments or war. This produces an acute and often sudden increase in the demand for credit on the part of government. Without controls, this usually results in inflation.[5]

When the crisis is over, aggregate demand is reduced and the slack in demand left by the government is not absorbed by the private sector, unless specific public action is planned and preparations are made in time. The result is often a lengthy period of severe economic instability, the outcome of which is unpredictable in a world subject to a continuous process of technological and social changes.

Like inflation, unemployment problems cannot be solved or alleviated unless the policies employed rest on a realistic foundation and a thorough understanding of all the facts. Economic policies should serve to create a more humane society in which large, defenseless groups will be spared the suffering and humiliation of unnecessary economic catastrophies.

Underemployment—Poverty through Inefficient Production

Over 90 percent of all working Americans are employees (about 10 percent are self-employed) and depend on the existence of jobs for their livelihood. These statistics are similar for many of the major industrialized countries. A relatively small number of people possess entrepreneurial abilities to the extent that they can *create* economic opportunities. The others—the large majority—remain unemployed if there is no demand for their particular kind of labor.

Unemployment is only part of the employment problem. Underemployment is equally serious. In some regions, it is even more serious than unemployment. Unlike unemployment, underemployment has not had the attention of most economists. Whether a person earns too little because of being overqualified for a job, or because the productivity of the job is so low that wages must also be very low, underemployment, as the concept is used here, refers to any job that pays wages below the subsistence level.[6]

In an economy that is privately owned and controlled, the subsistence level of wages is of no special concern to the people who make the economic decisions (that is, private management). The bottom line is profit—enough for survival and growth. If the productivity of some jobs is too low to pay subsistence wages, then the workers employed in such jobs have a serious problem. In a modern, socially progressive economy[7] this becomes a problem of the state, because there is generally very little that most underemployed or unemployed workers can do to provide a subsistence level for themselves and their families. That depends on the existence of jobs that add enough value to a product or service to permit the payment of subsistence wages. In many communities (even in rich countries such as the United States), there aren't enough jobs that pay subsistence wages or better to meet the needs of such people. This is a matter of education, training, economic development, opportunity, and guidance, which may be beyond many individuals' reach if society fails to come to their assistance.

Traditional economists as well as Karl Marx have defined productivity in terms of labor and capital. That definition is inadequate for explaining underemployment. Productivity has to be explained in terms of a job and *all* the factors that make a job productive or unproductive.[8] If we define productivity in terms of labor or capital alone, we create insoluble problems. Is a highly motivated, highly skilled carpenter productive when working with inferior tools such as a hammer with a loose handle? Or what about defective materials or structurally inadequate designs? Is a machine efficient if it is poorly maintained? Is a product efficiently produced if it is poorly marketed or unsoundly financed?

It is obvious that production is a cooperative effort and that the efficiency of any part of the process depends on the efficiency of every other part of the process. It is short-sighted to talk of the productivity of labor or the productivity of capital. It is meaningful, however, to speak of the productivity of a process or of a job in its totality.

Productivity in a modern economy depends on the cooperation of labor, capital, technology, management, marketing, finance, and other factors, depending on the particular process. Production in this context is used as it applies to either goods or services. It is misleading to say that wages are low because productivity of labor is low, although in some instances that may be the case. If wages are low, it generally means that the productivity of the total job is low. Underemployment then is a problem of job productivity. There are many examples. In some parts of the nation, warehousing and distribution are highly mechanized and automated, and job productivity is high. In other parts of the nation, similar processes are relatively primitive and inefficient, and job productivity is low. Wherever *job* productivity is low, there is likely to be underemployment—wages below the subsistence level. This is especially harmful in areas where a decent standard of living requires good wages. Low wages lead to slums.

Slums are only a part of the problem of underemployment and, for that matter, chronic unemployment. People who live in poverty (below subsistence levels) create an environment that is not conducive to wholesome human development. Children raised in slums become a part of the total labor pool. If they are ignored by society, they become the unemployed and the underemployed of the future. Underemployment has become an extremely expensive economic, political, and social problem—a cancer in our society.

One of the consequences of underemployment that has received much attention in recent years is transfer payments (in other words, income redistribution). Redistributing income is not a new political device. Charity is its oldest form. In many religions, it is made a part of the moral life. Political philosophers have explained that poverty is often the result of inequities built into the social and economic fabric. They have warned that political stability depends on the government's ability to reduce such inequities to a tolerable level. Income redistribution is one method, but broad-based economic development is another—probably better—method.

The tax mechanism becomes a vehicle for redistributing income when the objective is to reduce poverty and to alleviate inequities that to a greater or lesser degree become part of the economic and political process. A progressive income tax or special subsidies to the poor and underprivileged paid for out of taxes redistribute income. This method cannot be used indefinitely because a point will be reached when the taxes of the middle classes become so high that they become an obstacle to productivity and production. Eventually, if income redistribution is used excessively, it will merely shift the source of political instability from the poor and underprivileged to the middle classes.

When income redistribution is attempted via federal-budget deficits, other problems develop. If the deficit is financed from saving, it may have a crowding out effect on private investment, depending on the level of economic activity. Such deficits also redistribute income in the opposite direction in the future when the interest on the debt has to be paid.[9] If the deficit is financed with an increase in the money supply or with an increase in the rate at which money turns over (its velocity), the redistribution of income becomes inflationary unless, as in the 1930s, the economy suffers from a severe depression. At such a time, the redistribution of income becomes an economic stimulant.

The solution to the problems of unemployment and underemployment lies in the creation of economic opportunity and increased productivity, not in a reliance on income redistribution through transfer payments. One of the objectives of this book is to deal with that problem.

Supply-Side Economics—Another Miracle Drug?

The chief weaknesses of traditional economic theory lie in its oversimplified view of the causes of inflation and unemployment. It underestimates the vast gulf between a free-market economy and a predominantly privately planned economy. Keynesians tend to overestimate the role of aggregate demand in inflation and recession. They see fluctuations in profit expectations and their effect on aggregate demand as the cause of economic ills. The monetarists see fluctuations in credit demand and the willingness of the monetary authorities to accommodate them as the root of all economic evil.[10]

Structural unemployment and inflation cannot be corrected by a monetary policy divorced from the real problems of the economy nor by a Keynesian policy that does not give sufficient weight to structural problems.

There are numerous structural causes of inflation and unemployment that have already been described. The view that inflation can be cured with unemployment or vice versa is more in line with wishful thinking than economic reality. At best, such a simplistic policy can only succeed by temporarily concealing the real causes of inflation.

In the first half of the 1980s, a combination of monetarist and Keynesian economics was popularized under the banner of "supply-side economics" as a miracle drug for stagflation. Since stagflation is a combination of inflation and unemployment, it is believed they must be treated simultaneously. This involves the Keynesian remedy of lower taxes as a stimulant for combating recession plus the monetarist remedy of tight money and high interest rates for combating inflation. If the stimulant is to take the form of higher saving and investment, the supply-siders believe that business taxes should be reduced as well as taxes on profits of upper-level incomes. This theory is based on the belief that income redistribution in favor of the poor has gone too far and must be reversed if those who save and invest (largely corporations and the wealthy) are to be encouraged.

By adding the dimension of supply-side economics (which is based on the assumption that investment will be stimulated by lower taxes, deregulation, and reduced government spending), the supply-siders believe that they have conquered the economic ills spawned by the Keynesian revolution.

The idea of using monetary policy and fiscal policy simultaneously to combat stagflation has some attraction for economists who ignore the structural and institutional factors causing stagflation. Even so, high interest rates tend to have the opposite effect on growth investment from that of lower taxes, so that such a policy might cancel out its impacts. The unemployment created by high interest rates will discourage investment further through a decline in aggregate demand. In addition, it leads to deficits that will create future problems, either by crowding out private investment or by creating new inflationary pressures.

For an example that their theory is sound, supply-side economists point to the upturn in the U.S. economy that began at the end of 1982 and continued for over five years while the rate of inflation declined simultaneously. Actually, the upturn and the low rate of inflation were produced by a combination of fortuitous circumstances having little, if any, connection with supply-side economic policies.

The economic upturn was produced by unprecedented deficits that more than doubled the U.S. national debt in eight years from $1 trillion to $2.5 trillion. This was accompanied by a simultaneous drop in the rate of inflation and by a set of unusual circumstances described at the start of this chapter.

Although the economic upturn and declining rate of inflation are welcome changes from the stagflation preceding them, the unprecedented budget deficits, the high real interest rates (especially in the private long-term investment sector, the agricultural sector, and the consumer sector), and record trade deficits are problems that must be faced. In other words, there are only complex solutions to complex structural economic problems, and these are dealt with in later chapters.

Unfortunately, nations are tempted to create prosperity with military buildups and unsound monetary policies. Hjalmar Schacht, Germany's financial genius during the 1920s and later during Hitler's reign, manipulated his country's currency through a system of exchange-rate controls, called *Askimarks,* which gave Germany the foreign credit and hard currencies it needed to build up its war machine. The German people praised Hitler for the prosperity this created.

The U.S. armaments race with the Soviet Union has been financed with an extremely unsound monetary policy that differs only in detail from the methods used by Schacht. In essence it has mortgaged our future, has left an unconscionable burden for our children, and has jeopardized our economic independence. Yet it has produced a prosperity that has blinded people to the dangers of reckless living. It is doubtful that governments could pursue such policies if people really understood the folly of such actions.

Part II
How the United States Works and Consumes in the Nuclear Age and Space Age

---

6
A Human View of Production and Productivity

The Anatomy of Conflict—The Neglected Factor in Production and Productivity

The inherent interdisciplinary nature of the social sciences requires that economic phenomena such as productivity be analyzed in all their aspects and not merely from a purely economic point of view.

The classical system of economics is based on a simple concept of supply and demand in which conflict and compromise play no role. Production is determined by a price mechanism that allocates resources in line with a simplistic concept of supply and equally simplistic utilitarian version of demand. Supply is interpreted as the willingness of sellers to sell their products at different prices determined by the costs of production and subject to the laws of the market. Demand is based on a simple utilitarian theory in which buyers buy more as prices fall and buy less as prices rise. There is no conflict, only the aggregation of individual decisions.

In the actual economic process, there are many conflicting interests. They become a source of confrontation when there is no provision for reasonable compromise (as in most utopian and extremist doctrines).

Most traditional economists today still regard conflict as a social rather than an economic phenomenon. This is because the social sciences are too insulated from one another. Latent or unresolved conflicts, for example, affect productivity and must therefore be resolved before productivity can be functionally defined.

Conflict is an essential element in a theory of production because the sanity, emotional stability, and motivation of a worker are major factors in productivity. The total environment in which people live and work has an impact on their ability to produce. Yet traditional economic theory does not concern itself with the environment and its impact on productivity.

The process of conflict, compromise, and harmony is not limited to economic activity. It is a prerequisite for survival. In nature this process is automatic, and harmony is reflected in what is called the ecological balance. Humankind has recreated much of its physical and social environment and, in so doing, has left the world of automatic ecological balance or natural harmony. To survive, we must create our *own* balance and harmony.

In the past, our effort to survive has not reflected our willingness and ability to convert conflict into compromise and harmony. It has, instead, centered on the accumulation of power, the use of power for war, and the use of war for domination in the disposal of conflict. Such arbitrary domination is never more than temporary and has therefore never resulted in harmony. Today this process threatens humanity's survival.

Conflict is deeply ingrained in human life and human institutions. As Aristotle said, man is both an animal of habit and an animal of reason. This means that as an animal of habit, we are determined to keep the things we believe in as they are. As an animal of reason, we are willing to change in order to survive. In some people, habit has a stronger hold—in others, reasons. But no one is free of the conflict between the two.

The inherent conflict in humankind is overlooked by traditional economists. As a result, political and social institutions are left with little meaning because they are deprived of their real purpose—the achievement of harmony. This explains why some economists view the state (or society) simply as the aggregation of the individuals who comprise it. In fact, a *democratic state represents the institutionalization of the processes that lead to compromise and harmony.*

What is the nature and origin of conflict? It arises from the fact that human beings see themselves as the primary object in the drama of life. To the extent to which individuals believe themselves threatened by other individuals, to the extent to which information differs as it reaches different individuals, to the extent that values differ within an organization, within a community, within a nation, and between nations, to that extent does the basis for conflict exist.

The classical economists did not perceive conflict as inherent in the economic process. They regarded conflict as the unwillingness of some people to abide by the rules of the market, and they saw compromise as the abandonment of the principle of optimization. This followed from the belief that the free market optimizes the allocation of resources and that conflict arises from the desire to gain control of a market through arbitrary decisions. When that happens, the free market can not perform well. Conflict is therefore an aberration and an anomaly in the eyes of the classical economist.

Conflict exists in every area of social activity, and conflict between nations is an extension of the conflict that exits within a nation. The disagreements between nations are, however, more likely to lead to the use of arbitrary power and confrontation, since the concept of national sovereignty has been employed to dignify the use of arbitrary power as a vehicle for dealing with conflict.

In economic development, the use of land and capital has given rise to conflict. Since labor without land and capital is useless in all but the primitive stages of economic development, workers must sell their labor to those who own or control land and capital. In the entrepreneurial stages of capitalism, the work relationship exists between the owners of capital and the owners of labor. In the later stages of capitalism, the relationship is to a large extent between workers and those who directly or indirectly control the land and capital—the political or economic managers.

Power enters into such relationships quite naturally and gives rise to conflict. Those who own or control the land (including natural resources) and capital occupy a position of power vis-à-vis those whose labor is useless without land and capital. In the age of supertechnology, knowledge must be added to land and capital as a source of power. In the past, workers have tried to match such power by combining into labor unions and employing the strike as a weapon. Frequently conflict is not limited to workers and employers. Firms in the nineteenth century began to realize that their existence would be safer and their size and profits greater if they succeeded in taming competition. The more aggressive firms soon learned how to tame competition through the ingenious use of financial resources. The pure market of Adam Smith in the hands of such economic barons as Rockefeller, Carnegie, and Morgan soon gave way to monopoly and oligopoly.

The concept of free trade, an important part of the utopian dream of laissez-faire, is based on the belief that nations should not use power in their economic relations with other nations. The classical theory of international trade is based on the law of comparative advantage. A nation exports those goods in which it has the greatest comparative advantage or the least comparative disadvantage. There is, in the classical theory, no concern over conflict and the use of power, both of which are at the center of international relations in the real world. Conflict is inherent in a political system that divides the world into sovereign nations. In the absence of a better solution, nations make use of military and economic power to gain an edge in this conflict.

To resolve conflict with satisfactory compromises, three things must be known: the nature of the conflicts, the benefits to be derived from compromise, and a process capable of achieving compromise.

Such knowledge however is not enough. If the process of compromise is to be successful, it must become part of the culture and attitudes. If, for example, labor and management see each other as foes, the resolution of conflict is not likely to lead to harmony. It is more likely to lead to a flawed compromise enabling the firm to stay in business while sacrificing equity (fairness) and efficiency. If both sides see each other as part of the common good, their negotiations are likely to lead to a compromise that contains the elements of harmony.

Political Power in the Corporation

A modern corporation is a complex human and social institution. The decisions made are organized at different levels of the various phases of production. These decisions have a direct or indirect impact on human motivation and social relationships. They cannot be ignored or simply assumed to exist in any relevant analysis of production and productivity. Every aspect of production that has an impact on productivity must be specifically treated and ranked.

The traditional view of optimizing production is an extreme oversimplification that can be compared to biology before the invention of the microscope. Adding such concepts as conflict, power, time, motion, and relativity to the neoclassical model can do for economics what the microscope did for biology—improve the accuracy of analysis.

The Industrial Revolution set in motion three stages of economic development that are all classified as "capitalism," but that reflect a vital difference in substance and form. In all three stages, the firm plays a key role in production and provides the social framework for economic efficiency.

In the first stage, the market dominates the decision-making process of the firm. In the second stage, firms tend to dominate the market. In the third stage, firms are subject to external political and social influences separate from the process of economic efficiency.

Economic efficiency and profit is the exclusive objective and task of the firm in the first stage. The entrepreneur manages the process of economic efficiency and the worker performs the various tasks of production, which are relatively simple compared to the complex processes of high technology in the later stages.

In the second stage, firms emerge as large mechanized enterprises and their efficiency depends on the effectiveness of the internal political organization. Since organization involves many people, social relationships also become a major factor in production and productivity in this stage.

As the political and social organization of the firm evolves, the sources of conflict multiply as a result of increasingly complex human relationships. In the third stage of economic development, the basis for conflict widens even further as a result of external political and social influences.

In the third stage, economic development has progressed to a point where further growth depends on the ability of the corporation to organize and mobilize resources and markets domestically as well as beyond their own national borders. Research and development on a large scale and the ability to adapt to rapid change become increasingly important in this stage. Population pressures, depleted natural resources, and the uncertain and sometimes harmful consequences of scientific and technological advances make the protection of the environment paramount to survival and the quality of life. In this stage of economic development, externally determined political and social policies are added to the internal policies and decisions of the firm in the process of production. The evolution of the firm throws light on the sources of conflict in the process of production.

In the first stage, conflict arises largely from the relationship between the entrepreneur and the worker. In the second stage, the growth in the size of firms and the replacement of a simple technology with a sophisticated one give rise to the political and social character of the firm. The entrepreneur gives way to managers, while craftspeople and apprentices give way to well-trained, qualified specialists and a much larger number of workers with relatively simple skills.

Human relations in this stage are no longer limited to the entrepreneurs, the workers, the bankers, and the landowners, as they were in David Ricardo's days when he developed his theory of production and distribution.[1] Even so simple a social framework as that contained elements of conflict that were clearly seen by Ricardo and later Marx.

As the second stage progresses and the firm becomes a well-organized political and social entity, the opportunity for conflict expands. Conflict arises in the different divisions of a firm in this stage in regard to the allocation of resources, remuneration, and status in the decision-making process. A major source of conflict emerges between those sectors favoring a policy of stable and smooth growth and other sectors favoring a vigorous policy of innovation supported by substantial investment in research and development. There is conflict between those who favor a policy of maximum profits and growth and those concerned with the quality of life of the workers, the condition of the environment, and the long-run place of the corporation in society.

The chief sources of internal conflict in the process of production may be divided into three parts: threatened self-interest, conflicting information, and conflicting values. The simple traditional economic theories of production and productivity are examples of what happens to the scientific method when such important facts as political and social conflicts are left out of the analysis.

In the third stage, the emergence of political and social forces *external* to the firm add new sources of conflict that have impact on productivity. The interest of the consumer and the protection of the environment assume great political and social significance, and this leads to an extensive system of regulations that affects the operation and productivity of business enterprise. At this point in economic development, issues ignored in the earlier stages raise new questions in regard to human values and social objectives. The more enlightened economists have participated in this new dialogue, but it has not found its way into the mainstream of economic theory.

One of the great areas of conflict in a modern economy is the relationship between government and the private sector. More and more, the protection of the environment, the interests of the public, and the safety of the workers have become the concern and the objective of government. The conflict arises between those who regard the concern of government as an intrusion into the affairs of the private sector and those who believe that the public interest in a modern economy cannot be left to the discretion of the producers.

The conflicts generated in the later stages of development are far more complex than the earlier ones. The complexity of conflicts cannot be understood and the compromise cannot be discovered until the problems are analyzed in the light of social values.

A Theory of Production Based on Economic, Political, and Social Goals

The evolution of the firm began two centuries ago with economic optimization. About a century later it acquired an additional objective: *internal* political and social peace. Since the 1930s, two *external* objectives were added: environmental protection and the safety and welfare of the worker and the consumer.

This has affected not only production and productivity, but the entire economic and political process. These additional objectives acquired by the firm in the later stages have become the basis of

much dialogue, but have for the most part failed to affect significantly the essence of microeconomic theory.

In the evolution of the firm and the economy, economic decision
making progressed from a single-level to a multilevel system. In
classical theory, the single level consisted of a free, self-equilibrating
market conceived to be able to make all economic decisions and
regulate all economic processes. This was the unseen hand of Adam
Smith. It consisted of producers and consumers, and equilibrium
was reached when the supply of the producers equalled the demand
of the consumers. Actually, however, even in the early stages of economic development, there existed a second level consisting of a
number of public entities such as central banks and, in England, the
East India Company (a government-controlled international trading company founded in 1599).

Marxist communism is also a single-level economic system in
which the state "withers away" and the natural laws of a "just and
moral society" automatically lead to the right economic decisions.
Such utopian models do not reflect the real world, whether capitalist or socialist.

In the present U.S. economy, there are three levels of decision
making relative to the process of production. In addition, there are
sublevels that add to the complexity of the problem.

- The first level is the firm itself. In large corporations, there are
  the central corporate management, the domestic management,
  the international management, and the management of the subsidiary corporation.

- On the second level, there are the laws and regulation of government (federal, state, and local), which apply to the activities
  and operations of the firm. This includes all policies in regard
  to environmental protection, the public safety, and the public
  interest. It also includes resources made available for research
  and development and the numerous subsidies designed to facilitate production and productivity.

- On the third level are the various international agencies and the
  laws of foreign governments that have an impact on the activities of the firm. Firms operating globally are very much con-

cerned with the tax laws, labor laws, environmental laws, and safety laws of all nations. Many firms are concerned with the laws and regulations pertaining to international trade and payments and the various international and regional organizations created to facilitate them. The World Bank, International Monetary Fund, European Community, Organization of American States, and international departments of the major central banks are a few examples.

In the process of production, the various levels of decision making involve a complex structure of human relationships that must be identified as a prerequisite for finding the compromises required for preventing confrontation and alienation, which have a negative impact on productivity. A simple diagram will illustrate this point.

The shape of the curve in figure 6–1 indicates that productivity deteriorates progressively as unresolved conflicts arise, in spite of economic optimization. That is why the present approach to economic theory (which relegates the problem of conflict and alienation to the other social sciences and treats them as externalities) is inadequate for building a relevant theory of production and productivity. Conflict and alienation cannot be treated as externalities.

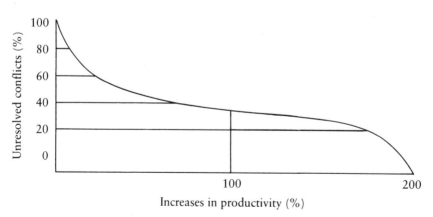

Figure 6–1. *Change in Productivity Resulting from Changes in Unresolved Conflict*

They are central to any useful theory of production and are as much a part of it as is the impact of technology.

In figure 6–1, no attempt is made to give an exact account of what happens to output and productivity when unresolved conflict is reduced or increased. Such data does not yet exist except in the form of rough estimates. Figure 6–1 makes only two points, both still in the nature of assumptions, but very logical ones. First, if the level of unresolved conflict reaches 100 percent, output is zero. Actually, zero output may be reached before the level of unresolved conflict reaches 100 percent, as a result of inevitable chaos. The other point is that output increases progressively as the level of unresolved conflict is reduced until such conflict reaches a relatively low level, after which a further reduction increases output at a decreasing rate. The reason for this is that at high levels of unresolved conflict, whether 70, 80 or 90 percent output will be close to zero as a result of a virtual breakdown in human relations. When unresolved conflict reaches low levels, such as 10 or 20 percent, a further reduction will increase output only moderately because human relations have already reached a realistic stage of cooperation.

Figure 6–2 shows a production possibilities curve that depicts a constant output with varying amounts of inputs (in this case, labor and capital). For example, at point A, the same output is produced with more capital and less labor than at point B. Output is increased, of course, when both labor and capital are increased or when one is held constant while the other is increased. In that case the production-possibilities curve moves up.

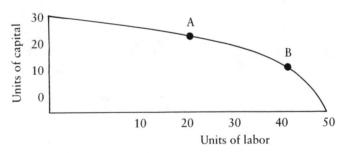

Figure 6–2. *The Production-Possibilities Curve*

Figure 6–3 shows the changes in the production-possibilities curve when unresolved conflict, the quality of inputs, and the state of technology change.

In figure 6–4, we can observe the complexity of relationships in a modern economy. The diagram is actually incomplete because behind all the formal organizations involved in the economic process are the pressure groups and covert relationships that have a considerable impact.

The fact that the modern social relationships of production are complex is no reason for ignoring them in a theory of production. In fact, in a number of countries such as Hungary and Japan, new theories of production are being developed that put the social relationships relevant to production at the center of theory and policy.

At the heart of any theory of production should be the principle of democratic organization. That explains why neither nineteenth-century capitalism nor twentieth-century authoritarian socialism can be employed successfully in the third stage of economic development. The modern world is radically different from the worlds of Adam Smith and Karl Marx. It is therefore vital that we re-examine such concepts as democratic organization and social harmony.

The conflicts arising in the process of production are inherent in the social organization and are, per se, quite natural in any society. They should not be regarded in a negative way any more than personal human problems should be. Primitive people regarded human problems and conflicts as the work of demons or the devil. We must not make similar judgments in evaluating the problems of economic activity. We should instead regard conflict as natural—to be resolved with compromise.

The structure of conflict is both vertical and horizontal. At the bottom of Figure 6–4 are listed the operational divisions of the firm. They are affected by relations vis-à-vis each other and by relations that go to the top management within the firm. They are also affected by the firm relations with the other levels and their subdivisions.

Horizontal conflict in production may arise between those responsible for the actual production of one or more products and those with responsibility for research and development. The former

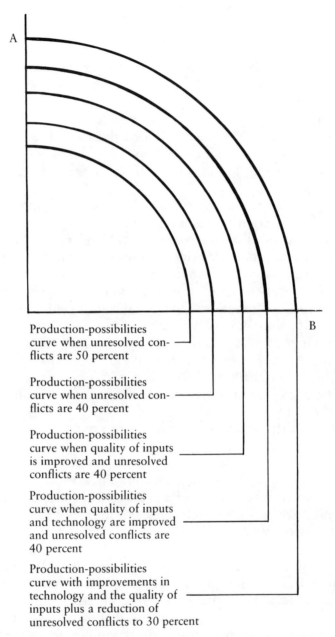

A

Production-possibilities
curve when unresolved conflicts are 50 percent

Production-possibilities
curve when unresolved conflicts are 40 percent

Production-possibilities
curve when quality of inputs
is improved and unresolved
conflicts are 40 percent

Production-possibilities
curve when quality of inputs
and technology are improved
and unresolved conflicts are
40 percent

Production-possibilities
curve with improvements in
technology and the quality of
inputs plus a reduction of
unresolved conflicts to 30 percent

B

Note: A movement outward of these production-possibility curves indicates how
output can be increased with the same input of resources A and B (in this case
capital and labor) when conflict is resolved.

Figure 6–3. *The Impact of Improvements in the Quality of Inputs,
Advances in Technology, and Changes in the Level of
Unresolved Conflicts*

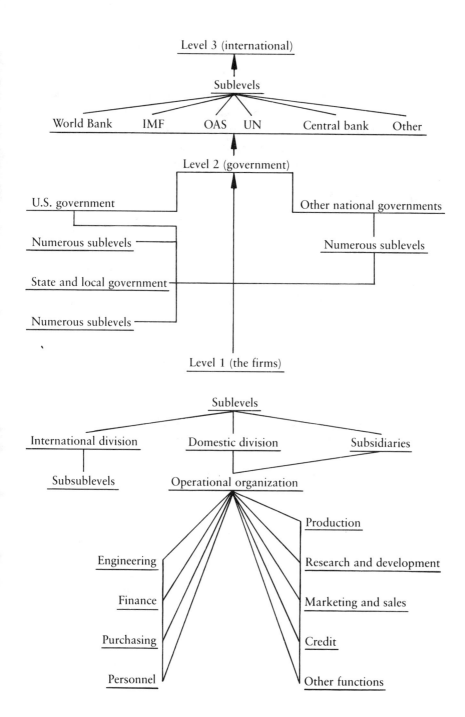

Figure 6–4. *The Decision-making Mechanism of a Modern Corporation*

are interested chiefly in the smooth flow of all inputs and a relative stability in output. Those responsible for innovative technology may favor writing off old techniques and processes to free resources for research and development. That explains some of the rigidities of large corporations, such as the auto companies, that waited too long to change from large to small cars in the 1970s during the OPEC oil crisis. This was a cause of the loss of markets by U.S. auto makers in favor of German and Japanese producers.

Those responsible for sales, and others responsible for credit and credit worthiness, will have conflicting views on operations. The sales division will regard a strict policy in regard to credit allocation and growth as unfavorable to sales expansion.

Those responsible for the financial stability of the firm may not see eye to eye with those in charge of human resources, who are concerned with workers' quality of life. The list of internal horizontal conflict is much longer, but the examples given should illustrate the point.

To this must be added the internal vertical conflicts between the subsublevels, the sublevels, and the top decision-making level of the firm. A corporate management may decide to follow policies that it regards as in the best interests of the firm as an entity, apart from the people who make up its social structure. It may decide to eliminate certain operations or transfer them to another part of the world because it regards such an action to be in the interest of its future growth and prosperity.

To understand the social impact of such decisions, it is necessary to view them in the light of the human relationships affected. The stockholders and top management may benefit. Some parts of middle management and certain groups of workers may be adversely affected. If the firm is large, whole communities may be affected by its decisions. The great global firms can affect many national economies with their decisions.

The impact of international decisions on the part of either national governments or international agencies can have a profound effect on the production and even productivity of a firm. The decisions of an international cartel such as OPEC affect production and productivity in many parts of the world. The decision of a national government to subsidize firms, restrict trade, or limit the export of its technology has profound effects on firms in other countries.

It is not difficult to imagine the opportunities for conflict and confrontation. The record of war and violence in human history reflects the breakdown of social relations within the firm, within the nation, and between nations. In light of this vast potential for confrontation and violence, it is strange, to say the least, that some economists can suggest that the quality of life will be enhanced by making each person "free to choose"—that is, to pursue the person's own selfish interests without socially desirable restrictions in this maze of human conflict. It is far more likely that under such conditions survival will become impossible.

Compromise as a Factor in Production and Productivity

It is the political and social organization of society as well as the individual that turns conflict into compromise or confrontation. From the beginning of the Industrial Revolution, the organization of the firm lent itself to confrontation rather than compromise and harmony. Often, confrontation was latent until it was met with the use of force.

Power became the basis of the organization of the firm. In the early entrepreneurial stage of development, the structure was simple: the owners, the supervisory employees, and the lower-level workers. The entrepreneurs or owners possessed the decision-making power of the firm. The supervisory employees helped to execute that power, and the workers obeyed—or lost their jobs. This relationship was considered fair by the firm insofar as it regarded the wage as compensation for labor *and* obedience.

The simple social relationships of the firm were to some extent inherited from earlier societies. Under the feudal system preceding commercial capitalism, each person had a place in society and the economy and the power of the feudal lord in his fiefdom was absolute and unquestioned. Conflict existed, but it was kept under control through the use of arbitrary power. Compromise was alien to such a system and was regarded as a sign of weakness.

As economic development progressed, firms grew in size and, as the earlier simple social relationships changed, conflict became more complex and more open. Arbitrary power in the firm was challenged by labor unions, labor laws, and other regulations. Often this challenge led to confrontation, but eventually some of the more extreme forms of conflict were resolved through negotiation and compromise. Such compromise, arrived at through the organization of countervailing powers,[2] was often resented by employers who believed that they gave too much and by workers who thought they received too little. As a result, the word *compromise* reflected a negative approach to social relations.

As economic development advanced further, the range of conflict became still more complex, involving firms and all levels of government. Finally, the relationships that gave rise to conflict extended across national boundaries, involving firms and governments globally.

Since the firm is organized on a foundation of private property, and workers are propertyless so far as the economics of production is concerned, the critics of capitalism have assumed that private property is at the root of conflict. However, conflict in human relationships also exists when the means of production are not privately held but socially owned.

The question of conflict does not center on public or private ownership but rather on the use of power in human relations. Power in the case of large U.S. corporations is generally vested in management and not in the owners of corporate stocks. In the Soviet Union, such power is vested at several levels, but not in the people, who (according to the constitution) own the means of production. It is true that under capitalism, private ownership often leads to the misuse of power. It is equally true, however, that under socialism, public ownership often does not prevent the misuse of power.

Compromise does not work well as a solution when it is built on dependent participation (as will be discussed in chapter 10). It is more likely to lead to confrontation. Human beings must be *willing* to cooperate; they cannot be forced to cooperate as a permanent solution. Since a modern economy is built on a process of social relationships, cooperation is vital for success. The unwillingness to cooperate is a cause and effect of alienation.

Participation in society can either be cooperative, creative, and satisfying, or it can be forced, sterile, and alienating. The latter is referred to as dependent participation because it depends on the use of arbitrary power by others. The former is usually referred to as democratic participation.

When social conflict is subjected to dominance with the use of arbitrary power, the alienated segments of society attempt to reject their dependent participation by shifting their focus from cooperation to animosity. This can exist in varying degrees. At one end of the scale is the violent confrontation between a few landowners in a Central American republic and the farm workers who are dominated with the use of power, supported by a military regime. On the other end is a relatively stable society in which alienation resulting form dependent participation leads to declining productivity.

Balance and harmony can result from compromise only when it is based on democratic participation. *Democratic* does not mean that everyone is equal. That can only exist in a utopian model of democracy. Democratic participation means that society is organized in such a way that people are freely willing to cooperate in achieving common goals.

The process of production cannot be limited to input-output analysis and technology. Individual motivation, political organization, and social harmony are integral parts of production. These are ignored in orthodox economic models of production and productivity—ignored because economists prefer to limit their analysis to quantitative variables, which can be treated with statistical and econometric precision.

Precision, however, does not lend itself to realistic economic analysis, for economics is an art and not a science. The process of economic efficiency can be treated as a science only when it is isolated from all other human influences. Economic efficiency, however, is only one factor in the study of economic behavior, and economic theory ceases to be applicable to the real world when it limits itself to that.

Combining economic efficiency with political organization and social harmony makes economics a social science, which it should be. When economics is viewed as a social science, it becomes clear that conflict and compromise are an integral part of its analysis.

In resolving conflict by means of compromise, which results in harmony in the economic process, it is necessary to have a clear understanding of the various factors involved. These include the dynamic nature of life, some common objectives, personal identification, alternative methods, limits of acceptance, time, and motion. If all factors become favorable, the economic process will move in the direction of balance and harmony, showing improvements as it progresses (as will be discussed further in chapter 12).

Before the process of compromise, balance, and harmony can be analyzed further, it is necessary to examine the process of distribution and consumption.

7
The Distribution of Wealth and Income

Wealth—Its Source and Distribution

The classical and most neoclassical economists had a simple explanation for the division and distribution of wealth and property. They saw humanity, whom they regarded as rational beings, in purely economic terms. They had very little to say about the distribution of wealth, but the political philosophers who influenced their thinking had a great deal to say about it. John Locke, for example, was a strong defender of private property, but he believed that what gave people the right to ownership of private property was the labor they spent on its acquisition and development.[1] Farmers working on their land are a classic example of this. A more modern example is the distribution of stock ownership to the employees of a corporation.

The actual ownership of private property has a varied history, much of which has little in common with Locke's view of private property. Although the question is largely academic today, there are interesting examples of how some property was privately acquired. In the seventeenth century, the first Duke of Marlborough, one of England's great military heroes, acquired a large part of Wales. The king gave it to him to soothe his feeling over matters involving the Duchess of Marlborough. In time it was discovered that this land possessed nearly half the coal in Britain.

A favorite pastime of those who possessed influence in the antebellum South was persuading their political friends in state capitols that they should be given a bank charter. Since supervision existed largely in name only, the lucky owners of banks could print bank notes, which they used to acquire the best land. This was usually done in the names of others and is called "wildcat banking" by historians. Another method of acquiring property, which strictly speaking does not fit Locke's definition of the "inalienable right of private property," is the purchase of land that is later found to contain valuable resources, such as oil, that bring wealth to their often surprised owners.

There are aspects of the question of wealth and its distribution that concern us here. The first is that its political and social nature requires value judgments that do not lend themselves to the economic interpretations that traditional economists use in their analysis. The second point of interest is that the *method* used in acquiring private property becomes an important factor in its *distribution*.

If private property is acquired as envisaged by Locke or as practiced under the Homestead Act, wealth is not likely to be concentrated in the hands of a few, with the great majority poor and propertyless, as is the case today in many nations of Latin America, Asia, and Africa. (The Homestead Act became law in 1862. It provided for the distribution of U.S. public lands, usually 160 acres, to anyone who filed a claim and who settled the land and cultivated it.) If, however, the acquisition of private property is divorced from the labors of those who acquire it, wealth is likely to become concentrated. In the case of the British nobles such as the Duke of Marlborough, the discovery of vast coal deposits had a profound impact on the distribution of wealth in Britain. Actually, the method of acquiring wealth becomes an important economic factor that is overlooked by most economists. The possession of wealth gives rise to power, and power is a major factor in the economic decision-making process.

Exactly what is wealth? Alfred Marshall, (1842–1924) the neoclassical economist *par excellence,* gave a comprehensive definition of wealth that is still useful as a starting point in analyzing it. Wealth is both internal and external; it is both private and public. In the economic sense, wealth is an economic good as distinguished from a spiritual good.[2]

To the classical economist, wealth is external; that is, it is in the form of land and capital and does not include a person's skill and knowledge, which constitute internal wealth and consist of what a person brings to a job. It is not clear why the latter should be excluded from the definition of wealth, especially since such internal wealth depends upon physical, mental, and emotional health—which are the ingredients of a sane and productive society—as well as training and experience.

The distinction between private wealth and public wealth is a matter of philosophy and law. Public wealth consists of collective goods that make up wealth from a social rather than an individual point of view. It is wealth owned by all members of a political entity—such as a city, a state, or a nation. Private wealth is all that is possessed by an individual or a group that is not a political entity.

It is not possible to say in absolute terms what is *inherently* private wealth; that depends on the value system on which the answer is based. In the United States, the bulk of wealth is in private hands. In the Soviet Union, the bulk of wealth is public.

If we view wealth as the source of a nation's well-being, then the terms *private* and *public* are less significant than they appear on the surface. More significant are how wealth is controlled and managed and how a nation's well-being is defined.

Neither private nor public ownership is necessarily a tool of exploitation, but both *can* be, if the exercise of power in the name of one or the other is arbitrary and undemocratic. (The exercise of power may or may not be derived from the ownership of wealth.) In nineteenth-century capitalism, there was a direct link between wealth and power. Men such as Rockefeller, Morgan, Vanderbilt, and Carnegie exercised great power over oil, finance, the railroads, and steel. Their decisions had an immense impact on the national economy and on the lives of millions of people, both directly and indirectly. They were men of great wealth and influence. Although they held no public office, they exercised enormous political power behind the scenes. They were the pioneers of capitalism, but real democracy was the furthest thing from their minds. This was especially significant at a time when the great majority of people had a political voice in name only. Workers were not politically represented, women had no vote, and ethnic minorities were effectively excluded from political participation. This was a period of private ownership and economic exploitation.

In the Soviet Union, power is not linked to wealth. The national wealth, according to the Soviet constitution, belongs to all the people. There is still very little private ownership of wealth so far as the land, its resources, and the means of production are concerned. Yet a man such as Stalin exercised great power, which his own successors condemned as arbitrary. Neither the classical economists nor their socialist critics such as Karl Marx fully understood the nature of power as reflected in both private property and that which is controlled by the state in the name of the people.

Is there an objective criteria that can be used for the separation of private and public wealth? The argument used by the defenders of private property—that public ownership leads to an excessive concentration of power that lends itself to arbitrary policies and abuse, as in Stalinist Russia—tells only half the story. It is also true, as claimed by the critics of capitalism, that private ownership leads to a concentration of economic power *directly*—and political power *indirectly*. This lends itself to arbitrary policies and abuse, as in the early days of Hitler's Germany and in other nations where the military governs in the interest of the owners of great wealth.

More important than the formal legal structure of the ownership of wealth are the participation of people in its use and how it is employed to satisfy the needs of people, the requirements of the environment, and the quality of life—both present and future.

The legal division between private and public wealth should reflect cultural values and attitudes. If private ownership is equated with the right of individuals to make decisions consistent only with their own desires, regardless of the impact on others, on the environment, and on the present and future quality of life, then the use of private ownership must be restricted in order to assure survival. If, however, private ownership is built on a foundation that recognizes and respects its impact on society, the conflict between private wealth and social needs is greatly reduced. In that case, private ownership will lend itself *in a socially acceptable manner* to most economic activity.

Alfred Marshall was sympathetic with this view of the use of wealth. "So long as wealth is applied to provide for every family the necessaries of life and culture, and an abundance of the higher forms of enjoyment for collective use, so long the pursuit of wealth is a noble aim; and the pleasures which it brings are likely to increase with the growth of those higher activities which it is used to promote."[3]

The forms of wealth have changed over time. Land and its improvements (agriculture, buildings and so on) constituted the first type of wealth when people began to make their living from farming. To that was added the domestication and breeding of animals for food and for farm labor.

The Industrial Revolution gave prominence to a new form of wealth—capital equipment or the means of production. This wealth was created by the capitalists, who organized labor to produce and retained part of the output as their profit, which they invested in the means of production. This process has to take place under socialism as well as capitalism if economic growth is to occur.

The accumulation of capital and the willingness and ability to save part of current income go hand in hand. Some economists are inclined to disregard taxes as a form of saving because taxes are presumed not to lead to the creation of productive capital and wealth in capitalist economies. This is far from true, as Marshall observed in 1791. "The most obvious forms of such wealth are public material property of all kinds, such as roads, canals, buildings and parks, gas works and water works ... But the Thames has added more to the wealth of England ... and ought for many purposes to be reckoned part of England's wealth."[4] To the extent that taxes are used to construct and maintain material things that provide needed and useful services and add to the productivity and quality of life—to that extent they should be regarded as savings that create wealth in both the private and public sectors.

One form of wealth that has become increasingly important is science and technology, which were not classified as wealth by most neoclassical economists because they did not meet their criterion that wealth is external to humankind. (This criterion excludes from wealth the knowledge that people bring to jobs.)

Science and technology—or knowledge—by becoming primary factors in the creation of income must be regarded as wealth. Is this a form of private or public wealth? Is it national or international?

It should be noted that people and nations are already arguing over property rights in regard to *knowledge,* as they once did over land and physical capital.

Since we cannot survive without a favorable environment, wealth must be used to encourage such an environment and to promote the physical, mental, and emotional health of humanity—or what Erich Fromm called the sane society. Wealth must be used in a socially constructive way or survival and the quality of life are endangered. It is futile to argue for individuals' right to choose if the social consequences of their choices and their prospects for survival are ignored.

Land, physical capital, knowledge—these reflect the evolution of wealth as the provider of income and the nourisher of the quality of life. Just as evidence of a democratic society was reflected in its distribution of land and capital in the past, so a society's claim to democracy must also be judged by the possession and distribution of knowledge among its people today.

Income—Its Source and Distribution

From a purely economic point of view, income is the reason for the accumulation of wealth. As inadequate as total or even average income is as a measure of either a nation's prosperity or the quality of life, it is a better measure than wealth, which is the source of income.

Wealth, as we have observed, consists of the means of production, of physical resources, of human beings who contribute mental and physical labor, of science and technology, and of experience and imagination. Income reflects more directly the satisfaction of human wants and needs, present and future. To really understand the social meaning of income, one must define it functionally in terms of its ability to satisfy wants and needs in the framework of survival and the quality of life.

To judge a nation's prosperity or the quality of life by the size of its gross national product (GNP) as measured today is not only inadequate, it is wrong. To measure GNP without regard to the *reason* for the existence of wealth and income is at best a measure of the process of economic efficiency without regard to social, human, and environmental needs. This, however, is exactly what is done today, because economics as it is practiced today reflects an abstract, quantified process rather than a social science or art.

Most traditional economists defend this narrow and abstract approach by claiming that economics as a science cannot be burdened with value judgments. Yet the assertion that so far as the GNP is concerned, more is necessarily better is a basic value judgment. It is also wrong, as Aristotle has shown with his examples of the golden mean. More, Aristotle pointed out, is only better when less is not enough.

It is actually not too difficult to measure the GNP in a socially constructive way.[5] If a nation's income is comparatively high and its level of poverty is also comparatively high, perhaps income distribution is at fault, but there may be other reasons that should be identified. The fault may lie in a system of education and training or an industrial structure that invites underemployment and low wages for too large a part of the population.

The health of the people is an important part of the quality of life. Medical delivery makes up a part of the national income. If a large percentage of the people are deprived of adequate medical attention, the quality of the national income must be judged by that.

The quality of life after retirement is also an important aspect of the total quality of life. If a significant part of the population lives in poverty after a life of useful labor, this too affects the quality of the national income.

Since most people must work to be able to live and to provide for themselves and their families without depending on the charity of others, job security is an important part of the quality of life. If, in the creation of the national income, a significant part of the population is involuntarily unemployed for a period of a few months to a few years, the national income, whatever its size, leaves something to be desired.

To relate the GNP to the quality of life, an index can be constructed that gives an indication of how the economy measures up to the human and social needs of people and the environment.

The GNP can be measured with a weighted index, not as an

indication that its numerical value can be exact, but rather as evidence that people's ability to judge the quality of life is based on human and social values and on experience. The factors that should be given weight should include the following: per capita income; income distribution; the percentage of families earning a below-subsistence income and requiring assistance; job security and unemployment; the percentage of income allocated to education and training; retirement income; the quality and distribution of health care; recreational facilities for everyone; the adequacy of maintaining the infrastructure (roads, highways, schools, and so on), the protection of the environment; research and development; and the availability of free or low-priced cultural activities to everyone. This list is, of course, incomplete, and depends on how the quality of life is reflected in the values and the culture of a people, as will be further discussed in chapter 15.

The main effort should be to regard the GNP in a broader sense and more realistically as a component of the quality of life, subject to its standards. Any other measure of the GNP is not likely to reflect the needs of people and the environment.

How is the GNP created? It is the product of a total effort in the production of goods and services. It involves the cooperation of all the people who contribute the various components of production. They in turn are the recipients of the GNP, which gives them a claim to the goods and services produced.

There is no doubt that those who contribute to the creation of the GNP are entitled to a share of it, but the question has provided one of the great controversies in the evolution of economic theory. The physiocrats (the French economists who preceded Adam Smith) believed that natural laws governing the rate of growth of populations kept the wages of labor barely at the subsistence level, with a few exceptions. They reasoned that similar natural laws governed the return on capital (profit and interest).

It was not until the time of the neoclassical economists of the late nineteenth and early twentieth centuries that productivity became a factor in wages. Wages were assumed to reflect the productivity of labor. Capital, too, earned a return equal to its productivity.

The neoclassical economists added an important dimension to wage theory in a world in which economic growth had a high priority. They based their claim that wages reflect productivity on the assumption that labor is mobile and that markets operate under natural economic laws that automatically correct any inequality between the supply and demand for labor.

Neoclassical theories of the distribution of income are based on the belief that all economic activity is controlled by market prices. Wages are the price of labor, and profits the price of capital, and each is subject to the productivity of the other.

In today's world, the price mechanism is only one of the forces affecting economic activity. Much of this activity does not respond to ordinary price adjustments. This includes political and social organization—internal and external to the firm—as explained in the previous chapter. It also includes the rapid and radical technological advances that bring about many structural changes to which adaptation is far from automatic, and should in fact be based on specific and relevant planned action. Such adjustments are beyond the abilities of the neoclassical market—even if such a market existed in the free and pure form that the neoclassical economists had envisaged.

If the neoclassical market does not exist, at least insofar as its ability to allocate resources and income is concerned, then how is income distributed?

Wages in Planned and Unplanned Markets

The division of income presents one of the sharpest areas of conflict. The neoclassical economists avoided dealing with this problem by assuming that the economic laws of the market, based on supply and demand, would lead to a "natural" division of income.

Marx attributed this conflict to private ownership of the means of production, which in his view led to a society subject to *class* struggle. His solution lay in the social ownership of the means of production and a classless society.

In any society—socialist or capitalist—the total value of income that can be distributed is determined by the total value of the goods and services produced. This in turn is subject to the productivity of all the factors that produce the goods and services. Although productivity controls the *total volume* of production, it does not control, as the classical economists believed, the *distribution* of income to the factors of production.

The missing links in traditional productivity theory are the extent to which the recipients of income possess power. In addition to that, there is no practical way to measure the productivity of labor. The productivity of labor depends on *all* the inputs required for producing a unit of output.[6]

In traditional productivity theory, the cost of every unit of the various inputs in production is determined by supply and demand. Productivity is merely *one* of the factors involved. The following example will illustrate this:

> The workers at company A are about as competent and as experienced as the workers in more efficient firms. So why is company A relatively inefficient; that is, why is its cost of operation higher than other firms'? The reason is that it is undercapitalized and poorly managed. Thus, productivity in company A is lower than in the other firms. Yet, unless there is a recession and unemployment, firm A has to pay its workers the going wage rate determined by supply and demand. It cannot pay a lower rate reflecting the firm's lower productivity because of labor unions. The wages, therefore, are not determined by the workers' productivity in each firm, but by conditions of the market for labor. Labor unions are only one of the factors that make up this market.

It is also clear that to the extent that one can refer to a worker's productivity, this productivity is determined by many factors external to the worker as well as by some factors internal to the worker. *The productivity of a worker is the product of a cooperative process,* as is the productivity of capital and technology. In a modern economy cooperation is the essence of productivity. Cooperation between workers and all the other factors of production, (management, investors, lenders, creators of technology, the owners of resources, and the public sector) is essential. This can be done by establishing realistic and viable social and political relationships for everyone involved in economic activity.

What are the conditions of the markets that determine the division of income? Markets may be *completely free*, with no one exercising power over price, output, wages, and so on (the laissez-faire market); they may be *partly free* and *partly planned by private management;* or they may be *planned* by the public sector.

The U.S. economy, like every other modern economy, is composed of all three types of markets. There are, however, important differences in the proportions in which these markets exist in different countries. The biggest differences lie in the supply side of the markets, but there are also differences in the way demand is exercised. In some socialist countries, such as the Soviet Union, the supply of producers' and consumers' goods is mainly in the hands of a central planning commission, with the help of regional and local planning boards. Such plans may be for five years or longer and are modified periodically to correct errors or for other reasons.

Consumer demand is "free" in the Soviet Union insofar as people can choose to buy the goods and services available—providing they can pay the price. When there are shortages in the more important necessities for which demand is fairly inelastic, long lines appear at stores, which may have sold out. There is still a market because transactions take place between sellers and buyers, and because consumers are free to choose, limited only by income restraints and available supply.

In the U.S. economy, there is a considerable amount of planning by that part of the private sector composed of oligopolistic firms and powerful labor unions. The supply of goods in the privately planned sector is determined to a large extent by managements in firms possessing power. The planning, however, is not as centralized as in the socialist countries.

The demand side of the privately planned sector includes consumers who are free to choose, subject to their ability to pay and the availability of goods and services. Since this market is largely privately planned on the supply side, it does not meet the specifications of the classical free and self-adjusting market.

The shortages in some of the Soviet Bloc's planned economies are not necessarily due to the fact that these economies are planned. The unplanned capitalist economies have also had serious shortages in various stages of their development. These shortages, however, were concealed by the fact that the prices of some of the most important necessities were above what the poor could afford to pay. The vast majority of the poor had far too little income for even the barest necessities. This did not result in shortages or queues in stores because prices effectively kept the poor from the markets for most goods and services, and they still do in 1988.

In the Soviet Union, moreover, the prices of necessities are often marked too low in terms of the income available to the masses. This results in both shortages and long lines. The prices of necessities are kept low enough by price setting for all people to be able to afford. The problem arises because of shortages. Many products are simply not available in adequate quantities, often as a result of priorities set by the government.

In addition to the privately planned market and the markets planned by public authority, there is the unplanned private market consisting of firms not large enough to possess power over the price mechanism. In the United States, this includes some of the service, agriculture, and manufacturing fields. The basic industries such as steel, other metals, energy, automobiles, utilities, and transportation consist of relatively few large firms that are part of the privately planned sector.

In the *unplanned* private market, wages are largely determined by factors outside the control of the firm. Although labor is largely nonunionized in this market, if a firm employs skilled labor, the wages it has to pay will often be influenced by union wages in the bigger firms and in other industries in the same region. Wages will also be influenced by the cost of living in the community. Power is not a significant factor in this market, and productivity is to a large extent only a long-run limiting factor in the wages the firm has to pay.

In the *planned* private sector, the firm and the labor union representing the workers possess power. Wages are determined by negotiations between management and labor. During the inflationary periods, money wages generally increase more than productivity.

Since this sector has power that it uses against smaller firms from whom it buys some of its supplies, it has an effect on the ability of these firms to pay wages, Hence the power of the big firms indirectly affects the wages of the firms in the unplanned private market. Frequently, the power of the large firm forces the smaller firm to compensate for its unfavorable terms of trade with the large firms by reducing its profits as well as the wages it pays.

Another result of the power factor in regard to wage determination of the firms in the planned private sector is the impact on prices and the price level. When management is able to shift the cost of wage demands of union labor to the consumer or to other firms that buy its products, it will do so to buy labor peace.

The neoclassical economists—building a system of economics on the hypothesis that wages are determined by the productivity of labor in a self-adjusting market, and ignoring the existence of power—created a vacuum in the theory of income distribution. If production is to be a cooperative effort leading to both efficient output and a regard for the individual and the environment, it must be based on a *realistic* theory of income distribution.

The present process of wage determination has several major weaknesses and leaves much to be desired. It discriminates against workers in the unplanned private sector, it is inflationary, and it alienates workers and management by making them adversaries in what would otherwise be a cooperative process.

Wage determination in the public sector of a private-enterprise economy such as the United States is in the hands of the Congress and the Civil Service Commission. The wages paid are not really comparable to those in the planned private sector. The president of the United States receives far less than the head of a major corporation when all bonuses, stock dividends, options, and other fringe benefits are considered. Cabinet members with great responsibility for and impact on the public welfare get far less than the senior managers of a large corporation. The same is true of the Supreme Court and the Congress.

At the professional staff level, the differences are just as great. The heads of marketing, engineering, and finance of the major corporations usually receive two to three times as much as the chairpeople of important agencies, such as the Federal Reserve and the Council of Economic Advisors. The top levels of the civil service system are equally underpaid compared to their counterparts in the private sector. This has resulted in a preference for the private sector on the part of the top graduates of colleges and universities and deprives the public sector of equal opportunity where excellence and talent are important and vital to the public interest. As a result, the public sector often has to employ people in the upper levels who are either underpaid or relatively less competent than their counterparts in the private sector. In the lower levels, public employees may in fact be overpaid compared to their private sector counterparts.

An exception to this is the influx from the academic community to the military sector, which is offering virtually unlimited funds for defense and space research. The salaries paid by the government in this area usually exceed academic salaries, and the research opportunities are a great attraction to research-oriented scientists.

Federal-government employees may belong to labor unions, but the unions have less power than those in the private sector. The strike—the union's strongest weapon—is forbidden to these unions. The theory is that it is illegal to strike against the U.S. government because it is a sovereign state.

Labor mobility does not tend to eliminate wage differences for similar skills in different industries and geographic regions. The differences are perpetuated through the existence of various degrees of power in different labor markets and through a deep-rooted bias on the part of taxpayers against the bureaucracy of the public sector. The existence of arbitrary power and irrational biases in the market for labor has created serious conflicts and widespread alienation. The solution to this problem is a prerequisite for economic efficiency and social harmony.

The Role of Profit and Interest

Profit is not merely one of several sources of income. It is the heart of the market mechanism. The classical economists believed profit to be the central factor that allocates resources according to the laws of supply and demand.

For profit to play this role, it has to be assumed that the maximization of profit is the dominant motive in production. This can be illustrated in very simple terms. The firm in order to maximize its profit has to change its price and output as dictated by changes in demand signalled to the market by consumers. (The consumer is assumed to determine output, this being consistent with the classical concept of free choice and Mill's principle of the greatest happiness for the greatest number.) Profit is payment to the risk takers who provide the capital necessary for production. In this role, it is a factor in the distribution of income.

The role of profit in classical economies, therefore, extends far beyond profit as a payment to the entrepreneur who plays the key role in the creation of wealth and economic growth. Its primary function is to regulate the market automatically, without external discretion, as the efficient allocator of resources.

Even today, most economists make the maximization of profit the primary motive in production. This is either a bias or a conclusion drawn from irrefutable evidence. Without this assumption, the equilibrium process of the market cannot be defended as it is in economic theory by traditional economists.

Since the early 1930s, economists have accepted the fact that in most industries, markets are far from perfect or pure. Theories of monopoly, oligopoly, and imperfect competition became an accepted fact in economic literature. In the eyes of the traditional economists, such industries simply became less efficient than they would be in a perfect or pure market. These economists did not question the profit motive as the dominant factor in production. They asserted that the market, though handicapped by imperfections, still reflected the wishes of the consumer.

The two questions to be analyzed at this point are how profits are determined and whether profits are indeed the magnet that draws production. Profit emerged in classical and neoclassical economic theory as the share of income going to those who assumed risk by investing their money in the capital fund of a firm. In the economic process, such money was converted into the means of production, such as buildings, equipment, and tools.

Prior to the rise of large corporations, this risk function was assumed by the entrepreneurs, who combined it with the management functions of the firm. They received two kinds of payments: wages for their role as a manager and profits for their assumption of risk. Sometimes their income, consisting of wages and profits, was carelessly referred to as profits only, but that is incorrect from a standpoint of income distribution.

With the rise of the corporation, the two functions of the entrepreneur were separated by the emergence of the stockholder (or risk taker) and the professional manager, who became the top employee of the corporation. Later, the function of manager was subdivided to cope with the problems of an advanced technology, and all upper-level managers jointly became the senior management.

In the planned private sector, the managers receive salaries, bonuses, and fringe benefits, and the stockholders receive profits in the form of dividends. The corporate stocks are bought and sold on the primary and secondary markets of the stock exchanges by individuals and organizations who want to invest their funds for income or capital appreciation.

The division of the entrepreneurial function has created a great distance between the owners (stockholders) and the management, which for all practical purposes is the real decisionmaker in a corporation. The management is controlled by a board of directors, which is theoretically elected by the stockholders, most of whom do not even know the names of top management, much less the names of the directors. Actually, members of the board are chosen by top management and the sitting members. The exceptions to this pattern are rare.

High technology has begun to change the pattern of ownership and profit. Knowledge has become the newest form of capital and it is not uncommon for people who contribute vital knowledge to receive stock and stock options in payment for their knowledge and technical skills. In many firms, knowledge is frequently rewarded with a voice in the decision-making process.

Profit in a corporate economy, especially a modern one, is therefore, a reward for knowledge as well as a return for risk. The possessors of vital knowledge become part of the decision-making process of a corporation, but not as stockholders, since they usually own too little stock for that in a large corporation.

In the sector of the economy in which firms are relatively small, the owner-manager still plays an important role. Even in small firms, however, if high technology is involved, the owners of financial capital more and more must share ownership of the firm with the owners of knowledge. So far as authority and participation in the management of a large firm are concerned, it is knowledge, and usually not stock ownership, that opens the doors of opportunity.

The role assigned by the classical and neoclassical economists to profit as the motivator of efficient economic activity and the key to a self-adjusting market, has to be revised in view of the changes that have taken place in the industrial structure. The changes in the role of profit are the direct result of the separation of ownership and management. The managers of a modern corporation are *personally* interested in profits only to the extent to which they own stock, which is usually small compared to their other benefits from the corporation. As *managers* they also have to be concerned about profits in order to satisfy the stockholders and thus keep the capital structure viable. This does not require the maximization of profits. It merely requires enough profits to match similar results of other corporations.

The managers and decisionmakers of a corporation generally benefit personally and directly more when they manage a large corporation than a small one. To the managers, growth is frequently a more satisfactory accomplishment than profit maximization so long as profits are adequate to satisfy stockholders in a competitive market for stocks.

The net revenue earned by a firm is often greater than the dividends paid out to stockholders. The difference is called retained earnings, which are invested in the growth of the firm. As the firm grows, its future becomes more secure and the rewards going to management increase. The stockholders get a certain dividend—if it is earned—the size of which is determined to a large extent by the market for equity capital. Beyond that, management can concentrate on growth.

It is more accurate to say that the dominant motives in the corporate firm are *adequate profits and growth,* rather than the *maximization of profits.* This challenges the assumption of traditional economists that the consumer rules in the capitalist marketplace (to be discussed further in the next chapter). The decision of a firm need not be dominated by changes in demand so long as profit maximization is not the ultimate aim. A firm may instead concentrate on mergers and acquisitions.

Interest, like profit, plays a dual role in neoclassical economics. It is one of the components of the national income paid to people who lend their funds to other people who use them in some economic activity. The question of ownership of such funds does not arise as it does with equity funds, stocks, and so on. Although the money made available to the users of capital by stockholders is for most purposes indistinguishable from that made available by lenders, the whole system of private ownership today is based on such a distinction. Frequently the lenders, if they are large financial institutions, have a far greater voice in the management of a corporation than all but very few stockholders; in some corporations no single stockholder has any real voice at all. The large lenders usually are able to participate in the affairs of their largest borrowers by putting one of their top officers on the board of directors.

Perhaps the chief difference between stockholders and bondholders (or lenders) is that dividends on common stocks are declared, not guaranteed. On bonds, the interest paid is an *obligation* of the corporation. The interest on all borrowed funds are a legal obligation of the borrower.

Interest, although it is one of the distributive shares of the national income, is determined, unlike wages and profits, by both the private sector and the public sector. Monetary policy (that is, Federal Reserve policy in regard to the money supply) has a direct impact on interest rates.

Like wages, interest is both a part of the national income and a cost of production. Interests rates are determined primarily by the supply of savings, changes in the money supply, the demand for credit, and expectations in regard to prices and economic activity. It is paradoxical that when the Federal Reserve attempts to combat inflation by restricting the growth of the money supply, interest rates rise, which increases the cost of production and puts pressure on prices.

In countries that rely heavily on monetary policy to combat inflation, interest rates are likely to be high during periods of buoyant economic activity. This serves to abort an expansion before inflation gets out of hand. A better way to combat inflation is to attack its causes. This approach is not likely to deprive a nation of steady economic growth and create unemployment as too great a reliance on monetary policy does. The preceding argument is more fully developed in chapter 5.

Although interest rates have an impact on the economy, that impact is probably much less than the neoclassical economists assume. If inflation or unemployment are caused by structural factors such as declining productivity, they are much less responsive to change in interest rates. Another reason interest rates are less important than assumed is that the planned private sector consisting of the larger corporations is much less dependent on external financing than it used to be. Today, a considerable part of corporate investment is generated by the price mechanism, which enables firms to finance themselves internally. This makes interest rates less important in their investment policies than if they depended entirely on external financing.

Wages, profit, and interest make up the national income.[7] They also play an important role in *traditional* economic theory as the variables that possess the magic power to keep the economy in equilibrium. The desire on the part of traditional economists to depict the economy as being almost entirely regulated by natural economic laws that help to achieve a stable equilibrium has caused them to imbue profits and interest with magic capabilities that, unfortunately, they do not possess.

The distribution of income today is not determined by pure market forces as the founders of the capitalist doctrine had invisaged. They perceived the distribution of income to be just, because they believed that it was determined by the unseen hand of the natural laws of supply and demand.

Income distribution has, in fact, become a matter of political power and social organization. Labor unions, corporate management, and the laws and policies of government are now superimposed on the economic market. The challenge today is to make the distribution of income fair as perceived by those who contribute to its creation. This is discussed further in later chapters.

8
The Role of Consumption in Satisfying Human and Environmental Needs

Consumption as the Road to Fulfillment

Consumption in the broad sense—all that we take in from the outside world—plays a vital role in human fulfillment. It shapes a person's ability to be creative and to enjoy life via the senses. In a very real sense, we are the product of what we consume, given our genetic and congenital factors.

In a psychologically healthy human being, consumption is essentially not an end in itself. It serves to satisfy human needs and to enrich life. But consumption must be limited or controlled to protect the needs of the environment so that future generations may live *their* lives. We do not own the earth. It is handed on from one generation to the next. The deeds of each generation thus leave their mark on future generations.

Questions concerning the quality of life have puzzled and fascinated many philosophers. The stoic philosophers saw happiness as the reward for self-discipline and the ability to accept life and its hardships. The utilitarians, who exerted a major influence on classical economics, saw it in terms of pleasure and pain. Reflection will show that actually both discipline and pleasure are necessary factors in happiness, no matter how it is defined.

It is a common phenomenon for human beings to have problems that need to be dealt with. Such problems have their origin in nature and evolution, and they are transmitted genetically, congenitally, and via the environment. The belief that problems are the result of imprudent living is far too limited a view to explain most problems.

Even so common a problem as insecurity has deep roots, which when ignored can become a source of pain and anguish. There are many problems that most, if not all, human beings face. Identity, acceptance, self-worth, recognition, building human bridges, guilt feelings, and the countless tasks involved in preparing for life are among the problems that must be dealt with as a condition for fulfillment. Since the human body, mind, and psyche and the environment are not perfect, only some problems can be "solved"; others require that we learn to cope with them.

Once humankind learns to deal with problems, the foundation is laid for greater human enjoyment and pleasure. At that point, what economists call consumption becomes a more important part of life. Some pleasures are a free gift of nature but generally involve some monetary expenditures. A trip to the Grand Canyon or the Canadian glaciers are examples. Pleasures such as books, toys, tapes, or attendance at a ballgame, symphony, or ballet are the creations of man. Still other pleasures are combined with the basic necessities of life, such as a home, furniture, clothing, and food.

Creativity is the act of self-expression that, together with the pleasures transmitted through the senses, forms the basis for human fulfillment. Creativity comes in many forms: the happiness we give to others; the personal dimension we add to knowledge and culture; the role we play in the environment of which we are a part.

Human preferences and culture, which play vital roles in consumption, are greatly influenced by the social institutions we build. Ideally, they should be concerned with the important needs of the human being and the human's environment. That is to say, the question of happiness and the quality of life should become more important in the selection and ordering of preferences.

Since income is limited for the vast majority of people, consumption should be consistent, in the economic sense, with a person's priorities. These should be clearly defined, and ideally they should have a high regard for basis needs and the quality of life. The basic needs of people are fairly standard: sensible nourishment, clean and comfortable shelter, adequate clothing, recreation, health care, education.

The quality of life leaves greater room for choice—work and hobbies that allow for creativity; the translation of compassion into action that enriches the lives of others; the enjoyment of one or more of the performing arts; stimulating reading, travel, and athletics; and other pleasurable activities. In order to get the most satisfaction from all the choices one has, it is necessary to list the activities of life in the order of their importance or to assign to them the priorities we want to give them. Since no one can do everything—because of time, income, and energy limitations—it is desirable to choose several activities to which we have given the highest priority.

The activities to which each individual gives the highest priority become that person's source of pleasure. But such enjoyment is not automatic. Most of us must *learn* to appreciate the things from which we expect to derive pleasure and fulfillment. We are not necessarily born with that ability. Even so natural a human relationship as sex requires knowledge, sensitivity, skill, and finesse if it is to be a source of mutual pleasure.

If consumption, in its fullest sense, is to lead to human fulfillment as well as to the satisfaction of basic needs, a person must be trained to appreciate the things that are capable of contributing to it. That is the essence of culture. If a culture is based on values that produce an appreciation for the things that lead to fulfillment through pleasures that stimulate the total person, such a culture contributes to human happiness. If, however, a culture is based solely on materialistic values that make the acquisition of wealth and power the central aim in life while neglecting to encourage an appreciation of intellectual, aesthetic, and physical excellence, it greatly limits the opportunities for human fulfillment.

This is not to say that money is not an important factor in the achievement of many of the things that lead to happiness. It should always be viewed, however, as a means to an end, never as an end in itself or as a substitute for the development of those inner resources without which life cannot be appreciated.

A person's selection of a career, income goals, and expenditure patterns should coincide with the priorities he or she has assigned to activities that will serve as the source of pleasure and happiness. The *long-run* consequences of decisions and choices are major factors in the achievement of individual fulfillment. The use of "free choice" as a tool for expressing an individual's perceived notion of self-interest is misguiding. Long-term concerns must *limit* present actions. The freedom to choose our limitations through a democratic process is a concept more likely to lead to happiness than the unrestricted freedom to choose regardless of the impact of the choice on others, on the environment, and on the quality of life in the future. Human wisdom dictates a balance and harmony between free choice and social culture.

If consumption is viewed in its total impact upon the individual and society, then the role of social responsibility in regard to such social ills as slums and unemployment becomes self-evident. Social responsibility does not begin and end with public expenditures. Transfer payments to the unemployed and subsidies and welfare checks to slum dwellers do not remove the harm done by these ills. They merely help to sustain life in the slums.

The environment created by slums, underemployment, and unemployment is as highly unfavorable to society (as a whole) as bruises are to an apple. For those directly affected by these conditions, it is not merely a question of economic poverty, but more importantly a problem of an unwholesome environment. Not only are slum dwellers and the underemployed often deprived of the basic necessities, but the environment does not offer them opportunities for developing an appreciation for the things that could bring them fulfillment.

Numerous economists have been so anxious to reject Marx's charges that capitalism inevitably produces socially undesirable *economic* crises that they have neglected the *qualitative* harm done by unemployment and underemployment. If economists are to deal with real problems and not just with numbers, they must combine their quantitative methods with qualitative evaluations. Although the *quality* of consumption cannot be measured like the *quantity* of consumption, it can be perceived and evaluated. If this is not done, conclusions drawn from the quantitative measures of consumption are less meaningful (a matter that will be discussed at the start of chapter 15).

The question of consumption has been made more complicated by the fact that humanity's social inventions, such as corporations and governments, have an impact on consumption that is often caused by other aims than the satisfaction of the essential needs of people and the environment. This is one more reason why the genius and curiosity reflected in our great scientific and social inventions must be carefully and wisely guided lest we lose control and become marionettes dancing to the music of a mad piper.

The Fiction of Consumer Supremacy

To the classical economists and their modern descendants, the consumer is supreme. The consumer's needs and wants—limited only by the scarcity of resources, human technology, and skills—determine what the economy produces. The producer, perceived under the illusion of the free and self-adjusting market controlled by no one, is merely a neutral unit who reflects the natural laws operating the market. If consumers' needs are not satisfied, it is their own fault, except at time when the economy deviates from equilibrium, which is not considered a serious problem since the market is assumed to correct itself automatically.

The illusion of such a market is not the only weakness of the classical theory. The truth of the assumption that the consumer could, by pursuing his or her own interest, create the greatest good for the greatest number depends on consumers' knowledge of the needs of their environment as well as of their own physical and psychological needs. It also depends on their knowledge of the impact of their current consumption preferences on their own futures and the future of the environment. If this assumption about the knowledge of the consumer is not made, it is absurd to conclude that by pursuing their own interests, they will, ipso facto, produce the greatest good for the greatest number.

Actually this theory was never tested because in the nineteenth century, before the advent of the great corporations, the large majority of people lived in or near poverty, having little free choice and doing their best to survive. The rich and near rich were able to pursue their own interests, but is is doubtful that this led to the greatest good for the greatest number, especially in respect to the needs of the environment and the quality of life in later generations.

The history of humanity provides ample evidence that the concept of free choice is an illusion. We may have left the Garden of Eden, but we are still very much a part of nature, which determines many of our physical and psychological needs that we can ignore only at our peril. This is hardly a case of free choice.

The situation is equally clear in respect to our social environment. We are taught that to survive, we have to live by rules. (The primitive religions and later most great religions based survival or salvation on rules.) Furthermore, not only survival but also the quality of life is based on rules that one may call a moral foundation.

Political organizations, too, are based on rules, which, in the writings of the great political philosophers, provide the foundation for such human goals as social justice and political stability. The point is not that rules or laws will guarantee survival and a decent quality of life; it is that the great religions and political philosophers understood the necessity for balancing individual freedom with social wisdom.

Today's culture is dominated by highly materialistic, technocratic values that find expression in consumption. Some of our most important values are shaped by this overly materialistic culture and the institutions it generates. Yet much economic theory, it seems, is still based on the concept of consumer supremacy. The producer is assumed to play a responsive role, the command coming from the consumer to the producer via the market.

In the world of today, the pattern of consumption is far more complex. Much of what is consumed in the broad sense of that term originates in the minds of scientists and other professionals long before its purchase. Contrary to traditional economic theory, it is the producer and not the consumer who generally initiates the process of consumption. The pattern of consumption is altered by advances in the frontier of knowledge. The new knowledge is converted into new products. By means of skillful marketing techniques, these new products usually enter the stream of consumption.

The modern corporation is organized to control a substantial part of the process of consumption through its management of science, technology, marketing, and finance. It must, of course, display these products in a way that will appeal to the consumer. It does this through its special relationships to the various media and through the massive use of advertising.

Since the producer is chiefly motivated by such goals as reliable and expanding markets, dependable sources of supply, and profitable operations, the question must be raised whether these goals lead to a pattern of consumption consistent with essential human and environmental needs. This is a vital question in the evolution of a sane and humane society and an environment in harmony with it.

To most traditional economists this question is of no special interest because they assume, as we have seen, that the producer is following the commands of the consumer. Consumers presumably satisfy their present and future needs and the needs of the environment by pursuing their preferences. The traditional economist regards this as a built-in protection for the consumer. In the modern world dominated by the needs and interests of the corporation and by an immediate satisfaction impulse on the part of consumers, (who all but disregard the long-range consequences on themselves, on others, and on the environment), the prospects for a sane and humane society are somewhat doubtful.

The assumption of consumer supremacy precludes a realistic approach to consumption. The considerable control the large corporation exercises over the prices of its products and its vast influence over the multimedia advertising machinery are only two problems in regard to consumption. If the producer had no power or influence at all over consumption, free choice and the pursuit of self-interest would not necessarily solve the dilemma. Inadequate knowledge on the part of most consumers regarding their own physical and psychological needs and those of their environment would still have to be overcome. The inability or unwillingness to take a *long-range* view of the impact of current consumption on the future quality of life is another flaw in the present consumption pattern.

Not only the pattern of consumption, but also the management of aggregate demand are of major concern to the producer of today. The huge outlays required for the developed of new products and the improvement of existing products require a steady flow of demand in order to make the operations profitable. In fact, satisfactory growth in the U.S. economy is a prerequisite for inducing the savings of the economy to be productively invested. If domestic markets cannot provide such growth, the producer looks to foreign markets and solicits the aid of government in the acquisition of such markets.

The producer, whose main goals are a growing market and profitable sales, has more important immediate concerns than the quality of life of the consumer and the quality of the environment. It is therefore not surprising that in today's economy, consumption is more likely to be based on the real needs of the producer than on the real needs of the consumer and the environment.

The main challenge in regard to consumption is how to organize it so as to make survival, a sane society, and the quality of life its *prime* goals.

Basic Needs and Social Responsibilities

> The dominant aim of economics is to contribute to a solution of social problems.
>
> —Alfred Marshall
> *Principles of Economics,* 1890.

The quality of life depends as much on physical, mental, and emotional health and a wholesome attitude toward life as it does on external possessions. Yet economists judge the *success* of the economy largely in quantitative terms that measure per capita consumption or the size of the Gross National Product.

When we consider an individual's total wealth, we should not ignore an extremely important part of wealth—collective wealth. Neoclassical economist Alfred Marshall pointed out that collective wealth is often the most essential kind of wealth. This becomes evident when we compare an environment favorable to human life with one that is hostile to it.

To the extent that an individual benefits from the environment, the environment should be counted as part of the person's wealth and income. The reason for including it is not merely that to do so is logical; it is necessary. If it is not counted as part of total wealth, it will not be considered to be that, which would be a distortion of real values. Some collective wealth is a free gift of nature. An important part of collective wealth, however, is created by people themselves.

The list of such collective wealth is far too long to itemize here, but a few examples will demonstrate its importance: a clean and healthy environment; decent housing at affordable costs; cultural enrichment; public parks and other recreational facilities; jobs and economic opportunity; a good educational system; and necessary social services.

If such collective wealth is available only to the privileged and the rich, the social and physical environment, from the standpoint of human consumption, is unfavorable for the large majority. This was the case in most countries experiencing industrial development in the nineteenth and early twentieth centuries. The economy was generally controlled by the rich and the privileged, most of whom believed that they had no responsibility to those in a less fortunate position.

The most advanced countries today accept at least some responsibility for using collective wealth to improve the quality of life for their people. They regard such collective wealth as necessary for basic human needs. In some of the socialist countries, responsibility for these needs has a high priority in economic planning.

In a favorable environment, as in the United States, such needs should never be regarded as luxuries: they should be treated as basic necessities. In an unfavorable environment, as in many developing countries, the best social effort may not be enough to produce such public wealth for basic needs. This failure may simply be a characteristic of early industrial development that can be overcome when economic capabilities improve.

The traditional market system exposes one of its most serious shortcomings in its neglect of collective wealth and social responsibility. Most traditional economists assume that individuals, following their own interests, will create a society that will satisfy all human needs as well as the needs of the environment. The problem is, in such economists' view, keeping the free-market structure intact—not the adoption of social policy.

The classical economists believed that consumption is the reason for production. They did not, however, realize that their market (or the invisible hand) had no way of making sure that production satisfied the essential *immediate* and *future* needs of human beings. That is one of the reasons why market theory has to be modified and made compatible with present-day exigencies.

The matter of social responsibility has become a major political issue in the United States and is a key controversy between the conservatives and the liberals. Whether an economy is capable of responding adequately to human and environmental needs depends on its economic capabilities in *general* and on the intelligent allocation of resources *specifically*. Excessive military expenditures and an obsession with luxuries may leave little room for the basic human needs without creating inflationary pressures, even in a relatively wealthy nation.

To what extent should the government accept responsibility for the satisfaction of vital human and environmental needs? Certainly, to allow them to go unheeded is to invite serious social problems in the future. A society may, for example, if it chooses, ignore the nourishment of its children. Or it may fail to furnish cultural and educational opportunities that prepare them for useful and creative lives. But such a society cannot escape the much greater costs of the resulting health problems, crime, unemployment, and underemployment that result from such a policy.

The relevant question now becomes: should society accept responsibility only when neglect leads to serious problems, or should it accept responsibility in the prevention of such problems? It can allocate its resources in a way that produces a healthy and productive population, or it can ignore such duties and later bear the prohibitive costs of its neglect and shortsightedness. *The market can react to the various price signals; it cannot create a motivated society! The reliance on the market for the solution of problems completely beyond its reach is one of the most serious shortcomings of traditional economics.*

The economic market is an essential part of a democratic society. Its signals are vital and should not be ignored. If, for example, the market signals that a third of the population cannot afford to buy or rent decent housing at existing market prices, social action is required to prevent slums and all the social problems arising from them.

There are several alternatives in dealing with such problems. One is to do nothing and shift the responsibility and costs to future generations! Another is to lower the costs of housing through a more efficient use of the resources involved. If the housing industry is already efficient, the remedy may lie in subsidies to the housing industry to meet the potential demand of the third of the population that cannot afford housing. The market cannot solve this problem efficiently because it is an income problem or perhaps a problem of an inefficient industry structure.

It would be incorrect to assume that society has no values except those represented by the interests of individuals, or that we are unaware or disinterested in the future or in the general welfare. But, historically, people and government have not awakened to the necessity for action until a severe crisis has arisen. Trying to deal with problems at this stage is fare costlier than the intelligent planning designed to prevent them. Even the best preventive planning cannot eliminate *all* future problems. One reason for this is that there are uncertainties in the future that cannot be anticipated; and in any case human error cannot be entirely eliminated. Nevertheless, social actions designed to anticipate and prevent problems *before* they arise are likely to be much more effective and economical than actions taken *after* the harm is already done.

Automobile and chemical manufacturers, for example, do not regard it as a matter of self-interest to protect the environment from pollution. On the contrary, they reluctantly adopt antipollution measures when they are required to do so by public authority. There are many cases of evasion, even when it is clear that such practices endanger human life! Although there is a cost involved in the *prevention* of environmental pollution, it is likely to be far less than the cost of *removing* the pollution from the environment.

Programs to correlate education and training with the kind of jobs available when a person is ready for employment involve costs, but such costs are far less than the cost of structural unemployment and underemployment. The rapid technological changes of a modern economy make planning absolutely essential in correlating the supply of labor with the demand for labor.

Many modern governments are already accepting the principle of social responsibility in varying degrees. Some governments concentrate on *preventing* problems in regard to basic human and environmental needs. Other governments intervene only when the problems already exist. Sometimes it is a question of poor economic planning; at other times, a matter of half-hearted attempts at planning.

It is obvious that social responsibility cannot be left to the market, although the market often plays an important role in identifying problems. As in all such matters, the question of where social responsibility begins requires a pragmatic answer. If a society knows its basic human and environmental needs, then social responsibility begins there. It is then only a choice between adopting policies that *prevent* human suffering (and make costly remedies unnecessary) or adopting policies that make the government responsible *after* the problems exist.

Should society study ways to anticipate and meet in the most economical way the needs of all its members, or should it postpone necessary action until the task is far more difficult and costly? Can civilized human beings allow their society to shirk its responsibility to improve the opportunities and quality of life for the least of its citizens? These are the decisions we must make. The price of ignoring them may be worldwide political instability and conflict in the future.

Survival and the Quality of Life as the Foundation of Consumption

The fact that the corporate sector largely controls the pattern of consumption has escaped many economists who still assume that consumer sovereignty governs production. This creates a serious problem because the needs of the producers and consumers are not the same, although many economists still construct their microeconomic models as though they were the same.

If the needs of the consumer and producer are significantly different, and the producer rather than the consumer and producer are significantly different, and the producer rather than the consumer has control over what is produced, the quality of life and even survival are jeopardized unless a way can be found to bridge the gap. The solution to this problem is extremely complex because it involves the whole pattern of values and culture.

One does not have to dig very deeply to recognize the connection between the economic organization and human values and culture. The need of the corporation to grow and to be profitable makes it necessary for consumers to develop a high degree of materialism in both their values and their culture. This becomes self-evident when we consider what the effect on the U.S. economy would be if consumers were to decide that one car and one television set per family were enough, or that it was not necessary to have the latest model in all their possessions.

The modern corporation depends on an insatiable appetite on the part of the consumer, and its uses every form of information media to influence that appetite. More and more, people's success is judged by their material possessions. For a brief period in the 1960s, young people rebelled against this crass materialism, but their rebellion lacked in judgment and organization what it possessed in heart. Since then, judging by the trends in career choices and the changed attitudes of students, materialism has returned stronger than ever.

The problem is not simply materialism; it is *uncontrolled* materialism. People must be materialistic to a certain extent to satisfy most basic physical and psychological requirements, but if we are not also *idealistic*, our materialism will ultimately hurt us. Greed is the product of uncontrolled materialism, and, like all extremes, it is self-destructive. It is devoid of balance, causing conflict and confrontation in the place of peace and harmony.

The economic structure that has evolved requires a materialistic culture, but it is necessary for humanity's survival that a way be found to make materialism consistent with survival and the satisfaction of essential human needs. That is the bridge that must be built between the producer and the consumer, and both must participate in building it.

The question must now be raised that if the corporation is to manage the demand for its products in a way consistent with its growth and profitability, how can it also be concerned with the physical and psychological needs of the consumer and the needs of the environment? At present, consumers are virtually brainwashed with the aid of modern advertising designed to appeal to emotions and immediate impulses. In fact, recent investigations have shown that much of media advertising is aimed at teenagers to prepare them for the role they must play in creating demand for the products of the corporate economy.

As a result of this one-sided approach to consumption, the future of humanity and the environment becomes a function of the growth and profitability of the corporations whose products we purchase. In recent times, a number of governments have intervened to protect the consumer and the environment from the extremes of corporate exploitation. There has developed, however, a countermovement, notably in the United States and Britain, that is attempting to reverse the role of government, returning more power to the corporation.

Political policies that are either procorporation or anticorporation are not useful in reconciling the needs of the producers with the needs of the consumers and the environment. To satisfy the essential needs of the consumer and environment without adequate regard to the needs of the corporation is self-defeating because the economy will be inefficient. To satisfy the needs of the corporation without adequate regard to the vital needs of the consumer and the environment is highly imprudent because the quality of life will suffer, and eventually survival will be threatened.

The problem offers an excellent example of the need for coordination and cooperation as an alternative to unilateral action and confrontation. The principle of cooperation and coordination, as it is used here, is based on an important assumption. The parties concerned must be secure in the belief that they will benefit from such a policy because it is unrealistic to build human and social relationship on pure altruism.

The concept of cooperation is one of the most basic ideas in the evolution of philosophy. Are people egocentric, subjectivist beings or cooperative ones? The early Christian doctrine and the church that embodied it accepted cooperation as the basis of a moral life. The struggle for the free market and emancipation from the church led to the growth of subjectivism and egocentric individualism, which have to a considerable extent influenced the development of modern western philosophy.

The struggle for a free market and the rise of egocentric individualism were accompanied by another development: science and technology. This helped us to change our physical environment and to improve the quality of life, which had been much more at the mercy of the world of nature. Before the advent of science and technology, in the world of Robinson Crusoe, individualism was more consistent with the requirements of life. *The power we gained through science and technology requires the cooperation of many individuals and a social organization (democracy) that allows different groups to function harmoniously.*

Science is morally neutral. It is also incomplete. It helps us to advance the frontiers of knowledge, but it does not by itself help to prepare us to find a life of peace and harmony. Science has helped to make the complex process of life more efficient and more skillful, but it cannot evaluate that process in terms of desirable human ends. For that, a moral foundation is required. The advancement of science and technology in combination with a philosophy of egocentric individualism and without a moral foundation must produce confusion. When this is combined with the power bestowed by science and technology, the result, as evidenced by conditions in our own day, can be devastating.

Traditional economic theory is based on a utilitarian version of egocentric individualism. Considering the evolution of science, technology, and power, it is no wonder that economic theory has become a source of confusion.

It is necessary to find an antidote against the dangers of combining science and technology with egocentric individualism. This antidote is cooperation and coordination. The social sciences must dedicate themselves to the task of developing a goal-oriented, interdisciplinary, rational approach to human activity, an approach dedicated to improving the human condition.

Part III
The Transition to a More Humane Economy

9
The Permanent Process of Evolution—A Matter of Challenge and Response

The Essential Balance between the Individual and Society

Humanity and the environment *depend* on each other for survival. In order for them to survive, such concepts as freedom have to be reexamined. If freedom is interpreted as all people having the right to pursue their own interest and whatever lies in their power without regard for the interests of others and the consequences on the total environment, our remaining days on earth are numbered.

If, on the other hand, freedom is interpreted to mean life within the rules of an authoritarian state, then our survival as creative, cognitive, and reasoning beings is endangered. A balance between these extremes should be considered a vital goal.

In the development of orthodox economic theory, economic activity has been divorced from moral considerations—especially in Great Britain and the United States. Individuals, it is assumed, are concerned primarily with pursuing their own preferences. The good of society is left to the market mechanism. In the words of Adam Smith:

> Every individual is continually exerting himself to find the most advantageous employment for whatever capital he can command. It is his own advantage, indeed, and not that of society, which he has in view. But the study of his own advantage rather necessarily

leads him to prefer that employment which is most advantageous to society. . . . In this case, as in many other cases, he is led by an invisible hand to promote an end which was not part of his intention.[1]

These words of Adam Smith have had the effect of isolating economics from moral and ethical philosophy as well as from the other social sciences. This seems strange in view of the fact that Adam Smith was a professor of moral philosophy (a term that, in those days, embraced what later became the various social sciences and other fields, as well). Yet, the explanation is simple enough. The father of classical economics believed that the natural laws of the free market would keep our baser instincts in check and serve as the guardian of social ethics in the economic process. Since humankind was conceived as the "economic man" whose morals could be left to the workings of the market, economics failed to develop as a genuine branch of the social sciences.

The self-regulating characteristics of Adam Smith's utopian market have evolved into a market structure entirely unforeseen by Smith. The decisions of the people who manage the big corporations are not regulated by an invisible hand. In numerous sectors of the economy, prices are administered and do not serve as an automatic adjustment mechanism. The present heirs of the classical economists looked to natural law to provide the moral and ethical requirements of a just society. Since the conditions required for such natural laws to function do not exist, it is not clear how the modern traditional economists visualize the transition from selfish private interests, freely pursued, to the moral and ethical requirements of a just society.

The fascination with natural laws in the nineteenth century gave birth, as we have seen, to John Stuart Mill's utilitarianisms. Mill believed that if all individuals, so far as their economic goals are concerned, are allowed to pursue their own interests *as they see them,* it will result in the greatest good for the greatest number.

At the other extreme was the doctrine of original sin. This doctrine was concerned with a solution to the problem of reconciling individual selfishness with social harmony. People were seen as being born selfish, self-centered, and incompassionate. If they went through life pursuing only their own interests, they would most likely destroy themselves and society. Original sin, therefore, had to give way to a higher purpose—God's law—if humanity was to survive.

Under this doctrine, humanity was not free to choose in line with its selfish interests. On the contrary, people were expected to live according to the word of God. Since the church was seen as God's representative on earth, individuals and society as a whole could be "saved" by following its rules.

Mill's utilitarianism and the doctrine of original sin formed the two extremes in the search for a solution to the problem of human selfishness and social harmony. The utilitarians underestimated the destructiveness of human selfishness and greed, and the doctrine of original sin underestimated people's ability to worship God while still pursuing their selfish and often antisocial ends. Between these extremes lies the evolution of the individual as a social being.

Survival requires that we evolve into successful social beings. We must establish relationships that facilitate the complex process of human interdependence. This is not a utopian dream; our primary instinct of survival requires it. Such relationships already existed at other times. Now the challenge lies in developing viable relationships for *our* time and *our* world.

Nature controlled the human population with disease and indirectly with various forms of self-destruction, such as war. A small percentage of humans reached adulthood when humanity's story began. Many did not survive the birth process; many more died in infancy. History reflects a continuous battle of people against nature. As our intelligence progressed, we tried to improve our chances of survival. Scientists are struggling hard in the fight against disease and the elements. How does this affect the ecological balance essential to our survival.

Since the "objective" of nature is to preserve the macrocosm through the ecological balance, our attempt to improve on nature's methods must not disturb that balance. For example, if the rate of population growth is significantly increased as a result of better prenatal care and the advancement of medical science, the population balance is disturbed and the individual and society are endangered by a population explosion. This is highly significant today when the ratio between people and the resources necessary to sustain them is increasing at a rapid rate.

Humanity can add its own dimension to nature's food supply, but the food produced by nature is attuned to the biological and chemical needs of people as a result of ecological evolution. The dimension we add must take into consideration the ecological balance between us and nature or the result can be disastrous.

It is clear that we are limited in our freedom to choose by the requirements of the ecological balance if we are to survive. If this balance is to be preserved, it is essential that we know what its limits are. In other words, when we substitute our will for the forces of nature, the ecological balance can be preserved only if we do not ignore nature's "objectives." This leads us to the awesome conclusion that growing knowledge must be accompanied by mature understanding of our needs and the needs of the environment if we are to survive.

We are subject to the requirements of both our physical environment and our social environment. In most primitive societies, social organization and relationships are simple. The "rules" existing to protect the social balance and stability become the culture pattern. As society becomes more complex and diverse and human activity becomes more interdependent, the survival of civilization relies more and more on the acceptance of constructive social relationships built on cooperation.

History records that our ancestors have created many social institutions in their quest for survival and security: the family, the tribe, the church, the school, the various levels of political entities, and many more. In the economic sphere, they created the farm, the factory, the shop, the office, and the corporation.

The early organizations were simple and required only a few people performing specific tasks. As science and technology began to make their impact, economic and political processes became more complex and the social structure became increasingly more interdependent. Our ancestors had to learn to coordinate their efforts with other members of their organizations and to work for commonly recognized objectives. Politically, this led from early tribal organizations to the development of the national state.

The process was frequently interrupted by violence of all kinds, because as soon as some people acquire power, they use it against others to further their own ends. Unrestrained power has had a most crippling effect on social evolution; such power retards the healthy development of society.

Like the political process, the economic process became increasingly complicated. The developed economies of the world have produced intricate and complicated organizations for the production and distribution of goods, services, and technology. These organizations depend on the careful coordination and close cooperation of the men and women who initiate and activate the economic process.

So important is coordination and cooperation in the corporate economy, that sociologists have invented a term, *the corporate norm*, to describe the written and unwritten rules that govern the relationship between the people who manage and operate the corporation. The corporation, however is more that the sum of all the people who work for it.

In the present corporate world, the people who work for the corporation have dual objectives as individuals. On the one hand, they need the opportunity to work and, if possible, to be creative. At the same time, they hope to earn enough to allow them to lead a financially unburdened life. On the other hand, the corporation must have as its objective sufficient profits to survive. To the worker as an individual, corporate profitability is not a primary objective. It becomes a primary objective of workers as social beings because only if the corporation survives can the workers achieve their objective as individuals. The workers can move on, but the same principle applies to all workers in all corporations.

Similar reasoning can be applied to the political process. As individuals, people may prefer to do as they please regardless of the needs of others. History is full of examples of people exploiting people, but the society or political entity of which the individual is a part has other objectives necessary for its survival. It must maintain at least an acceptable level of equity and opportunity in order to remain viable.

The utilitarian belief that the best society is one in which all individuals can pursue their own interests without regard to the needs and conditions of others is completely out of touch with a world in which the invisible hand was amputated long ago. The only possibility of survival for individuals and society in a world so well equipped for self-destruction is the acceptance of social relationships reflecting the maturing of the individual as a social being. We shall explore such relationships in the light of what has already been discovered in the social laboratory in which individuals and society leave their mark as they pass through history.

The Anatomy of Challenge and Response

What the quality of life depends on will become much clearer when we analyze the meaning of challenge and response. Challenge comes from the environment and from the requirements of the ecological and social balance. Our ability to react responsibly comes from our intelligence and from the recognition that we are a part of the environment. Reason and intelligence enable us to modify our environment, but our survival depends on our ability and willingness to preserve the ecological and social balance.

What are some of the challenges to which we must respond intelligently or invite disaster? Excessive population growth in the light of limited resources, environmental pollution, and disagreements between nations are some examples that demonstrate the vital points that our response to challenge determines the quality of life and ultimately our survival.

There is probably little disagreement in regard to the existence of challenge and the necessity for response. The disagreement arises chiefly over the type, quality, and degree of the response and how it should be implemented.

The pollution of the environment poses one of the most critical challenges of our time, equalled only by international conflict and world poverty. The last of these is closely connected with uncontrolled population growth. How does environmental protection respond to the classical definition of economics that has been cited as the foundation on which the quality of life is built? Even today, economic theory is still built on the classical trichotomy of optimization, market equilibrium, and individual preferences.

If the environment is polluted, we must respond. We do not

merely occupy a neutral position in the universe. The impact of our reason and intelligence on the environment influences our chances for survival. If our preferences as individuals do not coincide with the requirements of the environment, they must be modified. They must be adjusted to be in harmony with the environment in order to preserve life itself.

How does a democratic society, operating under traditional concepts of economics, respond to the challenge of environmental pollution? The political organization of modern democratic societies is composed of pressure groups exerting varying degrees of power and influence on legislative bodies charged with making the laws that govern people. Since environmental protection involves substantial costs, those who incur them might oppose legislation that would enforce antipollution measures. This might include pressure groups representing the chemical industries, energy industries, automobile manufacturers, and so on. It might also include consumers opposed to paying for the costs of environmental protection.

The values of those who oppose environmental protection may not have matured sufficiently for them to appreciate the long-range consequences of the harm to themselves and to future generations. The question now arises, suppose the preferences of the most powerful pressure groups are opposed to environmental protection and, as a result, the environment is exposed to lingering and damaging pollution. Members of weaker pressure groups, the apathetic, the uninformed, children below voting age, and future generations will be subjected to an environment that will threaten their existence. Of what merit is economic optimization (the essence of traditional economic theory) if the process optimized creates an impasse between people and the environment? Preferences and pressure groups are not sufficient to create harmony between the individual and the environment. There is a missing dimension, the essential human goals, that must be discovered if we are to survive.

Population control is another challenge. Our response to it is vital. Prior to the Industrial Revolution, most of the world was sparsely populated and life expectancy was low as a result of disease, wars, and other dangers that kept population growth in check. With the development of agriculture, pressure developed for a higher birth rate to satisfy the need for farm workers. Large families were encouraged because the farm needed many sons and daughters to satisfy the demand for labor, before that demand was greatly reduced by the introduction of mechanized farm equipment.

Large families were considered a virtue and sons were preferred to daughters because they were more useful on the farm, took care of their aging parents, and made better soldiers. Some of the major religions adopted policies putting God squarely on the side of uncontrolled population growth. This was an argument against human interference with the work of God and nature.

So long as disease and wars controlled population growth and before the introduction of farm machinery, the absence of birth control did not upset the ecological balance. As soon as human ingenuity improved the chances of survival, the old strictures against birth control began to threaten the environment with uncontrolled population growth. High increases in the rate of population growth in turn began to interfere with efforts to raise the standard of living through economic development.

The countries benefitting from economic development managed to keep their rate of population growth below their rate of capital investment. Only in that way were they able to raise their productivity. Some countries, for religious or other reasons, experienced population growth that far exceeded any practical rate of capital accumulation. This served as an insurmountable obstacle to economic development.

The history of population growth serves as an excellent example of the need for harmony between people and the environment. Some customs inspired by religion and culture to bring harmony between people and the environment serve to create friction and conflict after they have outlived their usefulness as a result of scientific, technological, or social evolution. Dietary laws and the prohibition of divorce and of birth control are examples.

Science, technology, and social evolution are the offspring of reason and intelligence. They have an impact on society and the rules generated by religion and culture must be relevant to these changes if harmony is to be achieved. As we change the social and physical environment, we must change the rules or we endanger ourselves and the world.

Unfortunately, a particular set of rules tend to create special privileges, wealth, and power. When changes create new conditions requiring new rules, serious problems arise. Changing the rules threatens the states quo or the privileges of those whom the old rules have made wealthy and powerful. As a result, powerfully positioned people often refuse to adjust to society and the world. The failure to adjust when necessary has had a dangerous impact on international relations. The practice of colonialism or imperialism imposed on Third World regions by powerful nations has greatly enriched some people. When this practice is challenged by revolution or other means, those who benefitted from imperialism will often resort to military power to prevent change.

The world's resources (including land, labor, capital, and technology) are not distributed in such a way that each nation has what it needs to make itself independent of other nations. So far as economic requirements are concerned, trade between nations became essential as soon as we advanced beyond the primitive stages of agriculture.

As a result of historical development, location and limited resources, all nations are dependent on other nations. They must import food, capital, resources, or technology—often all of these—to provide the requirements of economic development. To pay for imports, nations must export, which requires the availability of foreign markets.

We have already observed in an earlier chapter that the unseen hand—which, according to the classical economist, facilitates trade, both domestic and international—in fact gave way to monopoly and military power. Before human intelligence had created the economic and military capabilities for world wars and ultimately the possible destruction of humanity, the ecological balance did not absolutely require relationships among all the peoples of the world that encouraged harmony rather than conflict. As a result, throughout history man could, through his tribe, or city, or nation, pursue his own greedy interests without destruction of humanity and the environment.

Greed and selfishness, once encouraged, are difficult to control. Yet, our survival now depends on it and on the creation of cooperative relationships among all peoples. Aristotle said that man is an animal of habit. Whether we survive or not will depend on whether our instinct for survival and our intelligence can overcome the destructive habits we have acquired.

The Dual Roots of Humanity—Nature and Reason

"Things" are in the saddle and ride mankind.
                                        —Ralph Waldo Emerson

One of the fundamental weaknesses of the classical system of economics is its simplistic conception of humanity as the "economic man." As a result, the foundation of the classical utopia rests on assumptions having little to do with the reality of people as social, political, and psychological beings.

The classical economists had an extremely materialistic notion of life that all but ignored the noneconomic relationships between individuals and society. In the words of Erich Fromm: "Just as man transforms the world around him, so he transforms himself in the process of history. He is his own creation, as it were."[2] The greatest danger we face in our development as human beings lies in our lack of appreciation of the impact the things we create have on our sanity and on our integrity.

If we are to survive, we must learn to control the things we create. Humans, unlike any other animal, have transcended the natural course of events through the process of their evolution. The nonhuman animal lives unquestioning in harmony with nature. That is, such animals cope with the conditions in the environment with the response mechanism nature has provided via the slow-moving evolutionary process.

Humans have transcended the conditions of nature governing the lives of other animals through the development of self-awareness, reason, and imagination. Physiological needs alone are not enough for human fulfillment. People have higher psychic needs originating from the conditions of their existence that must be satisfied if they are to preserve their sanity in their search for happiness.

While our physiological needs are clearly defined by the dictates of the body (hunger, thirst, fatigue, and so on), our higher psychological needs require the guidance of principles evolved during the growth of culture. The reason for the need of cultural guidance for the satisfaction of psychological needs is that such needs are vague in comparison to the physiological needs. Normally a sane person does not take poison or abstain from sleep when it is needed. To distinguish between what is good and bad in regard to our psychological needs is far more difficult.

Why is it so important that our psychological requirements are satisfied? Having transcended the natural state of all other animals, we play a much greater role in the creation of our own future. We are able to create or to destroy; to love or to hate.

The seeds of humanity's development are sown in our culture and in our environment. From our culture we need guidance; from our environment, opportunity to love and to create. We are the only animal who is able to significantly influence and modify our culture which in turn influences and modifies our own development. The social, political, and economic organization that we create cannot help but have an impact on the condition of our lives. It influences our ability to create and to destroy, to love and to hate.

The classical economists, who saw humanity as the economic man, all but disregarded our psychological needs. They made the assumption about humanity that suited their vision of utopia. The drive for material gain, perhaps because it is necessary for survival, was the only drive the classical system was built on. Humanity was defined as an economic input and as a consumer of the products we produce. Humanity was seen as competitive and selfish, but the unseen hand of the utopian market would keep us in line. The classical system by restricting the social organization as a product of natural law (as in the case of nonhuman animals), created an economic system that ignored the noneconomic relationships between the individual and society and the impact each had on the other.

The classical system has undergone great changes since the days of Adam Smith. These were brought about by scientific and technological advances that radically changed the economic organization. Their impact on humanity was no less significant. Exploitation, destructive competition, authoritarian management, thrift,

and rugged individualism are beginning to give way to social behavior more consistent with high technology, although old ways are
very slow to disappear.

Cooperation becomes essential when people work together in
large groups or on high technology enterprises. Cut-throat competition becomes impractical and exploitation becomes an obstacle to
high productivity. Mass production needs expanding markets, and
thrift is replaced by more and more consumption. And so we are
changed by the things we have created.

Human beings have freed themselves to some extent from the
confines of nature to which all other animals are subject, but they
are in danger of being dominated by the things they created. In the
modern world of mass production and high technology, the division
of labor is carried to a point where people relate to each other and
to concrete things less and less. The world we live in has become
abstract and highly quantitative.[3]

Unfortunately, in the modern world of high technology, abstrac-
tion and quantification are essential. A person no longer makes a
pair of shoes, a piano, or a chair. Most workers are still cogs in the
wheel of technology and scientific management. The inability to
give expression to creative needs leads to frustration and, in some
cases, regression.

The psychological alienation of the worker is not, as Marx
thought, peculiar to capitalism. It has been inherent in all societies
in which technology and mass production dominate the economic
process. So far as the fate of human beings is concerned, ways must
be found that will enable us to control the things we create. Only
in that way is there hope that we will not become robots alienated
from ourselves.

The process of alienation has already gone very far as a result
of the excessive bureaucratization of society. Bureaucracy is a necessary part of a modern organization, whether it is a government,
a business enterprise, or a labor union. It does not depend on the
political, economic, or social structure, and it is equally at home in
capitalist and socialist societies.

So far as human alienation is concerned, the significant question
in regard to bureaucracy is whether a bureaucracy can exist without
manipulating people as though they were robots or "things." We

shall see later that this problem is receiving considerable attention in the more progressive economies in various parts of the world.

It is not only the workers who experience alienation; the "owners" of the large corporations are equally alienated. They no longer have any responsibility or direct relationship with the enterprise they "own." The value of their ownership does not depend on them but on others—the corporate bureaucracy—over whom the owners have little control. Personal effort and human contact are no longer part of the value of ownership. They have been replaced by impersonal relationships and financial manipulation.

Perhaps the most dangerous alienation is from the social forces that shape our lives and determine the prospects of our future. Wars and depressions are generated by forces that come into play long before they occur and of which only relatively few people are aware. The vast majority of people do not possess the knowledge, awareness, or opportunity to participate actively in the shaping of their destiny. Most catastrophies occur because we are not sufficiently aware of the consequences of the things we create. If we are to be less alienated from our environment and if we are not to be adversely controlled by the things we create, we must acquire a better understanding of our role in society.

People's habit of surrounding themselves with ideas unrelated to the realities of life creates some of the conditions leading to alienation and "things" in control. Utopias, idealistic slogans, and strong passions are unacceptable substitutes for mature, carefully thought out ideals and a realistic knowledge of the world. A case in point is the economic systems dominating the world today. They are loosely referred to as "free-enterprise" and "authoritarian" systems. In the free-enterprise system, the responsibility for economic decisions is left to "the market" and the natural laws of supply and demand. In the authoritarian system, responsibility is largely left to rules made and executed by political leaders. In either case, the vast majority of people are not involved in the decisions affecting a vital part of their lives.

Alienation has produced conformity in both authoritarian and so-called free-enterprise economies. In the authoritarian society, conformity is achieved through rules that are effectively enforced. In the "free societies" of today, visible authority is supplemented by an anonymous and invisible authority, which may be referred to as, "it." We are expected to conform to "it" or suffer the consequences. Examples of "it" are invisible sources of rules such as the social norm and the corporate norm. In free societies, governments rotate, but the "invisible authority" (like the invisible hand) is unassailable. It is far easier to attack overt authority than the invisible "it."

Neither the free-enterprise societies nor the authoritarian societies are organized today to free us from the alientation we suffer. This will happen only when we become actively involved in the decisions affecting us. (This is discussed more fully in later chapters.)

The Ability to Adjust—A Challenge For Humanity and the Environment

I have maintained that the quality of life and humanity's survival depend on harmony between people and the environment. Some earlier political philosophers understood this very well and based their theories of government on it. Unfortunately, all such theories had serious shortcomings and were eventually discarded.

Saint Thomas Aquinas' essay on geometric justice portrayed a world in which every individual, from the lowest serf to overlord, played a role prescribed by God. If people performed well, they were rewarded with salvation and the "system" prospered and survived.

Thomas Hobbes and Thomas Hooker, the seventeenth-century political philosophers, portrayed harmony in the form of a social contract between God and monarch. The monarch ruled the subjects according to this contract, which in theory meant justly. A ruler who failed to live up to this contract would be removed by God. In practice, it did not work that way. Nevertheless, the doctrine was based on the search for harmony between individual and society.

The old Chinese monarchs ruled with a "divine" understanding between God and themselves. If, for example, a famine resulted from their failure to irrigate adequately, God gave the people divine consent to remove the ruler. This was a theory of revolution, but it was also a recognition of the need for harmony between humanity and the environment.

Although these doctrines saw the necessity for harmony between the individual and society, they failed to produce harmony because the rulers tended to exercise ruthless power instead of the "will of God." Since then, political and social philosophers have concentrated their efforts on ways to control ruthless power.

Harmony is a matter of balance. It is balance between freedom and coercion, between the individual and the group, between the various pressure groups. This is clearly a recognition of the need for social harmony, but to what end? If the democratic process, as a result of well-organized pressure groups, leads to so much pollution that the world becomes uninhabitable, it may still give the appearance of social harmony, but certainly not for the purpose of preserving the environment, which, if we want to survive, must be our ultimate goal. Social harmony is not enough. What is missing in this case is harmony between individuals and the environment.

St. Thomas, Hobbes, Hooker, and the ancient Chinese understood the need for rules that protected society and the physical environment from short sighted greed, but their theories were vulnerable to ruthless power and tyranny because democracy was still in the future.

Locke, Rousseau, and Voltaire waged a brave battle against ruthless power and for freedom of the individual. In the first case, the concern of philosophers was with society and in the second case with the individual. In the first case, it was assumed that if society was protected by the proper rules, the individual would thrive. In the second case, it was assumed that if the individual was protected by the proper rules, society would thrive.

The shortcomings of both approaches are that they fail to recognize that ecological balance and social harmony require rules for both society and the individual. These rules must be based on realism generated by experience, scientific fact, and a clear understanding of goals and the difference between ends (goals) and means.

To accomplish this, we must build bridges linking opposing sides in the place of worshipping the past, which is a form of idolatry.

The ancient seers who denounced the heathen religions did not do so because they believed that worshipping several gods instead of one was the problem that created idolatry.

The prophets of monotheism denounced the heathen religions because they created material idols that the faithful worshipped and that in Emerson's words were "things" that "ride mankind"—in other words, the substitution of symbols for substance. Religious idols are not the only things that alienate people from themselves. Secular idols do the same—the "free and self-adjusting market," "the communistic classless society," "the corporation," "the labor union," "the fatherland." *Blind* loyalty to any of these is a form of idolatry.

In order to minimize alienation, a way must be found that allows for some direct participation by all members of a group in the decision-making process. The mere fact that people are allowed to vote for representatives who make decisions for them based on facts and relationships outside the voters' awareness is part of the process of alienation rather than a safeguard against it. In a society as large as ours, involvement in the decision-making process does not mean that everyone is involved in making the same decisions. That is obviously impossible. Decisions, however, are made at every level of human activity, and everyone should be involved at some level, depending on her or his position in the economy and in society.

It is unrealistic to assume that any organization could exist very long if its members were not loyal to its objectives and if they refused to abide by its rules. Loyalty as such is not the cause of alienation. However, *blind* loyalty to an organization or group in which most members do not participate in the determination of the objectives and rules tends to alienate people from character-strengthening values and consequently from the system to which they belong.

If we are to become fully developed as individuals, we must participate in our affairs rather than be ruled by them. Likewise, society cannot survive without rules designed to preserve it any more than individuals can survive as human beings without rules designed to satisfy their physiological and psychological needs. The answer lies in the process of adjustment: the individual adjusting to society and the social organization adjusting to the needs of the individual.

10
Freedom, Authority, and Motivation

The Role and Limits of Freedom

How much freedom do people in a democracy possess in determining their own destiny? Actually very little, at least so far as the great majority of people are concerned. The investments made by corporations and financial institutions all over the world help to determine a nation's global interests. The course of industrial development with its dependence on resources and markets is a major factor in the shaping of foreign policy. The flows of private trade and investment determine a nation's balance of payments position, which has an important impact on domestic economic policy. All these things play a major role in the development of international relations without involving the electorate. The factors encouraging peaceful relations or conflict are generated by processes involving few of the people affected by them. In other words, even in democracies, most people do not participate in making decisions that profoundly affect their lives.

The classical economists had a unique perception of freedom, and their utopian theories reflected it. They believed that each person contributes to the greatest good for the greatest number by freely pursuing his or her own interests. They assumed an economy governed by natural laws in which no one possessed arbitrary power. The freedom to pursue individual interests was in their view the means to an end, the end being the greatest possible satisfaction for the whole population.

The classical concept of freedom was not freedom for its own sake, but freedom leading to a democratic process of choice and satisfaction. The key classical concept of freedom is constraint by the natural laws of the free market rather than by government.

The freedom that existed during the heyday of laissez-faire was quite different from what the classical economists had envisaged. Those who possessed economic power enjoyed the freedom to pursue their own interests, usually at the expense of those who lacked economic power. For the masses, the freedom to pursue their own interests became academic; they were busy struggling for survival.

The classical economists understood that freedom becomes a foundation for social justice only if there are conditions favorable to its existence. Their utopia, built on natural laws, free from arbitrary power, was indeed an ideal environment for freedom to thrive in. Laissez-faire was built on assumptions, however, that unfortunately did not reflect the real world.

The rebirth of arbitrary economic power in the nineteenth century and the distinct delineation between those who controlled capital and those whose labor was sold for wages made the environment in which economic freedom thrived unfavorable for the large majority who could not benefit from it. Marx saw this as an inherent flaw in capitalism, and today's antisocialists see similar conditions in socialist countries as an inherent flaw in socialism. A great deal of misunderstanding and much antagonism could be avoided if the absence of social justice were regarded as a flaw in the developing stages of any nation.

The economic freedom of the classical economists did not lead to social justice because the environment in which it existed did not lend itself to that. In socialist economies in which private ownership of the means of production has been abolished, but in which bureaucratic values dominate the environment, social justice has also made little progress. An excessively bureaucratic environment is no more favorable to freedom in a socialist economy than in a capitalist one. So long as the creation of wealth and military power dominate the economic process in such a way that human and environmental needs are subordinated to it, a favorable situation is impossible, regardless of the name of the system.

The lesson to be learned from the past is that such splendid vehicles of humane living as freedom and democracy can reach their destination only if the environment is favorable. When the conditions for their existence are unfavorable, freedom leads to exploitation and democracy degenerates into the covert rule of the powerful. Aristotle knew as much over two thousand years ago.

Social justice is only one of the possible results of freedom; frustration is another. Many nations take pride in the laws giving citizens the freedom to choose their own line of work, the freedom to work where they choose, the freedom to express their own thoughts on all issues, the freedom to vote for political candidates of their choice, the freedom the live wherever they choose, and so forth. If the environment does not create opportunities to allow all people to exercise their freedoms, then those who cannot exercise them will suffer the additional pain of frustration.

Freedom and opportunity go hand in hand. It is morally unconscionable for a state to create fictitious freedoms when at the same time it creates an environment that makes it virtually impossible for large segments of the population to enjoy the fruits of their freedoms. An individual cannot prevent the conditions that create unemployment. If unemployment cannot be successfully avoided by social action, it is counterproductive to create the illusion that all people have freedom of choice in the economic sphere of their lives. The need to work and to earn income is the most important economic choice of most people. To create the illusion of economic freedom when the opportunity to exercise it is greatly restricted for millions of people can only create frustrations, guilt feelings, and ultimately psychological and social breakdowns.

Freedom is also greatly restricted when people are forced to take dangerous jobs, regardless of working conditions, in order to survive. About 90 percent of all people in the industrialized world work as nonmanagement employees. Their ability to work and earn an income is subject to being employed by those who own or control the capital required for the employment of human labor. In the nineteenth century—the height of laissez-faire economic freedom— most workers were compelled to work regardless of working conditions, or face starvation. Today, as a result of labor unions and more enlightened political intervention, more workers have greater freedom in regard to working conditions.

In the world of the future, the proper use of freedom will mean the difference between social justice and social entrapment even more than in the past. What is the proper use of freedom? If all people are free to pursue their own interests selfishly, freedom self-destructs, because those who possess power will control those who do not. The concept of countervailing power is of little help because different groups pulling in different directions do not neutralize power; they merely prevent the establishment of viable relationships between individual and society.

How free are we from the laws of nature and from the environment that we helped to create? How free are we to create the kind of environment that will not only satisfy our physical and psychological needs, but that will help us to evolve into civilized human beings capable of living in peace? Until these questions are answered, there is no point in discussing freedom in either normative or pragmatic terms.

Unfortunately some writers who have had a great deal of influence (from John Stuart Mill to Milton Friedman, including the libertarians) have romanticized freedom to a point where it ceases to have any practical application. Such concepts as democracy have been blown out of proportion by the fiction that free people can vote for the kind of life they want. People can no more vote for the kind of life they want than alcoholics can solve their problems with a New Year's resolution. This does not mean that *freedom* and *democracy* are empty terms. Far from it. It does mean, however, that they cannot be created simply by the passage of laws.

If it were possible for individuals to be free from any link to nature and from the constraints of their physical and cultural environments, they would not be free, they would be lost. In fact, insane individuals lack the ability to build adequate bridges to link them to their fellow human beings and to their environments. They are lost and seek refuge in the fantasies of their minds.[1]

Freedom does not mean that people are free to do as they please. There are, after all, the constraints imposed by nature and the environment. Nor does it mean that each individual is able to participate in changing the constraints of nature and the environment. That is an absurd view of democracy. The constraints of nature can be modified only through the application of reason and science. They cannot be overcome merely by means of the electoral process. The Nuclear Age and the Space Age came upon us through advances in science and technology; people were not free to vote for them or against them. Once science and technology became a part of the human life process, their advance could not be determined by democratic action. Scientists are free to advance the frontier of knowledge; most people not trained in science are not free to do that.

Science and technology have had a greater impact on humanity than any other phenomenon in modern times. Yet only a few have had a voice in shaping its course and in determining its impact.

How free have people been in determining their political destiny? Of all human relationships, war has been the most destructive. Today, the future of life on this planet depends on our ability to prevent war. In democracies, people are supposed to declare war democratically through their properly elected representatives. Even that is no longer adhered to, as in the case of Vietnam and the Middle East. On closer examination, we discover that only a few people participate in the process that *leads* to war.

The major reasons for modern war are economic and geopolitical. Nations require access to raw materials and to markets where they can sell their exports. Superpowers such as the United States and the Soviet Union are concerned about their relative power and influence in the world, and they create alliances along geopolitical lines. Geopolitics is the "art" of combining economic, demographic, geographic, and political factors in such a way that power is balanced. The problem arises from how powerful nations *view* balance.

To what extent then can people have the freedom to shape their own destinies? As the world is now organized, few people have that freedom. In the case of war, the seeds are sewn long before conflict becomes virtually inevitable. By the time a parliament approves a declaration of war, the scenario has fully matured.

If most people do not have the freedom to determine the course of science and technology or the essential relations between nations—two factors that together have a vital impact on the quality of life—then who or what shapes their destiny?

In an authoritarian government, perhaps no more than several dozen political, military, and industrial leaders, by exercising various degrees of power, make the really important decisions that determine the quality of life for the people. These leaders are increasingly dependent on the men and women who possess the vital scientific, technical, and administrative skills necessary in the Nuclear Age.

In today's democratic societies, the decision-making process is becoming increasingly authoritarian, chiefly as a result of the technological and structural realities of the modern world. People elect their leaders democratically, but they do not participate in the vital decisions of modern life. They cannot participate in the scientific, technological, financial, and corporate decisions of today's world. By the time the electorate participates in the decision-making process, the vital factors that they did not help to create are already in place, and their freedom to really affect the course of destiny is either greatly restricted or nonexistent.

The vital question in this respect is how the people can gain control of their lives in a world that now excludes most of them in the really vital decisions. In other words, how can we adapt to the vast technological changes that have taken place so as not to lose control over our own destiny by leaving it to those few who now create the essential conditions of our environment?

Traditional democracy and traditional economic freedom in today's superpower, high technology world have left the vast majority of people behind in the decision-making process. Professor Friedman is quite wrong in suggesting that by returning to the old techniques of laissez-faire, we will regain our freedom and be once more free to choose our own destiny. This cannot happen because adapting to the world of the past makes no sense whatsoever, and, furthermore, the vast majority were not free to choose during the height of laissez-faire.

We can regain freedom in the modern world only if we adjust the structure of freedom and democracy to fit the reality of today. We can preserve our freedom only if we continue to make such adjustments as the world changes.

The Role and Limits of Authority

Clearly, freedom is influenced by the condition of the social and physical environments. As the creator of science and technology, we have had a profound effect on our environment. We have created great material wealth and have greatly improved our chances of survival in our fight against disease. We have also learned more about ourselves and the universe.

As the creator of our environment, however, we have made life far more complex. This has reached a point where most people have lost touch with the vital aspects of the economic and political decision-making process which has alienated them from many of the personal relationships between the individual and society.

If the quality of life is to improve significantly in the posttechnocratic or enlightened age, a major effort must be made to involve more directly the large majority of people in the decisions that affect their lives. To do so, we must understand the relationship between the relatively few in authority and the large majority of people who carry out the decisions made by others.

To involve people more so that they will be well-motivated citizens it is necessary to humanize authority. This is especially important in a complex environment, characteristic of the posttechnocratic age, in which authority plays a vital role.

Erich Fromm, whose writings reflect great insight into what constitutes a sane society, divided authority into two categories: rational and irrational. He cited the relationship between the student and the teacher as an example of rational authority, and the relationship between the slave and the master as an example of irrational authority.[2]

The teacher has authority over the student but the interests of both coincide. The teacher educates the student and the student's life is enriched through education. They succeed together.

The slave owner's interests, on the other hand, is based on the exploitation of the slave. Their interests, therefore, clash. Slaves are treated like machines to be used until they have outlived their usefulness.

In the case of rational authority, the gap between teacher and student narrows as the student becomes more like the teacher. The authority of the teacher helps the student to satisfy physical and psychological needs.

The slave owner, through the use of legalized power, is superior to the slaves and uses authority over the slaves to exploit them rather than help them. Fromm called this "irrational" authority because the gap between master and slave is widened as a result of the exploitation.

Rational authority tends to *narrow* the gap between those in authority and those subject to authority. In the case of *irrational* authority, the gap is *widened*.

Authority is indeed a necessary part of a high technology, complex society. The more complex the world becomes, the less possible it is for all people to be equal. Under the conditions created by today's high technology environment, equality is impossible. Actually even in primitive societies equality is not possible. The intelligent thing is not to seek equality because that is futile. Our effort should be directed at creating the conditions necessary for the exercise of *rational* authority in a sane way. The humane society *must* be built on a foundation of rational authority. In the nineteenth century, authority in the developing economies was increasingly based on the ownership of capital, just as it was based on the ownership of land in the feudal period. The worker had to obey, because without capital or land, there was no work. Just as loyalty and obedience were rewarded with the promise of salvation by the church when feudalism reigned, so loyalty and obedience became the foundation of the material reward system in the first stages of modern economic development.

Economists have not been concerned with such problems as the nature and use of authority because they regard it as a social or political problem and not an economic one. This is strange, because the central economic problem is efficiency in the use and allocation of resources. The way authority is structured and used has a critical impact on efficiency.

From the purely economic point of view, efficiency is the heart of the problem. From the purely political and social point of view, political and social harmony and stability are the key objectives. From the psychological point of view, a sane society is the goal. The relationship between those who exercise authority and those over whom it is exercised is vital to the achievement of all these goals. It will become clear that over time all these goals—economic, political, social, and psychological—have to be achieved simultaneously or not at all. This is only one example illustrating why the social sciences cannot be studied in isolation from one another.

When authority is so structured that both parties to it benefit because their interests coincide, the chances of achieving the various goals simultaneously are probably very high, because society is built on a foundation of rational authority. When, however, authority is exercised in such a way that only those who exercise it benefit from it while the others are either exploited or alienated by it, it is irrational because the basic human goals cannot be achieved.

Historically, authority became irrational because those who exercised it were motivated more by power and wealth than by the achievement of social goals and harmony. In the early stages of economic development, irrational authority leads mainly to exploitation but also to alienation. As economic development succeeds in producing wealth, irrational authority produces chiefly alienation, but exploitation continues—although on a lesser scale. There is ample evidence that this is true in both capitalist and socialist societies. The labor-union movement at the turn of the century in the United States and current Solidarity in Poland are examples of that.

We have already observed that in the early stages of economic development, the worker is exploited because no better way has been discovered to generate the capital necessary for economic growth. This exploitation appears to be more severe when foreign capital and technology are not available for internal development. To the extent that foreign capital came to the United States in the nineteenth century, it served to reduce the pressure for domestic savings to finance railroads, canals, and so on. This left a larger share for consumption without sacrificing economic growth and development. In the Soviet Union, on the other hand, foreign investment has been scarce because Soviet doctrines are unpopular in those countries that have surplus capital. As a result, the standard of living of the worker has probably been poorer than if foreign investment had been available. Perhaps the greatest exploitation of the workers occurs in Third World countries that are subjected to economic imperialism by foreign powers.

Since growth in the early stages of economic development seems to require the exploitation of the worker,[3] and since the worker can be exploited through the exercise of authority, how can such authority be called irrational if it leads to economic development? If we define irrational authority as Erich Fromm does (as authority used to exploit or to widen the gap between those in authority and those subject to it), then the authority that exploits the worker is irrational.

This creates a dilemma: the authority that exploits the worker cannot logically be called irrational if the goal is economic development, because it achieves the goal. This dilemma can be resolved, however, if it is recognized that there exists a conflict between two important social goals—economic development and social harmony. The authority that exploits and alienates people is irrational in terms of a sane society and social harmony. It is rational, however, in terms of the early stages of economic development.

This is not a play on words; it is an important fact. The job before us today when so much wealth has already been produced, is to reconcile economic development in the developing countries, and economic activity in the developed ones, with social harmony based on rational authority. In the developed countries, economic exploitation is declining although it still exists among the poor and among women. The more significant problem is alienation.

Whereas exploitation reflects an economic relationship, alienation comes from social relationships in which people without authority are made dependent on people who possess authority. Alienation does not preclude the participation of the alienated in organizational or administrative matters, it merely precludes them from the vital decision-making process.

In the economically developed countries, the majority of people are no longer exploited nor do they suffer from severe economic poverty. The disease replacing exploitation is the conformity to authority—visible or hidden—that produces alienation. The old class struggle has given way to a new social struggle. The new struggle is between those in authority who make the important economic and political decisions and the large majority outside the decision-making process who are reduced to dependent participation and are expected to conform.

Alienation is generated by two separate developments. Sophisticated technology has reduced many people to a robot-like work pattern. Shoemakers of old could take pride in their work because there was a direct relationship between them and the shoes they sold and the people who bought and wore them. This process offered great satisfaction to the skilled craftspeople.

Today the work pattern is entirely different. Except abstractly, no one in a firm of any size has any direct contact with the entire production of a product or the people who use it. Even executives have only an abstract and partial contact. Marketing, finance, and accounting executives can relate to a product only in abstract and quantified terms; the personal relationship of the craftspeople of another age is gone.

There are a few exceptions even in this highly technological age. Entrepreneurs still have a place in the development of innovative enterprises that allow them to experience the satisfaction of direct and complete relationships. The successful enterprises, however, are absorbed by the big corporations or become big corporations themselves, and the personal relationships are transformed into the abstract and quantified relationships of bureaucratic management.

In addition to technology, the management of authority as it is practiced today also produces alienation. In the United States, genuine participatory management allowing workers to engage in the decision-making process is still frowned upon. In countries such as West Germany and Hungary, some progress has already been made in the creation of rational authority.

Even on a larger scale, nations can become alienated. This happens under colonialism, neocolonialism, and modern imperialism. The satellite territories are made dependent on the decisions and goals of the superpowers.

Why is it so important to solve the growing problems of alienation? Obviously to improve the quality of life through social harmony. There is, however, a more immediate problem that must be solved. The motivation of people to work has been seriously affected by alienation and the problem is growing. The impact on the economy and on the tranquility of the social system is producing great concern. The question is how were people motivated before and how can they be remotivated now?

The Anatomy of Alienation—Its Impact on Motivation

The classical economists saw work as inferior to leisure, and money wages as the factor that motivates people to exchange leisure for work. Their view of life, so far as the creation of wealth is concerned, appears to be based on what Nietzsche called the *cash nexus* of nineteenth-century capitalism.[4]

This narrow view of work, unfortunately, remains part of traditional economics in spite of the fact that for the worker, "leisure" generally meant idleness and poverty during the nineteenth century. As a matter of fact, workers were more than willing to exchange leisure for work at the basest subsistence wages because they preferred poverty to starvation. The threat of starvation motivated workers to submit to the unquestioned authority of the employer until the Great Depression, when the industrial labor union began. The crafts union came into existence in the nineteenth century, but the anti-union sentiment in the Congress made it virtually powerless.

With the advance of economic development and the gradual evolution of democracy, which gave the worker a greater political voice, starvation became less of a threat and lost some of its power as a motivator of labor. That fact plus the alienation of the worker, produced by a rapidly advancing technology, is creating an urgent need for a more enlightened approach to motivation.

Motivation is generated either by compulsion, by identification and adaptation, or by the interest in the work developed through active participation in the decision-making process. The lack of motivation all too often goes hand in hand with alienation—a problem that is now reaching large proportions. It is a serious problem because the alienated worker becomes a factor in unsatisfactory economic performance.

If workers have no alternative, even poverty-level wages motivate them to work. Their desire to survive needs no other motivation. That is the reason why some employers still believe that "a little unemployment is a good thing." In the early days of capitalism, compulsion provided the only motive for work for virtually all the workers. Today there are additional motives.

Workers whose only choice is conformity will usually conform to the authority exercised by the employer, but they will be alienated by such authoritarian compulsion. Such a system is unstable and will eventually evolve into something more acceptable to the worker or it will self-destruct.

Much has been written on the subject of identification, adaptation, and participation by psychologists such as Erich Fromm and management experts such as Peter Drucker and James O'Toole. Economists generally have failed to integrate the new knowledge gained in the field of human motivation into their formal microeconomic theories, which are still based on archaic assumptions about work and workers.

Identification and adaptation as a source of motivation occurs when an employer adopts policies with which workers can identify and to which they can adapt. Alienation still exists if the worker does not participate in the process by which the policies are chosen, but the alienation will not be hostile as in the case of authoritarian compulsion.

Identification and adaptation are usually more common among executives and highly skilled employees, who can identify more easily with the objectives of the corporation because they usually benefit handsomely from its success. Even among such employees, there is dissatisfaction when the standards adopted by the corporation depart too much from their own system of values.

Although Milton Friedman, as he discussed on the TV series "Free to Choose," believes that the great virtue of free enterprise is individual freedom and free choice, the essence of corporate capitalism is the coordination of effort. Employees of the corporation are expected to subordinate their own values and goals to that of the corporation. The corporate norm describes the values and behavior patterns to which employees are expected to conform if they expect to keep their jobs. This is especially true of employees who hope to move up the corporate ladder. The corporation that adopts standards and values that are generally acceptable to the community encourages the process of identification and adaptation.

For the non-unionized blue-collar and clerical worker[3], identification has usually not provided the motivation that it has for the better rewarded professionals and corporate executives. The former are too far removed from the center of activity, their work is usually uninteresting and their reward is frequently not sufficient to generate loyalty and identification. It is one thing to hold on to a job for lack of alternatives, and quite another to hold on because of a reward system that generates loyalty and identification.

The industrial countries in both capitalist and socialist worlds are in the grip of revolutionary changes, forcing them to take a new look at problems of production, consumption, and distribution. Rapid technological advances and the inability of political and economic policymakers to effect the necessary adjustments are creating widespread alienation. This is happening at the same time that workers have gained greater political power, freeing them from the prospect of starvation as an alternative to objectionable and degrading work. If positive steps are not taken to reduce significantly the alienation of the worker, the economy will face mounting problems resulting from declining productivity and unemployment.

In order to deal effectively with the rapidly growing problem of alienation and new methods of motivation, we must fully understand all the causes of alienation so that steps can be taken to humanize the motivation to work. The present state of human frustration caused by the rapid growth of an impersonal technology plus almost equally impersonal corporate and government bureaucracies is creating neuroses threatening the future of capitalist and socialist systems alike.

Alienation can result from a variety of causes. Whatever its cause, however, it interferes with the development of a sane society and an efficient economy. *Efficient* does not mean simply a higher ratio between output and input as it is defined in neoclassical microeconomics. It also means in the human sense the production of material things in a way that satisfies the important needs of humanity.

The term *in a way* is all-important. *How* we go about producing the things that are to satisfy our needs is as important as *what* we produce. It is the "how" that creates alienation. Both the "how" and the "what" are, however, vital factors in the creation of healthy individuals and a sane society.

Workers are alienated from their jobs if their relationships to these jobs are very insecure. Workers who regard jobs as "theirs" are likely to identify with such jobs much more than those who know that they may lose their positions at any time because profits are declining or because a machine or robot may replace them. To most workers, a job is the only source of income that furnishes the economic foundation of their lives. Income to the worker from a job is as essential as the dividends to the person who lives on the income produced by invested wealth. A person whose wealth can be confiscated by those in authority will be alienated from the system that allows that. A worker whose income can be stopped by those in authority is likely to be as alienated as the person of wealth who suffers confiscation.

Alienation also results from the inability to participate in the decisions affecting a worker's income, working conditions, quality of the product produced, or future of the firm. Stockholders have become alienated from ownership because the vast majority cannot realistically participate in the decision-making process that determines corporate policy.

Consumers, too, have not escaped alienation. Although in a market economy, they have the opportunity to express preferences, advertising has been employed to appeal to the most vulnerable human temptations. Today, much advertising focuses on teenagers and young adults who have little opportunity in an overly materialistic culture to develop sound values necessary for physical and mental health.

Advertising controls the voice of today's culture—the media. People are not born with the ability to make decisions that will help them to lead a sane and healthy life. They acquire their values from their culture, and today's culture is greatly influenced by corporate advertising via the electronic and print media.

Technology, the foundation of material success in today's highly sophisticated economies, is in itself a source of alienation. The organization of high technology firms is of necessity complex and decisions are based on information supplied by many individuals who specialize in specific aspects of production, marketing, finance, and so on. The chief executive officer, usually with the assistance of a board of directors who know much less than the CEO about the operations of the firm, makes the difficult, important decisions.

The degree to which a chief executive relies on the advise of subordinates varies, as does the extent to which the CEO allows them to make decisions. But decisions that are comprehensive in scope cannot be left to experts or executives in charge of specialized functions.

Except for a few employees at the very top, the vast majority of a staff are strangers to almost everything that goes on in the organization of which they are a part, except the minute area their job occupies in the total structure. For the most part, they have been alienated from the human aspects of work to which the craftspeople of old had access and could relate.

Such alienation may be even more pronounced in certain socialist countries where the decision-making process is even more centralized than in modern corporate capitalism. Fortunately, the solution to alienation does not lie in returning to the world of the past, because that is not going to happen. But it is possible to humanize technology and motivation, and some attempts have already been made.

Involvement as a Motivator in a More Humane Society

Alienated people become strangers in the drama of life. They dance to a tune that they did not compose and to which they cannot relate in a meaningful way. There is a clash of rhythm that leads to resentment or withdrawal.

Existentialism, which came to full bloom in France at the end of World War II, concerned itself chiefly with the problem of alienation. It was a natural reaction to a period in history when authoritarian dictators took the reins in a number of countries left helpless by the consequences of wars and depressions. In the case of many European nations, this reflected the failure of democracy under monopoly capitalism. In Russia, it reflected the breakdown of a semi-feudal society.

Jean Paul Sartre, perhaps the best-known French existentialist, coined a phrase that best describes this philosophy: "existence precedes essence."[5] In other words, the meaning of life (essence) results from the world as it is gradually recreated by people (existence and experience). Essence is not pre-determined to be acted out by people. On the contrary, humanity is perceived as its own creator, so far as the meaning of our lives is concerned.

Sartre believed that this process of creation must not be left to a few who dominate the rest of humanity, such as Hitler in Germany and Stalin in the Soviet Union. To be deprived of involvement in the continuous process of creation is how the existentialist perceives alienation. The answer lies, Sartre asserted, in feeling the anguish of alienation and responding to that with full involvement in the process of living.

Although psychologists and sociologists have also warned that what we produce and how we produce it have profound impact on individual and society, many economists have regarded such concerns as outside the field of economics. Herbert A. Simon, however, received the Nobel Prize in economics for his work in human motivation in a highly industrialized world.[6]

Simon stressed the importance of four factors for reducing alienation and increasing motivation: (1) the individual's respect for the integrity of the organization, (2) the ability of the organization to satisfy the needs of the individual related to the person's work, (3) the opportunity to establish frequent interaction between all the individuals of an organization, and (4) the ability to keep aggressive competition among the members of an organization to a minimum.

The point made by Professor Simon should be of interest to everyone in a world in which the size of the GNP has become more important than the methods by which it is produced. He emphasized that if we are concerned about achieving our economic objectives, we must do more than optimize numbers. We must look at the needs of people who create the numbers.

The idea of involvement or participation has received considerable attention from European scholars in the post-World War II decades. They focus much of their attention on the humanization of the economic process. A more popular approach to this problem appears in the widely read books by Alvin Toffler, *Future Shock* and *The Third Wave*.[7]

Experiments in other countries are throwing much light on the problem of humanizing the economic process. It is too early to predict which methods will prove most successful. It is very likely, however, that not all methods will work especially well everywhere since conditions vary from country to country. The main factors that should be considered in any attempt to humanize the economic process are a people's history, culture, and stage of economic development. The approach to this effort should, therefore, be pragmatic rather than utopian or ideological.

The Japanese model for humanizing the economic process is

somewhat unique, as indeed we should expect it to be. Japan is the only Asian nation that has reached an advanced stage of industrialization (though Korea and a few others are not far behind). China still has decades before it can match Japan's level of per capita output. Japan's per capita income matches that of the Western World.

The Japanese industrial system demonstrates an important element in the motivation of labor. The workplace in Japan reflects the cultural and social values of the men and women who work there. Identification is considered a humane approach to work, which is regarded as vital to any relevant theory of optimization. Output cannot be optimized when the most important input, people, is alienated.

Family life in Japan is based on a high degree of loyalty and on the identification of the individual with the family group. The pattern of industrial organization parallels the basic cultural values of family life. New employees are accepted as lifetime members of the organization and are as loyal to it as they are to their own families. The firm in turn is concerned for the employees' welfare and accepts responsibility for decent housing, recreational facilities, health care, and further training and education. Both the firm and the employee regard a job as permanent, layoffs are extremely rare. Workers who are laid off are guaranteed an income comparable to their wages.

Japanese employees are closely identified with the firm they join immediately upon completion of formal education. Because they presumably enter the firm for their entire career, if they want to change jobs, they are suspected of having been problem workers. Moves can be done, but the system discourages them. As a result, employees regard the success of the firm they work for as necessary for their own success. Such motivation is regarded as a vital part of productivity by the Japanese.

It also serves as a form of motivation for the firm to live up to its responsibilities to the employee. If employees leave a firm, its reputation in regard to its responsibilities is questioned. Japanese firms are anxious to avoid labor turnover.

Labor unions in Japan also follow the family-oriented culture. Unions are "enterprise" unions, not craft unions. A firm is unionized rather than the special skills of the worker. Labor unions do not exist to protect jobs since the jobs belong to the worker. They represent the worker in a system in which labor, management, and the government cooperate to encourage productivity. Unions bargain for higher wages but within the framework of economic capabilities. Strikes are rare and the cost measured in terms of time lost is only about 2 percent of what it is in the United States.

The job security in the Japanese system is not only a factor in labor motivation, it also affects willingness to adapt to change. The introduction of new technology is not resisted for fear that it may result in job losses. The Japanese system is committed to protecting workers' jobs as long as they perform within reasonable standards. This requires the cooperation of government, the firm, the labor unions (where they exist), or the workers (where unions are not involved). (About 30 percent of all workers are unionized.)

The Japanese system has been criticized for its lack of labor mobility. The fact is there is considerable mobility within the Japanese system, but it is intraenterprise rather than between firms. The basic industries in Japan consist of only a few large firms as in the other highly industrialized countries. These firms operate all over Japan and in many other parts of the world. It is a policy of management to give their employees an opportunity to expand their knowledge and experience by encouraging them to work in various parts of the enterprise.

The Japanese organizational structure is also somewhat unique in another way that bears on motivation. Decisions are based on the cooperative deliberations of committees rather than on one-person decisions. Such committees exist at all levels of operation and deal with technical issues, social issues, the reward system and all other areas in which people are involved with one another.

This approach to decision making is rooted in the Japanese custom of family councils in which the entire family participates in forming decisions. Historically this approach is also deeply rooted in the Japanese village councils in which all families participated.

The Japanese system of security, identification, and participation, which has humanized motivation in that country, does not coincide with the cultural pattern of the United States. In the American culture, individualism predominates and the group is played down. Although Christianity is the predominant religion, average Americans do not consider themselves to be their brother's keeper.

Social and organizational relationships are largely contractual rather than familial as in the case of Japan.

To humanize motivation in western culture requires methods that have their roots in that culture. This issue is analyzed in the next chapter with special emphasis on the U.S. economy. At this point, it is useful to briefly look at other examples of attempts to humanize motivation and to increase productivity.

Yugoslavia serves as a good example, not because it has been successful in creating a humane economy, but because, rejecting Stalinism on the grounds that it represented arbitrary authority, the nation followed a different approach to socialism. It's longtime leader, Marshal Tito, regarded Stalinism as a breach of Marxist-Leninist socialism. The important point is that the Yugoslavs searched for new answers to escape from the threat of arbitrary authority that they regarded as inconsistent with their socialist aims.

New slogans began to emerge and a new law was enacted by Yugoslavia's National Assembly in June 1950. This law has become known as "the law on workers self-management." The Yugoslav theoreticians seem to be convinced that "the state should wither away" in line with the Marxist formula. Their theories are a form of laissez-faire socialism, but (unlike the capitalist mode) they are not based on natural law and equilibrium theory.

The new slogans sound almost utopian, but they are more than that. "Debureaucratization," "decentralization," and "workers self-management" in 1950 may have contained more idealism than realism, but they also demonstrate a recognition of the relationships between human needs and economic goals—a recognition that the end does not justify the means, under either capitalism or socialism.

There are conflicting reports as to how well this system works. It is probably no more than a beginning, and if it succeeds at all, it will undoubtedly have to go through many changes. In terms of human and social evolution, it is a case study from which we can learn.

As we observe how different nations deal with the problem of involvement, we must bear in mind that all people are not equal physically, mentally, emotionally, or in terms of training, experience, and leadership qualities. Therefore, involvement cannot be the same for everyone. The important thing is that everyone should be involved in a meaningful way at some level of the decision-making process so that work becomes a genuine human experience and not a mechanical performance.

11
Adaptation in a More Humane Society

Human Values and Social Goals

Such values as freedom and justice are meaningless if they are conceived in an ideological vacuum. Just as the individual and society are interdependent, so values and goals have a mutually significant relationship. If human values evolve that lack adequate regard for the well-being of society, they endanger the future of humanity. On the other hand, if social goals are determined without sufficient regard for the physiological and psychological needs of the individual, we will regress as human beings.

The nineteenth century produced economic theories woefully lacking in an understanding of the vital relationships between the individual and society. As a result, values and social goals developed haphazardly and irrationally. The social goals of laissez-faire, for example, assumed that the world, including the economy, was governed by natural laws that somehow satisfied humanity's needs. The same natural laws were assumed to be capable of constraining people from any harmful interference with their social and physical environment.

If the relationship between the individual and the physical and social environments cannot be entrusted to the natural laws of the market, then how is it to be determined? In other words, how are values and social goals to be selected so that they will produce a wholesome balance? That is the essential question, and the answer lies in our knowledge of humanity and the environment.

A fundamental characteristic of the process of evolution is the matter of adaptation or adjustment. An organism's chance of survival depends on its ability to adapt to changes in its environment. To the extent that the environment changes over time, the organisms that reproduce themselves with significant variations have a better chance of survival—as a species—than those that cannot adapt. In the process of natural evolution, the microcosm has to adapt, if it can—not the macrocosm.

Humanity has added its own dimension to the natural process of evolution. Human society and culture are dynamic in contrast with the cultures of other animals. The latter are static and change only with the natural processes of evolution. Whereas the life problem of other animals is centered on their ability to adapt to changes in the environment over which they have *no* control, the life problem of humanity is far more complex. We do have considerable influence on our physical and social environments. In order to survive as human beings, we have the dual task of adapting to increasingly rapid changes in the environment, for which we are responsible, and *controlling* these changes so that they will harmonize with our physiological and psychological needs.

Like all animals, we have inherited impulses. We are both individuals and social animals. Frequently our impulses as individuals and as social animals conflict, creating problems that are peculiarly human. Our impulses in regard to self-preservation, hunger, and physical pleasure may be in direct conflict with our social impulses of family life and community relations. We can only do well as human beings if we can learn to balance and harmonize our individual and social impulses.

The utilitarian belief that if all individuals are allowed to pursue their own interests the result will be the greatest good for the greatest number is either completely wrong or an enormous oversimplification. The greatest good for the greatest number could only result from this theory if it is also assumed that a person's impulses as an individual and as a social being are naturally in harmony.

Conflicts between individual and social impulses are present in every social organization. Such conflicts exist in families, in economic organizations, in political organizations, in social groups, and in religious organizations. If each person is allowed to pursue individual impulses without conforming to the constraints imposed by the group as a whole, hostile relationships dangerous to the individual and to the group arise.

The group or organization has a life of its own apart from the life of the individuals comprising it. A family unit of two parents and two children is made up of four individuals, each possessing personal and social impulses. If these impulses are channeled into constructive, cooperative relationships, both the individual and the family unit survive—in fact as well as in law. If, however, individuals are allowed to express impulses without constraint, conflicting impulses may break up the family unit—in fact, if not in law. Although its members continue to exist, the family unit no longer functions and its benefits are lost—whether or not there is divorce.

Since the family unit and all other human organizations are the product of human design, we must always be aware of the need for mutual adaptation. We must also be aware of the *consequences* of adaptation. If we want to survive as human beings, rather than, let us say, as semirobots, we must take great care to understand the organizations we create and to which we must adjust. *It is fundamental to the survival of humankind as individuals that we create organizations that adapt themselves to our physiological and psychological needs. It is equally important that we adapt ourselves to the requirements of the organization in which we expect to thrive.*

These ideas are not limited to social organizations; they apply to the physical environment as well. The Nuclear Age and the Space Age are monuments to our success as reasoning beings, but we may create for ourselves a Waste Age if we fail to protect our physical environment from harm.

Humanity adopts values and social goals in its struggle for survival and, beyond that, the good life. These values evolve over time and are based on experience as well as on hopes and dreams. The value which we inherit from our natural evolution as an animal is survival. As a reasoning human, we have, however, modified the natural process of survival. As we have gained control over our environment, we have added other values to basic survival. When we create wealth and build social, political, and economic organizations, we adopt values that reflect our views as to what is "right" and "wrong" in regard to all our relationships with others as well as with our environment. Such values relate to health, work, pleasure, wealth, family relationships, social responsibility, citizenship, and so on. Ideally they should serve to improve the quality of life.

Hard work and thrift played an important role in the creation of wealth in nineteenth-century capitalism. Protestantism became the progenitor and advocate of these values that created a surplus that was converted into the means of production, which became the source of economic growth and wealth.

Hard work and thrift did not apply equally to all members of society. The upper class was not expected to practice it. It was expected to provide leadership. The lower classes were not expected to practice thrift except to the extent that it enabled them to survive. They were unable to practice thrift beyond that. They were expected to work hard, but generally did so only because they had no choice if they wanted to eat. Since their wages were generally barely adequate for subsistence and not infrequently even lower, workers regarded hard work as less of a virtue than did their employers. The middle class of old, the "knights" of capitalism who bravely fought its battles, practiced hard work and thrift so ardently that they became the prime virtues of the age.

The upper classes and the middle-class entrepreneurs benefitted from these goals and values, and their needs were satisfied. The lower economic classes, who made up the bulk of the supply of labor, did not fare so well. Low wages, job insecurity, boredom, and almost no opportunity to be creative left the psychological needs badly neglected. Whiskey frequently took the place of a wholesome existence.

The environment in the nineteenth century produced hostility between workers and employers. The system survived, however, because in the twentieth century it adapted itself, to some extent, to the needs of the workers. The rise of the modern corporation and the modern labor union brought about changes that reduced hostility and extended the benefits of economic development. Also the entire economic pie grew. Despite efforts to improve the situation, some problems remained, however. The majority of workers still suffer from boredom and have little or no opportunity to be creative. Their physiological needs are better satisfied now, but their psychological needs remain unheeded.

Unsatisfied psychological needs, combined with job security resulting from the government's assuming greater responsibility for the public welfare, has created new problems. Workers can no longer be *coerced* to work hard and long hours, because survival no longer depends upon it. As a result, new ways have to be found to motivate people to work hard and efficiently if real economic growth is to continue.

Just as the managerial class is motivated by such psychological rewards as decision making and the opportunity to be creative and innovative, so ways now have to be found to motivate workers by satisfying both their physiological and psychological needs. In many countries of the world, experiments are conducted with the aim of finding solutions to the problems of human motivation.

It should be obvious that harmony between the individual and society can exist only if values and goals are so determined that relationships between the individual and society are *mutually* satisfying. Individuals must find physiological and psychological nourishment from society, and society must be sustained by human values. Only if they support each other can society and the individual live in lasting harmony. This is not yet the case today. As a result, active or latent hostility stands in the way of harmony.

The Role of the Market

The classical economists recommended that all individuals be allowed to pursue their own interests within the confines of a free market. They underestimated the importance of human values and social goals in the creation of harmony and balance. The only values and goals they recognized were those that related to the process of economic optimization. Even in that respect, however, they failed to consider realistically the impact of the economic process on individuals and society. Some of the classical writers were aware of the problems arising when these are treated as economic entities without adequate regard to noneconomic needs. Unfortunately, this awareness did not find its way into orthodox economic theory and policy.

As a result of the narrow approach to life that traditional economics represents, a large part of the world lives under the illusion that selfish, irresponsible interests, freely pursued, without constraint, could lead to human progress. This strange conclusion is based on the belief that natural law, operating in the form of a free market, could automatically create social harmony.

The free market could not deliver the promise made by the classical economists, nor were the natural laws able to protect its purity. As a result, the opponents of capitalism cast their scorn not only on the abuses of capitalism, but also on what they regarded as the foundation of capitalism as well—the market system.

Although the market plays a vital role in the process of adaptation, a reliance on it as the prime regulator of the economic process prevents the achievement of vital social goals and harmony. As the market functioned in the nineteenth century, the law of the jungle became supreme. The concept of pure competition was based on the naive belief that power plays no role in the economic decision-making process. As a result, employers exploited workers and firms exploited each other in the name of competition.

The market as the prime regulator suffers from a serious drawback that is harmful to the individual as well as to society. The individual and the firm lose control over economic decisions when the market is allowed to set the pace. As Andrew Carnegie said, not to expand means to regress in an economy in which the market makes all decisions.

If any firm in the market is set on expansion, all other firms must follow suit or they will eventually be eliminated through what is called monopolistic competition. This is, of course, exactly what happened in most of the major industries in which only a handful of firms survived.

One of the dangers of a system that has no social goals transcending the market is that individuals lose control of their destiny and are forced to play roles determined by market forces that are aloof to the noneconomic needs of individuals and society. In such a world, we become the agents of progress measured in purely physical terms, which leaves our other needs as human beings unsatisfied. As a result, we become incapable of dealing intelligently with the needs of the social and physical environment of which we are part.

The fact that the market is incapable of satisfying all the essential needs of the individual and society does not mean that human interests are best served by a nonmarket economy. The traditional concept of a market economy, however, is naive and unrealistic.[1] A few economists have begun to look at market functions in a new and more sophisticated light. Whereas the traditional economists still believe that the self-adjusting market is a superior alternative to human decisions, a more realistic interpretation of market functions is that they should play a major role in the regulation of economic activity, but that they are not, and should not be, the *only* regulator.

To what extent can economic decisions, adjustments, and human and social adaptation be left to the self-adjusting market? At what point does judgment become the regulator? These are fundamental questions in an economy whose objective is to produce harmony between the individual and society by democratic means.

We must look at the evolutionary process in nature to find the answers to these questions. Before humanity as reasoning animals, appeared in the process of evolution, all adaptation occurred naturally without any interference from living creatures. Nature has no regard for the individual and sacrifices it to preserve the species. (Creatures devour each other). Even species perish when their natural ability to adapt to change is inadequate.

In the nonhuman animal, all signals originate in the natural process of physical life. The signals reflecting deviations from a norm lead to natural responses that either restore the norm or kill the animal. This is nature's way.

This concept found its way into classical economics and describes the classical market. The norm in this market was automatically restored either by resolving the problem through adaptation or by forcing the demise of the unhealthy economic unit (the submarginal firm).

In transcending nature, humanity has added a new dimension to the process of deviation from the norm as well as to the response mechanism. We have added specific psychological needs to our physiological needs, and we have created our own process of adaptation and destruction. The modern market reflects this. It is not a pure and natural market, but a market made by us that responds, not to natural laws, but to the environment that we have created.

When we evolved as reasoning humans we developed the skills to improve upon nature so far as the quality of life was concerned. Today, nature and humanity in partnership determine the quality of life. Each has a function that must be understood in the interest of survival.

What are these functions? The human body is usually capable of making automatic adjustments to *normal* deviations from the physiological and psychological balance called good health. The body gives out involuntary signals such as a fever or a rash that warn a person of deviations from the norm. If the signals are not signs of a radical deviation, the body can normally make the necessary adjustments. The body cannot, however, make the necessary adjustments when the deviations are *radical*. Examples of this are bacteria to which the body cannot develop immunity. The loss of a limb in an accident is another type of radical change.

Just as we find normal and radical deviations in the physiological and psychological functions of an individual, so we find similar deviations in social, political, and economic functions in society. In both cases, the approach to normal deviations and to radical deviations require different methods.

In a market economy, some of the signals in regard to deviations from the norm originate generally through the market mechanism. Sometimes the signals indicate normal and expected deviation; sometimes they indicate radical deviations and serious problems. How are such signals identified? The market uses such variables as prices, output, profits, and interest rates for this purpose.

Not all deviations from the norm can be identified by these typical market signals. Some of the deviations from a norm—such as an increase or decrease in federal budget deficits—are not signalled by the usual market variables in the economy. In his *General Theory*, Keynes defined these as autonomous, nonmarket variables.[2]

The modern market is still a market, however, and it plays a role in the process of adaptation. It performs badly when either more or less is expected from it than it can do. In the United States more is expected from it—and in the Soviet Union less—than it is able to contribute to the well-being of society.

What can the market do and what can it not do in the process of adaptation? The market sends out signals when there are deviations from the norm. Sometimes, when the deviations are mild, the market can generate a process of adjustment.

There are deviations from the norm that are autonomously generated rather than induced by market forces. Keynes' profit expectation (the marginal efficiency of capital) is an example of that. It is influenced by factors outside the market, such as wars, other international developments, political developments, international competition, significantly changing productivity, and rapid technological changes. These are events produced by humanity and our efforts to control nature in the creation of our own environment. The "pure and natural" market could not help even if it existed, because the deviations are caused by factors outside the market.

Although the market cannot cure such autonomous deviations, it is helpful in signalling their existence. This is vital to the process of adaptation. When the deviations from the norm are radical in nature, the market is not able to generate a process of adjustment, whether the deviations are caused by market forces, by autonomous factors, or by a combination of both. If, for example, rapid and radical changes in technology distort the relationship between the supply of and the demand for labor, market forces will signal this by reducing the demand for workers whose skills have become obsolete due to radical and rapid technological changes. At present, there are millions of workers unemployed as a result of such a radical deviation from the norm.

Market forces cannot make the necessary adjustments within a reasonable time span and probably cannot make them at all. Human progress is too fast for the long periods required for adaptation when the process is left to each individual pursuing his or her own ends. Adjustment under such conditions may never occur, because the problems or deviations are replaced by new problems before old problems become solved.

Humanity, as the creator of its environment, cannot afford to leave the outcome of scientific and technological revolutions to chance or fate. That is how Dr. Frankenstein's monster destroyed its creator.

Rather, we must learn to use our reason and intelligence to foresee the changes that will occur in the future as a result of our scientific and technological advances. Many of these changes are predictable. The ability to adapt the environment to humanity, and humanity to the environment, depends on our willingness to plan and prepare for the future.

The Role of Anticipation and Planning

Why, therefore, despite all these efforts should the system be spinning out of control? The problem is not simply that we plan too little; we also plan too poorly.
—Alvin Toffler, *Future Shock*

Planning exists both in the Soviet Union and in the United States. In both nations, there are serious obstacles to its success as a vehicle for humanizing life. In the Soviet Union, the main obstacle is the absence of an adequate and effective market system signalling information to the planners, without which successful planning is impossible. In the United States, planning is jeopardized by an emotional attitude that rejects social planning as a proper method for preparing for the future. It reluctantly accepts planning as a necessary evil for dealing with problems that have reached overwhelming proportions. Such problems are usually the result of not having planned for their prevention.

Slum clearing is an example of planning after the harm is done. Slums are not merely composed of dilapidated dwellings. They are the habitat of human degradation and can even be described as a social disease. Slums are the result of economic decisions motivated by a shortsighted concern for costs and benefits. For the sake of maximizing profits immediately, costs that will arise in the future are ignored. If slums are to be avoided, economic decisions must be based on long-term plans that take future social costs into consideration.

Once the slums exist, the problem to be solved is far more complicated than the process designed to prevent them. Preventive medicine, intelligently applied, is far less expensive over time than a system allowing disease to develop in an uncontrolled manner and then responding with expressive treatment that is often too late to prevent permanent damage.

Once a slum exists, planning designed to clear it is handicapped. The economic problem has become entangled with serious social and political complications. People who live in slums are generally less healthy, less educated, less trained, less motivated, less prepared, more hostile, less politically aware, less community-oriented, and more prone to break the law than other citizens. Many slum inhabitants become permanently tuned in with life on welfare because they are not trained in any skill and are not prepared physically, mentally or emotionally for a life of productive work.

To be successful, slum-clearing programs would have to involve social planning designed to rehabilitate the people who live in them and prepare them for an active and useful life. After the harm is already done, it is often too late for rehabilitation; more often rehabilitation is not even attempted. As a result, many slum-clearing programs end in failure. The dilapidated buildings are replaced, but there is little or no rehabilitation and few economic opportunities. Slum-clearing produces new buildings, but the human degradation remains. Even the buildings deteriorate again in five to ten years because slum dwellers are unable to take care of them any better than they take care of themselves.

Many social programs meet the same fate as slum clearing because we plan too late and too little. There is, however, another factor that has in the past virtually ruled out intelligent long-range planning for the humanization of society. The Industrial Revolution was accompanied by a philosophical and social development, called technocracy which is primarily dedicated to the production of material wealth. Human values and needs are often subordinated to that, in practice if not in theory.

It can be argued, as Marx did explicitly and Ricardo implicitly, that human development has to be preceded by a period in which the creation of wealth is given the highest priority. This does not mean that the abuses of nineteenth-century capitalism and twentieth-century socialism are a necessary part of the creation of wealth. It does mean, however, that according to Marx, genuine human development has to be preceded by a system such as capitalism in which the creation of wealth predominates.

Although the dictionary defines technocracy as management by technical experts, a functional definition of technocracy is a social structure that is dedicated to the creation and maximization of wealth. Technocratic planning is not adequately concerned with the humanization of society and the creation of a balance between individual needs and social needs necessary for the preservation of the individual and society.

The twin objectives of the technocracy ushered in by the Industrial Revolution have become the creation of wealth and military power. Its indifference toward human needs is not its only weakness. Its emphasis on maximizing wealth is so overpowering that it ignores the impact on the future of humanity. The time span of its concern is very short and its social conscience nonexistent. This philosophy worked its way into neoclassical economics, which excludes time from its models. It also regards all value judgments pertaining to the individual and society as aberrations that have no place in economics. As a social science, economics reached its lowest point when it built its theories on the principles of a technocracy.

Technocratic planning also suffers from a third inherent flaw. Being indifferent to human and environmental needs, it encourages a bureaucracy in which the planners, whether socialist or corporate, pay too little attention to those whose lives are being planned. To plan successfully, it is necessary to accumulate information from the consumers, the local community, the workers, and people in other parts of the world on whom the plan has an impact.

The market, if it operates efficiently, produces feedback from consumers, which helps the producers to respond to the material needs of the people. This is consistent with the technocratic goal of maximizing wealth in capitalist countries where the products produced have to be sold to consumers willing to buy them and also in the Soviet Union, where the planners cannot be aloof from the wants of consumers or they produce too little or too much of the things consumers buy.

The equally important psychological needs of the people are ignored by the typical technocratic bureaucracy. Planners concentrate on output rather than the needs of workers and consumers. This, until recently, has been true in many capitalist and socialist countries because both have been committed to the ideals of technocracy.

In recent decades, some desirable changes have occurred that point in the direction of a greater emphasis on human and environmental needs. These have been inspired by two major developments. First there is now an awareness in some quarters that technocratic planning with its neglect of the psychological needs of people and the environment in the midst of rapid change has brought us perilously close to losing control of the decision-making process.

A second development that has made the world more aware of the technocratic dilemma is the great technological advance that has brought in the Nuclear Age and Space Age. We have acquired the ability to destroy anything within our reach, including humanity and the environment. At the same time, we have neglected to create political relationships that can help us to control the power we have created. Uncontrolled, such power can only destroy. Controlled and humanized, it can become the source of a much better life.

There are signs that a change in attitudes may make the Technocratic Age obsolete (as indeed it is on moral grounds) and usher in a more humane approach to the production of wealth. Some of the top universities have institutes devoted to finding solutions to the problems created by the neglect of human and social needs. They have only begun to scratch the surface, but there is at least an awareness.

In some Western and Eastern European countries, and in Japan, experiments are going on in what is called participatory democracy. In France, Germany, Yugoslavia, and Hungary, greater attention is paid to the psychological needs of the workers and people in general than has ever been the case anywhere since technocracy took hold of economic development.

In the Soviet Union, significant changes have taken place since the Stalinist era. There is greater decentralization in the economic decision-making process and more attention is paid to feedback from local communities.

What specific events have led to a virtual revolt against the technocratic power structure in many parts of the world? The mind-boggling advances since the 1930s have made the Industrial Revolution look like yesteryear's horse and buggy. The sun and the atom have become potential sources of unlimited energy; new scientific discoveries allow us to look into a new world of time and space; new theories in quantum electronics and information gathering and programing have revolutionized the decision-making process; the oceans have become a source of energy and resources of the future; genetics and genetic engineering are beginning to have an impact on human development and food production; and, finally, scientific discoveries still in the blueprint stage will alter in one way or another most traditional methods of production and distribution.

The immense new and better resources and the greatly improved methods of using them that lie on the horizon will give us the opportunity to advance a great ideal—the humanization of life and the creation of an enlightened society.

Our main problem is that we must manage to survive until that happens. Our chances of survival and humanization will greatly improve if we use the market system and planning in such a way that human, social, and environmental needs receive a high priority. Humanity must advance beyond technocracy as soon as possible.

The Market and Planning in the Posttechnocratic Society

The struggle for the market—the right to buy and sell without interference from the state or church—was the overriding political objective of the merchants and entrepreneurs who "fought" the Industrial Revolution. The economy evolved from the stage in which the market played a very minor role and consumers produced most of their own goods and services, to the stage where the market became a vast worldwide network bringing all people of the earth into direct and indirect contact. The producers and consumers were separated into two distinct groups, and then they were brought together again by a complex market network.

The market emerged as the structural foundation of western culture and politics. The concept of the market became confused when classical economists attributed qualities to it that it possessed only under very special conditions.

Although the market did not live up to the expectations of the classical economists who saw it as the manifestation of economic laws having their roots in nature, it became the structural foundation of economic development in both capitalist and socialist economies. This fact becomes apparent when we abandon the nonfunctional classical definition of the market.

Production may be structured in a variety of ways. It may be planned by a central government and executed by paid managers; it may be planned by corporate executives on a global scale in industries that their firm alone (or with very few other firms) dominates; or it may be planned by managers in small firms in a decentralized industry. No matter how it is structured, the market serves as a point of contact for the producers and the consumers, which is essential in economies based on specialization and trade. It is difficult for some economists to concede that a planned economy such as exists in the Soviet Union is built on a market structure.

The market is far more complex than the oversimplified version found in traditional economic theory. To be understood, it must be analyzed in terms of its social, political, economic, and psychological impacts. This can be easily demonstrated when we consider the following. Households supply workers whose physical, psychological, and mental needs must be reasonably met if they are to play a useful role as producers.

Firms supply products and services that have an impact not only on consumers but also on the environment and on future generations. Producers and consumers make up the electorate and the taxpayers, who have an impact on the quality of government. Government, in turn, has an impact on producers and consumers and on the environment as well as on the quality of life in the present and in the future.

The investments U.S. global corporations make anywhere in the world have an impact on our future—not merely our economic future but that affecting the total quality of our lives. Such corporations invest to secure resources, markets, and production facilities. The political and economic impacts of such investments commit future generations to accept responsibility in the name of patriotism for fighting wars, cleaning up the environment, or paying the debts of past generations.

Such economic decisions on the part of global corporations also affect the people in the region where the investment is made. It frequently affects their social and political structures as well as their cultural attitudes. This in turn has an impact on the politics of the nations in which the investing corporations reside. By omitting all such interactions and the social costs generated over time, the basic concepts of traditional economic theory have become woefully obsolete.

If economics is to play a helpful role in directing our future, it must be built around the actual relationships between households, firms, the government, and the environment—including international relations. It must regard humanity not merely as economic, but as the social, political, economic, and psychological entity whose survival and quality of life depends upon our interaction with the environment and our global interdependence.

Traditional economics does not consider the impact on humanity and the environment of production, distribution, consumption, and public policy except in purely economic terms. Are the firm and the industry profitable? Is there full employment, are prices stable, and is the economy growing? Old-line economists will argue that they must concern themselves only with economic issues and that psychological, social, and political problems belong to other disciplines. Such arguments have made economics very nearly useless as a social science! The fact is that there *are* no economic problems as such! There are only human and environmental problems.

Before developing theories and policies designed to cope with economic questions, it is necessary to accept the fact that economic decisions *do* have an impact on the social, political, and psychological behavior of people and that these in turn have an influence on economic decisions. Once this simple fact is fully appreciated and built into economic theories and policies, planning and preparedness as necessary steps in the evolution and adaptation of humanity and the environment follow quite naturally. Planning, however, is merely a tool in the process of reaching objectives. In a technocratic, planned society such as the Soviet Union, the psychological needs of people may be just as effectively ignored as in a so-called unplanned, technocratic society such as the United States.

For planning to adequately serve the needs of the people and the environment, it must be based on a great deal more than the principles of maximization on the use of human and physical resources. It cannot be measured simply by such indexes as the Gross National Product and price levels.

The enlightened economy will have as its objective much more than the wealth of nations. It will link people, production, and the environment in a new type of input-output relationship in which holistic human decisions will form the input, while the quality of life will be the output.

12
The Dynamic Economy

Time and Relativity in the Dynamic Economy

At the time of Adam Smith, the world that mattered in the economic sense was a very small part of the planet Earth and change took place slowly and predictably compared to today's world. This had the effect of making time and relativity seem less important than they actually were, and far less important than they are today.

No attempt should be made to interpret social, political, and economic development on the assumption that it follows the time-space-relativity pattern of the universe, which is known as Einstein's theory of relativity. Any attempt to do that would simply lead to a new economic theory of "natural law" far more sophisticated than the classical theory, but subject to the same shortcoming—not being realistic.

The universe was not created by people, as was the social, political, and economic world we live in. The same "laws," therefore, do not apply to both. It is, nevertheless, possible to learn something from the new concepts of time and relativity because they are the foundation of the dynamics of reality.

The real world of economics cannot be understood if we abstract from time and relativity as the classical economists have done. Classical economics followed the course of Newtonian physics, which did not include time and relativity in its theory of space and motion relative to the universe.

The concept of time and relativity can best be understood if we conceive of life and everything in the universe as being in constant motion. The reason we cannot observe motion is that the point of reference (the earth) is moving at the same speed as we are. Einstein

extended Newton's point of reference and we must do that in economics if we want to be in touch with reality.

What does that mean in regard to the universe and in regard to
economic theory? To understand motion and relativity, it is necessary only to realize that it is impossible to "drop anchor" in the
universe. We are not standing still, even when we think we are not
moving.

In the universe, two observers will see the same event at different times and places depending on their points of reference in regard
to motion (the earth, the moon, another planet or another solar
system). The earth rotates around its own axis and revolves around
the sun, and it moves with the sun in relation to its galaxy, which
is a small part of the universe. This simple phenomenon involves
three different rates of motion. The universe is made up of things
that move at different speeds up to the absolute limit in the rate of
motion, the speed of light (186,000 miles per second.) Time and
distance, or space, can only be measured in terms of events as they
are observed from different points of reference. That is the essence
of the theory of relativity. It can be illustrated in simple terms if we
imagine an object moving in a lake and three motor boats (A, B,
and C) racing toward it and then returning to their points of origin.
All three boats can be assumed to start at the same distance from
the object. Boat A is moving at one-half the speed of boat B, which
is moving at one-half the speed of boat C. The person operating
each boat will observe the moving object at a different place on the
lake, and at different times, from the people in the other two boats.

This is the meaning of time and relativity in today's theories of
the universe. How does this relate to economics? If all economic
activity is perceived from a single point of reference, it becomes a
logical process governed by the data pertaining to that point of reference. That is a description of a static model with the point of
reference called *equilibrium.*

Equilibrium is a point of reference toward which all the factors
constituting supply and demand gravitate. Economists have invented an economic law of gravity for the purpose of making corrections when the factors of supply and demand fail to meet simultaneously at the point of equilibrium. The equilibrium point is
called the market price and it is the only price at which all the factors of supply and demand meet.

The traditional market is one in which price serves as a self-equilibrating regulator of supply and demand. What are the "things" that move toward equilibrium to form market supply and demand, which determine what an economy produces for consumption, economic growth, and military purposes?

The most important factors of supply include technology, human labor of varying skills and many categories (a stock concept of labor), the education and training of human labor (a flow concept of labor), producer's goods (capital), nonhuman resources produced by nature and by people, laws and regulations in regard to production, international economic and political relations, and war and preparation for war.

The demand factors include the size and distribution of income, the system of values, customs, and culture, the massive use of advertising, public social programs and all other public nonmilitary expenditures, and military expenditures.

Equilibrium implies that all the factors of supply and demand arrive at a given point of reference at the same time. It has already been pointed out that if they do not, the market price acting like the law of gravity (an economic magnetic field) will pull all the factors toward the point of equilibrium. That is the traditional view of the market.

To picture a perfect market equilibrium, we need to assume that all of the factors of supply and demand move at the same rate of motion toward equilibrium and meet there at the same moment of time. In a less than perfect concept of equilibrium (which is the case in business-cycle theory), it is assumed that these factors do not meet at the point of equilibrium at the same time. This may happen either because the factors meet obstacles on the way toward equilibrium (one or more drop out as a result of supply shortages or sudden shifts in demand, as in the case of war) or because some of the factors continue in motion past the point of equilibrium as a result of mistaken expectations. In traditional economics, shortages and mistaken expectations are short-run phenomena that are self-correcting in the long run through the price mechanism, which is to equilibrium theory what gravity is to Newton's laws of motion.

Since disequilibrium is considered an imperfection rather than a normal phenomenon, time plays no significant role in traditional economics. Equilibrium is the normal state of the economy and disequilibrium is automatically corrected by a price mechanism. Time is, therefore, not an inherent part of equilibrium theory, except as an adjustment device.

If the factors of supply and demand change in one of the countless markets, this change is reflected in a change of the market price. If the price rises in one or more of the micro markets in this way, the prices in some of the other micro markets could change in the opposite direction to maintain general or overall equilibrium. The magic of automatic supply and demand adjustments is supposed to accomplish this in the world of laissez-faire.

A genuinely dynamic theory, reflecting the experiences of the real world, must treat the different rates of motion of the factors of supply and demand as rational responses to the continuously changing conditions of the economic universe, not as aberrations that can be explained with business-cycle theory. The vast and rapid changes of the Industrial and Technological Revolutions require that the political organizations that manage an economy be dynamic. Realistic economic theories must reflect this if they are to serve a useful purpose. The factors of supply and demand function in a way that makes relative time and motion a vital part of their normal behavior.

Since relative time and motion of the factors of supply and demand are normal phenomena of the economic universe, equilibrium should be replaced with a dynamic concept of stability: *balance*. Economic balance is consistent with continuous change and the discretionary human management of economic affairs, while equilibrium theory is not.

Time and Structural Change as Part of Economic Theory

The factors of supply and demand have a "life" that moves through time. Like human life, these factors undergo changes during the course of their existence. These changes are not automatic, but are motivated by the conditions of their environment, which are to a considerable extent influenced or determined by human decisions.

In primitive economies, change is virtually nonexistent, or it progresses so slowly that it is not observable except over long periods of time. The factors of supply and demand in such economies are for all practical purposes "timeless." Human labor remains unchanged, and culture patterns (the main factor of demand in primitive societies) are virtually cast in stone. A primitive market based on barter facilitates the exchange of the simplest of goods and services. Such a market can easily be imagined to be in a state of equilibrium because there is rarely any tendency to deviate from that single point of reference.

In the early stages of economic development, time still does not play a significant role. Commercial capitalism in the seventeenth and eighteenth centuries in Britain is an example of that. The factors of supply and demand changed very slowly when technology was in its simplest stages. Money replaced barter, but change was still slow enough not to disturb the concept of equilibrium—at least as a theory based on the conditions of the time.

As science, technology, and economic development evolved at increasingly rapid rates, the factors of supply and demand were subjected to fast-changing conditions. When conditions change, these factors must adapt in order to remain viable. Not all factors can adapt to change in such a way that the adaptation occurs simultaneously. On the contrary, the rates of adaptation are likely to vary significantly, and if conditions change radically or rapidly, the variations in the rates of adaptation are likely to be great. The factors of supply and demand do not all meet at the same time at a common point of reference called equilibrium. Their rate of motion varies; therefore, *disequilibrium is a normal condition*. In most cases, adaptation is not automatic and requires a catalyst—human intervention.[1]

In nineteenth-century United States, the factors of supply and demand did not move automatically toward equilibrium (or from equilibrium to equilibrium) to facilitate economic growth. After the Civil War, when economic development became a national objective, free markets gave way to economic concentration. By the turn of the century, men such as Rockefeller, Morgan, Hill, Carnegie, Vanderbilt, and Guggenheim were already directing a significant part of the market economy.

The giants of capitalism operated in a market system, but it was not the free, self-equilibrating market given birth by the fertile imagination of the classical economists. In the economy that began to develop after the Civil War, the market system was largely directed by discretionary human decisions. It was no longer a question of equilibrium, because time and motion became significant and there were no convenient laws of nature to coordinate their movements automatically. Time and motion were directed to facilitate growth and profits without regard to balance. The inevitable disturbances were interpreted as short-run disequilibria that would correct themselves in the long run.

Exactly how do time and relativity enter into an explanation of such disturbances as inflation and unemployment? The factors of supply are activated by a variety of uncoordinated decisions. The net birth rate and the educational system determine the availability of the various categories of labor. The net birth rate is affected by the birth rate, longevity, wars, and so on. The supply of skilled or even semi-skilled labor in all its forms cannot, therefore, be greatly increased or decreased without a good deal of preparation. The demand for labor is affected by changes in the demand for goods and services induced by economic development, aggressive advertising, and other things.

The "rate of motion" of the supply of labor and the time in which it moves toward the demand for labor if left to itself will most likely be different from the rate of motion of the demand for labor and the time in which it moves toward the supply of labor. As a result, there will be either unwanted surpluses or unwanted shortages of labor.

Traditional economists believe that such discrepancies will be automatically corrected via the affected price mechanisms in the long run. Such an adjustment assumes that the economy is standing still,[2] waiting for all the factors of supply and demand to fall into place at the point of reference (equilibrium).

If the point of reference is in fact not standing still, but is moving at increasing rates of motion as a result of technological changes, then the likelihood of an automatic adjustment is nil. This means that the concept of the long run is not applicable to an economy subject to an infinite pattern of change in the factors of supply and demand.

The rates of motion of most economic variables are dependent on the conditions of the environment in which they exist. (All factors of supply and demand are referred to as economic variables.) Their time and motion in one nation is therefore relative to their time and motion in another nation, and the degree of relativity depends on conditions in the total environment of each nation.

This principle of relativity is an important one in evaluating the performance of two separate economies. Economic variables will move at lower rates of motion in an economy where the population is large in relation to the size of the economy and where there is a dearth of natural resources, than in an economy in which the opposite is true. Climate, political stability, commitment to economic development, and the ability to import capital are other factors influencing the rate of motion.

Economic development is part of the total development of the individual and of society, so political, social, and cultural development must be viewed in terms of the impact economic development has on them. It is therefore impossible to "export" a political system as though it existed in a vacuum. *Time and relativity rather than absolute, timeless, motionless values are essential in understanding the world in which we live.*

As technology moves with an increasingly rapid rate of motion, economic balance becomes more difficult to achieve and the past is less and less able to serve as a guide for the future. This is the warning of Toffler's *Future Shock*. The intelligent application of time and relativity can, however, help to light the way to balance.

The Meaning of Balance in an Economic World of Time and Structural Change

As I have already said, the concept of equilibrium was invented to provide a theoretical base for an economic system built by the classical economists on a foundation of natural laws to match the orderly system of Newtonian physics. Unfortunately the economic world humankind created does not match the orderliness of the physical universe, which was not created by us. As a result, the concept of equilibrium is in itself the source of a disorderly economic world because it ignores the time and motion pattern of the factors of production.

The classical economists were able to adopt the concept of equilibrium by ignoring much of what is vital in the real world. The classical market could be in equilibrium at any given level of income and income distribution. People without incomes or with incomes inadequate for even the barest level of subsistence had no bearing on equilibrium because poverty and starvation were not considered in the development of economic theory.

Workers who are idle because they have not adapted to changes in demand in the various categories of labor are outside the framework of the theory of economic equilibrium. In the modern world in which change is so rapid and radical, many economic problems tend to be structural and would not respond to changes in prices even if the price mechanism worked as the classical economists had envisaged it.

Declining productivity, which has plagued the United States since the early 1970s and nearly all industrialized nations since the late 1970s, is a factor in both inflation and unemployment. Three of the most important reasons for it have been radical disturbances in the price and output of energy (due to quasi-cartels), worker alienation, and declining incentives for productive investments—all structural causes.

How does the concept of balance differ from the concept of equilibrium? Balance, unlike equilibrium, is not based on a system of economic laws patterned after the physical laws of nature. There is, therefore, no general self-equilibrating adjustment process in a theory of balance as there is in economic theories based on equilibrium.

Economic balance exists when the economic factors of supply and demand are in place so that the results reflect at least the high-priority objectives of the people whom the economy serves. The central problem in achieving balance is adaptation.

In the classical system, adaptation was automatic and was reflected in equilibrium. In a modern economy, automatic equilibrium is inconceivable because of the complexity of the time and motion problems of the factors of supply and demand.

Economic variables do not all respond equally to the challenge of adaptation. There is, first of all, the question of time and motion. The length of time involved in adaptation varies considerably. If the length of time is very great (five or ten years), timely adaptation can generally not take place without considerable advance preparation, the reason being that the conditions existing at a particular time do not remain constant for many years. Without preparation, adaptation can in some instances take so long that before the process is completed, great new problems that could have been avoided through timely preparation come to the surface.

An example of this is the energy crisis. The U.S. economy was built on the assumption that energy would continue to be plentiful and cheap. Part of the energy used came from abroad and, by means of a special brand of neocolonialism, it remained very cheap until the emergence of OPEC as a political force. Cars, factories, homes, and virtually all other facets of the economy were designed to waste energy, which was regarded as a cheap input.

Then, almost as though the crisis were unexpected, energy became scarce and expensive in 1973. This resulted partly from the anticolonial actions by OPEC and partly from the fact that the exploration and production of energy became increasingly more expensive. The United States and other industrial countries were caught off-guard, although they had possessed confidential information for decades in regard to the inevitable energy crisis. There were no adequate viable plans to deal with it and no preparations had been made for developing safe and economically sound alternative sources of energy.

As a result of this lack of adaptation the world economy was pushed farther away from balance. The Third World countries, with the exception of the energy producers, were unable to advance their economic development because of the prohibitively high energy costs. The United States experienced unprecedented trade deficits. The combination of these forces had a stagnating effect on the world economy.

The factors of supply and demand in the case of energy crises need two kinds of stimuli to initiate and execute the process of adaptation. One is the price mechanism, which signals the need for change. The other is research and development, which paves the way to adaptation.

Research and development is a long-term project. In the case of energy, it involves enormous outlays of capital and also requires policies favoring new sources of energy over high-priced existing sources. The question of whether research and development can be better accomplished by the private sector alone or whether the input of the public sector is also required need not be answered here. The important point is the element of time.

The economic development of the Third World, which was held back by the energy crisis, is vital to the market-expansion requirements of the developed nations. Without the creation of new geographic markets, the industrial nations are likely to compete too aggressively for existing markets. In addition to that, hunger and poverty in the Third World are likely to create obstacles to world peace.

Energy is a major factor in the structure of supply and demand. If the market signals are jammed or ignored, or if inadequate action is taken with regard to research and development, time and motion become factors in creating serious imbalances. Whereas economic equilibrium is based on the belief that the process of adaptation is an automatic market phenomenon, in the concept of balance the market plays an important but more limited role. Human decisions based on an accurate understanding of the conditions pertaining to the factors of supply and demand within the relative framework of time and motion become paramount. The elements of time and motion are so vital in the achievement of balance that adaptation cannot be left to chance if balance is to be achieved.

Balance as a Realistic Alternative to Equilibrium

The concept of equilibrium is not a mere theoretical whim. It is the heart of the utopian structure of laissez-faire. It is considered by its adherents as a preferable alternative to discretionary human decisions.

Equilibrium theory and natural law go hand in hand. The belief that we can rely on the laws of nature for the well-being of our economic life is at the heart of equilibrium theory. Equilibrium is divided into two parts, general equilibrium and partial equilibrium, which a few of the great classical economists correctly perceived as being inseparable in the laissez-faire economy.

General equilibrium theory is concerned with overall economic equilibrium. Partial equilibrium deals with parts of the economy, such as a firm or an industry. A firm or an industry, according to traditional economists, is in equilibrium if it can earn "normal" profits without deviating from its course. Many of today's economists no longer emphasize or even deal with general equilibrium. They concentrate instead on partial equilibrium because they regard that as more obtainable. They either ignore or do not realize that a theory of partial equilibrium cannot be separated from the concept of general equilibrium—a fact that the great classical economists understood very well and did not ignore.

The reason for the inseparability of partial and general equilibrium is rather obvious. Since changes in the condition of the overall economy affect the activities of firms and industries and all other microeconomic segments, partial equilibrium cannot exist without some assumptions about general equilibrium or the condition of the overall economy.

Actually, apart from the present tendency to concentrate on partial equilibrium, the whole concept of equilibrium is unsatisfactory in a world in which so many economic variables of the nonmarket variety affect economic activity. It is also inadequate, as we saw, in a world in which time and motion play an important role in the process of adjustment.

The essence of general equilibrium theory is the assumption that a market economy is inherently stable and requires no external assistance to move toward full employment and price stability in case of temporary inflation or unemployment. Prices, in all the forms in which they exist, are considered to be the only things that motivate people, and markets adjust automatically because there are presumed to be no structural obstacles to reaching equilibrium. The economy is assumed to be static or to change predictably within a market framework. All variables in the economy that make up supply and demand are assumed to move simultaneously toward a single point of reference—equilibrium.

Modern monetarists are still greatly influenced by the "neutrality" concept of money, which became a part of the general equilibrium theory. The neutrality of money is based on a so-called homogeneity postulate or a homogeneous mathematical function. This simply means that a change in the money supply affects the prices of all goods and services uniformly or homogeneously. For example, if the money supply is doubled, all prices in the goods-and-services sector will also be doubled. Since people have twice as much money as before prices doubled, their real cash balances are unchanged. Hence, money is regarded as neutral. The homogeneity postulate was discovered to be wrong, because an increase in the money supply does not affect all markets uniformly. In fact, there is *no* uniformity in the economic process of a modern complex economy. Other attempts to save the concept of general equilibrium also failed, and most traditional economists today limit themselves to partial equilibrium theory, ignoring the vital logical relationship between general equilibrium and partial equilibrium.

The problem with traditional general equilibrium theory as well as partial equilibrium theory is that they are far too limited as concepts. The world is not an economic world but a holistic one. Survival and the quality of life depend on much more than economic optimality regulated by a price mechanism. Equilibrium theory was the logical result of an overly simplistic interpretation of the world.

Equilibrium theory assumes that the only relevant information needed for economic rationalization is price information. Time plays only a peripheral role and the long run is the time necessary for the self-adjusting movements to stabilize the economy with an invisible hand. Although general equilibrium theory does not explain economic activity and stability in the real world, it cannot simply be rejected as it is by today's adherents to partial equilibrium. They are concerned only with the microeconomy, as though the macroeconomy did not exist. This is remarkable in a world in which much economic activity and many economic problems are of a societal nature.

If general and partial equilibrium theory do not explain the real world and serve no really useful purpose, then what does? If we discard the notion that economic variables follow simple natural laws and move automatically toward equilibrium, then we are dealing with a world in which such variables respond to discretionary decisions as well as to nonmarket forces. In such a world, balance is a much more realistic objective than equilibrium.

If we want to replace equilibrium theory with a theory of balance, we must guard against the common error in the past of accepting a simple fantasy in place of a complex reality as well as the present day error of accepting precision in place of accuracy.

In equilibrium theory, the relationship between the assumptions made and the conclusions drawn from them is based on a simple logic. Such a simple logic will not produce a relevant theory of balance because the assumptions we must make about the economy, if empirically accurate, are far too complex for that. They are so complex that we should not expect either simple or completely accurate answers to economic questions.

Alfred Marshall, the great neoclassical economist, saw at least some of these fundamental shortcomings of equilibrium theory when he referred to the neoclassical theory as a first approximation that had to be made more realistic to be useful. Most of the economists who followed Marshall lacked his insight, which has reduced the usefulness of traditional economic theory still more.

Professor Marshall was unable to make equilibrium theory more realistic although he tried to do that for more than thirty years after the publication of his *Principles* in 1890. Near the end of the twentieth century, economists are still using equilibrium as the nucleus of economic theory!

In summary, equilibrium in economic theory suffers from the following false assumptions previously referred to: (1) all variables involved in the economic process are of an economic nature responding to market forces, (2) market prices are free and unimpeded, and (3) all factors of market supply and demand automatically meet at the same time at a single point of reference.[3]

In an effort to rationalize the inherent instability of a system left to chance, economists developed a variety of cyclical theories that depict an economy fluctuating around long-run equilibrium. Although economists are still concentrating on equilibrium and business-cycle theories, the governments of all the so-called market economies have found it necessary to intervene. In some cases, such intervention is limited to monetary and fiscal policies and to subsidies and other forms of income redistribution as a remedy for problems that were not anticipated or not prevented in time. In other cases, such intervention also involves a certain amount of anticipation and planning.

Variables that do not respond to prices and that are subject to a relative time and motion pattern and to a complex structure of multiple points of reference will not conform to equilibrium theory. Supply and demand, however, redefined to reflect the physical, social, and dynamic forces of the real world, are part of a theory of balance.

It is not difficult to comprehend the impossibility of a traditional equilibrium theory in a world in which variables, moving at different rates of motion, are subjected to unpredictable and rapid change. Let us consider the simplest form of equilibrium. It is defined as all variables that make up supply and demand meeting at a single point of reference at the same time. Let us concede for the sake of this example that an imaginary firm is at a point of equilibrium and that there are no inherent tendencies for the firm to move from this position. As a result of external forces, such as radical and rapid changes in science and technology, the firm experiences disturbances reflecting the end of its equilibrium. The economic variables—the factors of supply and demand—are changing. The type and quality of labor, management, and physical resources suitable for the old conditions are no longer satisfactory for the new conditions.

In this example, there is no anticipation and no preparation, only a reliance on market forces. In order for the firm to reach a new equilibrium, it must be assumed that all the variables making up supply and demand will meet simultaneously at a new point in time. Such an assumption is completely inconsistent with the known facts. Indeed, it can be shown that a reliance on market forces to restore equilibrium can only promote chronic disequilibrium, a more accurate term for which is *chronic structural imbalances*.

The simple diagram in figure 12–1 illustrates this point. The diagram illustrates the different time intervals involved in getting the variables that make up supply ready for the new conditions in the economic process that were set in motion by an external force,

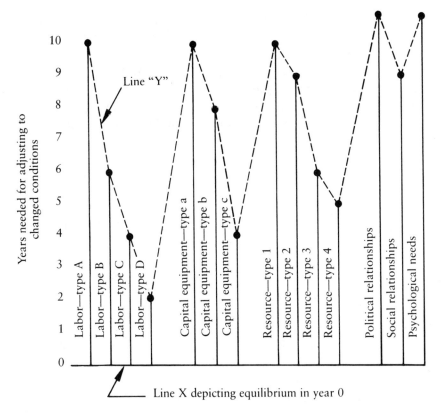

Line X depicting equilibrium in year 0

Line X indicates that all factors of supply and demand have come together at the same time in year 0. There is no inherent tendency to deviate from that position, which is called equilibrium.

Line Y shows the chaotic conditions that result from leaving adjustment to chance or to the market, which cannot operate effectively when changes are structural and of a radical nature.

Problem: The introduction of a radical change in technology—for example, the introduction of computers—creates pressures external to the industry that disturb equilibrium. Adjustments in all the inputs (labor, capital, resources, and so on) have to be made before the industry can once more meet the demand for its products. Since the time necessary for adjustments for the various inputs can vary considerably, serious disturbances can be avoided only if allowances are made for these differences in planning the adjustments. (See figure 12–2.)

Figure 12–1. *Deviation from Equilibrium and the Process of Adjustment*

such as a radical change in science and technology. If we assume, for the purpose of illustrating a point, that equilibrium exists at time X, then it is obvious that if we allow the variables to proceed without a time and motion plan, they cannot meet at a new equilibrium at the same time. That is why the assumption of equilibrium does not meet the requirements of logic and reason.

It is clear that an analysis based on equilibrium must ignore the complex time and motion patterns of economic and social variables (except when the out-of-phase pattern is very small and infrequent), which is only possible if it is assumed that these variables respond to the natural laws of a unique market that somehow synchronizes everything. The rationalization that the difficulty of synchronization can be overcome by the assumption that variables never reach an equilibrium, but only move toward an equilibrium, is no better than the assumption of equilibrium.

In figure 12–1, line Y, which connects the time pattern of the variables, shows the chaos resulting from the absence of anticipation and planning. In figure 12–2, we can see how planning helps to solve the problem of time and motion and multiple points of reference. Here, each variable has its own point of reference or starting point, rather than the single point of reference reflected in equilibrium X in figure 12–1. By giving the proper recognition to the time and motion differences of economic and social variables, it is possible to approach balance in the economic process, as indicated by line Y in figure 12–2. In order to reach balance at line Y, it is necessary for each variable to have its own starting point, or line of reference, as indicated by line X.

It is, of course, not likely that all the variables will be perfectly coordinated at the point of balance, but it is obvious that the result of anticipation and preparation is far better than leaving the economic process to chance. It is well worth repeating that my concept of balance is quite different from what economists mean by equilibrium.

Balance is the goal of anticipation and preparation, and it results from successful human action in the adjustment mechanism of the economic process. Equilibrium, on the other hand, is based on automatic market forces assumed to make the necessary adjustments when economic variables are set in motion by error or chang-

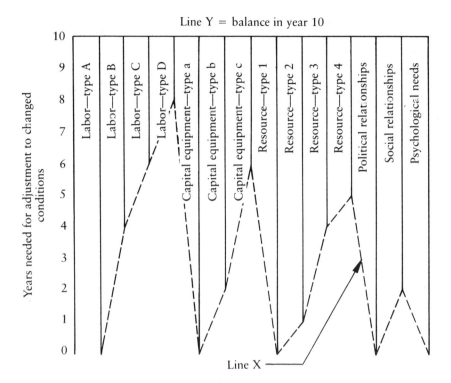

Line X connects the different starting points of each variable. These variables reflect individual time and motion patterns. This approach allows all variables to reach the point of balance (line Y) at the same time. In reality, errors will make the point of balance only approximate.

Problem: New conditions resulting from structural changes in the industry or the economy require adjustments of the inputs (labor, capital, resources, and so on).

Figure 12–2. *The Movement toward Balance When Structural Changes Disturb Existing Conditions*

ing conditions. An analogy may help to illustrate this difference more dramatically. Equilibrium is akin to Christian Science teaching, which relies on the self-healing properties of the body for the treatment of disease. Balance is more closely related to the art of medicine, which is based on anticipation and prevention of disease and discretionary treatment when disease occurs.

Anticipation and preparation are already firmly established in

those industries in which large firms dominate output. This, however, still leaves those economic and social variables over which the
firm has little or no control to chance and to a philosophy of equilibrium. Replacing equilibrium with balance allows economic theory to deal more effectively with the social dynamics that control
the economic process.

Part IV
Humankind in a
More Rational Society

13

Humankind as the Focus of Economic Goals and Policies

Beliefs and Value Judgments

If we are to survive and improve the conditions of our lives, we will have to be more pragmatic and less emotional. Our lack of realism is at least partly due to the lack of objectivity in the social sciences.

The influence of the social sciences is probably much greater than most people realize. Their effect is reflected in the value judgments and beliefs of people rather than in the actual solution to problems. Such social inventions as laissez-faire capitalism and utopian communism appeal to the value judgments of people in different parts of the world and are employed by them because they believe them to be true. In the solution of problems, however, these theories are not always useful, because the value judgments on which they are based are often unrealistic.

Beliefs are what people think to be factually true. Value judgments are what they think to be right. This distinction becomes clear when we examine some of the value judgments expressed in the Declaration of Independence, in the philosophy of laissez-faire, and in Marxist communism.

"We hold these truths to be self-evident, that all men are created equal, that they are endowed by their Creator with certain inalienable Rights, that among these are Life, Liberty, and the Pursuit of Happiness." These value judgments are expressed near the opening statement of the U.S. Declaration of Independence.

In the laissez-faire doctrine, the utilitarian value judgment adhered to is that the goal to be sought in economics is the achievement of the greatest good for the greatest number. This is supported by the assumption that this is only possible if all individuals are allowed to pursue their own interests.

Marxist communism is based on a number of value judgments. Cooperation and sharing are held to be superior to competition and private property, especially in the case of the means of production. The ideas in regard to wages ("from everyone according to his ability—to everyone according to his needs") and in regard to power (the state should "wither away") complete the trilogy of indispensable value judgments in the pure Marxist communist society.

The "self-evident truths" expressed in the Declaration of Independence were intended as a vital value judgment in a period of revolution, not as a literal belief. The assumptions expressed in laissez-faire and in the utilitarian doctrine that form the basis of the free-market economy are other examples of a contradiction between value judgments and actual belief. It is an essential assumption in laissez-faire utilitarianism that all participants in the free market are more or less equal in size and possess no arbitrary power. The entrepreneurs who enjoyed the greatest success as the economy developed did not really believe this. They thought that the success of the economy and their own success depended on the opposite of the value judgments underlying these doctrines. They did everything they could to gain control over markets and resources while praising the virtues of laissez-faire.

Some of the Marxist value judgments have been seriously challenged by actual experience. The prospect of the abolition of private property and subsequent withering away of the power of the state remain slim, and workers do not seem to be motivated by the pure Marxist reward system.

The development of the social sciences, as reflected in these utopian economic and political doctrines, produced many contradictions between value judgments on which the doctrines stand and the real beliefs of those who make the political and economic decisions. This lack of objectivity in the social sciences is dangerous, because it has a great impact on what people believe to be true. The value judgments on which traditional economic theories are based are rarely exposed to examination and, more often than not, are simply taken for granted. Traditional economists keep what they call value judgments out of their theories. They believe that this guarantees objectivity.

Such a claim to objectivity should be questioned if economics as a social science is to serve a useful purpose. It conceals inevitable biases, thus making economic theories less relevant. By ignoring value judgments, such theories produce confusion between fact and fancy in the mind of the public.

The biases that affect economic research are partly due to the fact that economists are heir to the philosophical ideas of the past. The influence of natural law and utilitarianism is obvious in traditional economic theory. Biases are also generated by cultural and social norms that underlie the reward system.

The problem of avoiding the contradictions between value judgments and actual beliefs cannot be solved unless social research rests on a realistic foundation. At present, as during the nineteenth century, many economists still take great liberties in their treatment of reality. They do this because the problem of what is real, and therefore possible, does not arouse their curiosity as it did that of the great philosophers of the past and as it does the best minds of today in many fields.

What we consider real comes from the outside world into our minds just as what we see comes from the outside world to our eyes. After reaching the mind, the information received is interpreted with the help of past experience. What we think of as "real" is, therefore, a combination of external a posteriori experience and internal a priori interpretation. A posteriori means inductive or what is actually observed. A priori means deductive or how we interpret what we observe.

The quality of the mind, or the deductive part of knowledge, is as important to the correct interpretation of reality as the quality of the lens of the eye is to interpreting visual reality. This becomes obvious when we compare what primitive people perceived as real with modern humanity's conception of reality. The difference lies in experience.

The Australian bushman who has never seen a modern jet airplane is likely to perceive it as something quite different from the person whose mind has stored numerous experiences of a similar kind. Primitive people attribute supernatural qualities to everything they cannot explain with experience. In this way, they replace experience with illusion in their interpretation of the unknown. Imagination without adequate experience leads to fantasy. Imagination based on experience advances the frontiers of knowledge. An appreciation of this truth is essential in objective research.

The utilitarian–laissez-faire doctrine stating that if all people pursue their own interests, the result will be the greatest good for the greatest number was not based on experience. Marx's description of pure communism also had no basis in human experience. It is a case of assuming that what *ought* to be *can* be. In all these cases, the value judgments that are still accepted as being true by millions of people are based on deductive reasoning inspired by pure imagination divorced from experience.

What would have been the result if inductive experience had been subjected to deductive reasoning built on adequate stored experience? The great statesmen who wrote the Declaration of Independence would have observed inductively and reflected deductively that never in human history were all people created equal. Some were born into wealth and power, others possessed qualities enabling them to acquire it, while the vast majority were excluded on both counts. To say that all people are created equal is to deny the facts of human experience that show that inequality results naturally through heredity, the environment, and the existence of wealth and power.

The proper application of inductive and deductive experience would have made it clear that to back up the statement "All men are created equal" would require control over hereditary influences as well as equality in regard to wealth and power. Even a modified version that claims that all people are equal under the law assumes that all laws are just, and it further assumes that the execution of the law is the same for the rich and powerful as for the poor and powerless.

In the case of laissez-faire utilitarianism, the proper application of inductive observation and deductive reasoning would have shown that the greatest good for the greatest number would result from all people pursuing their own interests *only* under very unrealistic and nonexistent conditions. It has to be assumed that power plays no role in human relationships, that everyone has adequate knowledge about human and environmental needs, and that everyone is fully rational and able to act upon that knowledge!

In the case of Marxist communism, the proper application of inductive experience and deductive reasoning would show that the power of the state does not wither away merely because one system gives way to another, even if we assume that the new system is superior so far as equity and justice are concerned. The new state is also built on power, and human experience has shown that, because of many complex circumstances, power does not simply evaporate.

The liberties many social scientists have taken in treating fantasy as reality have produced theories reflecting normative values (or wishful thinking) rather than realistic conditions. Since the claim of social scientists has been that their theories are designed for the real world and not a hypothetical one, the mixture of normative assumptions with pragmatic claims has created much confusion and skepticism.

It must be remembered that what we deduce from what we observe is our interpretation of reality. The laissez-faire free-market economy is an excellent example of the misuse of the deductive method. The value judgments on which this doctrine is built cannot be empirically defended. This has caused some of its present-day proponents such as Milton Friedman to declare in its defense that the assumptions underlying the doctrine do not matter so long as the conclusions are accurate and true. He regards that as a form of pragmatism.

Even if the conclusions of the free-market economists had been true, which they were not (when did laissez-faire ever lead to the greatest good for the greatest number?), the suggestion that basic assumptions about humanity and the environment can be disregarded in the construction of economic theory rejects the most elementary process of rational thinking in the search for knowledge.

What is needed to give relevance to economic theory is not a rationalization of indefensible assumptions. On the contrary, the construction of economic theories must be subjected to the most critical tests—in regard to both the inductive and the deductive sources of knowledge. Value judgments must not be adopted as assumptions unless they have a basis in fact. Value judgments that are merely idealistic dreams cannot be treated as assumptions if the resultant theory is to be relevant and realistic.

Objectivity in the development of economic theory and policy involves a series of indispensable steps that must distinguish carefully between what ought to be and what is. Both the inductive part of theory (what we observe) and the deductive part (what we deduce or how we interpret what we observe) involve substeps in the construction of objective theory.

In the inductive process, we must collect data from the world *outside* of our own mind. This means we must abstain from fantasy. The data must then be subjected to the scientific method, which attempts to disprove it by all the relevant available data. If we cannot disprove it, we have a hypothesis.

The hypothesis must then be interpreted, and conclusions can be drawn from it. This completes the task of constructing a theory. The steps of interpretation and conclusions involve deductive reasoning. Mistakes can easily be made. The primitive Australian bushman may observe a jet plane far above him. He has many times seen birds fly far above him, but he has no way to test what he observes so he may establish a faulty hypothesis that the jet plane is a large, fast, and therefore, powerful bird. He can now deduce from this that if he could invent a bow and arrow powerful enough to reach this strange bird, he and his family could feast on it for weeks.

This primitive and faulty process of thinking contains two serious mistakes. In assuming that the jet plane is a large, powerful bird, the bushman reveals his inability to test what he observes. Without that, inductive error is almost inevitable. He has made a second mistake of deducing that the large bird could feed him for a long time. He has had no experience whatever with such birds and has no way of knowing that a dead bird as large and powerful as the jet plane would not kill him if he ate it. It could after all contain chemicals that made it so large and powerful, but that are deadly if consumed by humans.

This example may be far-fetched, but it contains elements of error also to be found in a considerable body of economic doctrine. In the laissez-faire free-market doctrine, the market is observed as consisting of many small buyers and sellers who possess no arbitrary power. It is deduced from this that if all participants in the market were allowed to pursue their own interests, this would result in the greatest good for the greatest number.

The period observed by Adam Smith and the early classical economists was the eve of the Industrial Revolution, before firms became large and powerful as a result of economies of scale (mass production) and before the emergence of corporations. The laissez-faire free-market doctrine has nevertheless been adopted by later economists, long after the conditions on which it was based had radically changed. This is a clear misuse of the inductive method.

The deductive method was also misused. Even if the free-market doctrine had been scientifically observed, there was no evidence whatsoever, based on experience, that this would automatically lead to the greatest good for the greatest number. This deduction was made without any experience and was therefore based purely on imagination.

Keynes' *General Theory of Employment, Income and Money,* too, was based on faulty inductive and deductive reasoning. He assumed that the micro-sector of the economy was in equilibrium. He further assumed that the reason unemployment existed was that aggregate demand was inadequate. A closer look at the actual world in 1936 would have helped him to observe that firms and industries were in chaos rather than in overall equilibrium, and that there were other causes besides inadequate demand that brought about unemployment.

Based on his assumptions, he concluded that to restore full employment required only an increase in government spending to fill the gap of "inadequate demand." There were at least two major errors in the conclusions he based upon his faulty observations. Increased government spending would not by itself produce remedies for unemployment for causes other than inadequate demand. If, however, inadequate demand had been the *only* cause, it is not likely that it would have been distributed evenly throughout the economy. In that case, increased government expenditures would have had to be directed to specific areas of unemployment, and the simple Keynesian solution would not have applied.

Marx was much more accurate in what he observed, but in his

deductive reasoning he too became victim of imagination without experience. His theory of communism was a product of pure imagination rather than a conclusion drawn from solid inductive and deductive reasoning. It should be remembered, however, that he did not have the benefit of pragmatism and empiricism which are the products of the twentieth century. They contributed greatly to the application of the scientific method.

The task of observing accurately the world in which we live and forming conclusions only when our deductive reasoning is based on at least a modicum of experience should be the standard adopted for the construction of relevant and realistic economic theories. Since the world in which we live changes constantly, and we continuously enlarge on the body of experience that forms the basis of deductive reasoning, no one should attempt to lay claim to theories alleged to have universal and permanent relevance.

A Realistic Application of Individual and Social Rights

Of singular importance in the whole discussion of freedom in modern society is the question of the "rights" of an individual and the "rights" of society. Social rights emerge from social values, which in an authoritarian society originate from upper levels of the political structure. In a democratic society, they reflect the values of the people who are governed by them. Social values serve as a foundation for the laws and regulations that restrict the actions of individuals and groups in order to produce optimal freedom (which can be called equity). If all individuals are allowed to do as they please, the strong will enjoy maximum freedom, while the weak will become oppressed and exploited. To avoid this, laws based on social rights should aim for optimal freedom for all instead of too much freedom for some and too little for others.

The question of social rights is a very real one and not merely an exercise in abstract logic. This becomes obvious when a nation is threatened. It has become a generally accepted principle that a nation has the right to draft its citizens for military duty during a war. This is a case in which people are asked to give up their lives, if necessary, for their country. It is not a question of whether a government should have the right to make that demand. Different answers can be eloquently developed on both sides of that subject so long as it remains on an abstract level.

If the world is organized in separate, sovereign political units, the question of survival becomes a very real one. There has been no shortage of "good causes" that can be claimed by one nation in defense of a military action against another. In the name of such causes, which are always an element of national security, nations have legitimized the power of drafting people to fight for their country or of taxing people to pay for weapons that may ultimately destroy them.

So long as each nation places its interests ahead of all other nations, without the constraints of international law, it is academic to question the right of a nation to draft its citizens for military duty. In case of a war that is not too unpopular it will do so. This is necessary because in a lawless international environment each nation is potentially in danger.

The question of social rights can be realistically answered only if we examine the conditions of the environment in which they are to be exercised. If we want to live in a world in which a government does not have the right to draft its citizens for war, we must first find solutions other than war in case of serious international disagreement.

Is the right to jail people who break the law a legitimate social right? So long as only a small percentage of the people break the law, society will protect itself from the lawbreaker in one way or another. Jails are one answer. If the laws are broken by a majority of the people, either the problem has deep social roots that need to be corrected or the law must be changed or simply not enforced. Jails will not provide an answer very long in that case.

Social rights are simply ways of dealing with social problems. If they prove more or less satisfactory, they will not be seriously questioned. When they no longer solve problems, they cease to be regarded as social rights.

In cases where the government does not represent all the people, eventually the question of social rights takes on another dimension. In the nineteenth-century women, workers, and minorities were not represented in our legislative chambers. As a result, those who had political power believed they had the right to exclude these groups from the privileges they themselves enjoyed. Women were deprived of equal opportunity and were excluded from the political process. Labor was not permitted to form effective unions, which were outlawed by the anticombination acts. Black minorities were brazenly exploited as slaves in the first two-thirds of the century and as second-class citizens thereafter. The social rights existing under these conditions were based on arbitrary power, despite our "democratic" form of government.

The question of social rights falls naturally into four parts: Are social rights necessary? Are they democratically or arbitrarily established? Do they deal effectively with the problems for which they were designed? What are their limits?

The necessity for social rights originates from the inequality of power and the need to protect people from the abuse of power, internally and externally. If, as the classical economists assumed, all participants in the economy possess equal power (that is, they cannot impose their will on anyone else), then, ipso facto, the need for social rights exercised through government can be assumed away. Such assumptions are absurd, however, in the modern world. If fairness is to prevail, social rights must be exercised in all areas where inequality of power lies. The existence of social rights weakens greatly the utilitarian belief that if all people are allowed to pursue their own interests, the result will be the greatest good for the greatest number.

How social rights are established is of vital importance. If they are not democratically established they themselves become a source of inequity. Although nineteenth-century Britain and the United States had governments based on law, the laws were based on social rights that were not democratically conceived. The majority of the people these laws governed had no real political power.

The effectiveness of social rights establishes their acceptance. Abstract dialogue about social rights, based on normative assumptions ("what ought to be"), is of no value. The justification for social rights lies in their ability to deal effectively with problems in which the inequality of power is a factor. If they can do so, they are justified; if they cannot, normative defenses are irrelevant.

Finally, the limits of social rights and the limits of individual rights must be agreed upon if authoritarianism and great inequality are to be avoided. Logically, the limits of social rights cannot be defined until the question of individual rights is settled.

The rights of individuals fall into several categories: the freedom they possess in pursuing their own interests and impulses, such as choosing a profession; the rights they have that define the privileges they enjoy as members of society, such as visiting a national park; and the rights they have in participating in the decisions governing their lives and the lives of others, such as the role they play in electing a government.

In the case of an individual, as of society in general, it is academic to discuss the question of rights in a vacuum. What they *ought to be* requires a utopia. What they *can* be requires an understanding of the world in which we live.

The question of rights is more complicated when arbitrary power is involved. Can society grant all of us the right to freely pursue our own interests if people are unequal in regard to their size, power, and ability to impose their will on others? The classical economists avoided this problem by ignoring the question of arbitrary power. In the real world, the question of power cannot be ignored. It plays too vital a role in the behavior of people and their chance of survival.

Society attempts to protect the individual from the abuse of power with laws and regulations based on social rights. Society does not prevent adult professional football players from playing football. That is considered their right. It imposes regulations, however, that prevent such a team from opposing one made up of school children, except possibly under the strictest conditions. In this case, society relies on a social restraint that denies the powerful the right to bring injury to the comparatively weak.

If all people in a nation had equal power—that is, if they possessed no arbitrary political or economic power that could bring harm to others in any way at all—they could still harm others inadvertently. Driving under the influence of alcohol is an example. Polluting the environment is another. Irresponsibility in regard to contractual obligations is a third example. There are many others. People try to protect themselves from such harm through laws based on social rights. Such rights have deep roots in the history of civilized societies.

Not only economists, but even governments have refused to deal adequately with the question of power and social rights in regard to the economic organization. That is why many economists concentrate on economic abstractions instead of on the political economy.

Antitrust law, as conceived in 1890 with the passage of the Sherman Antitrust Act, reflected the U.S. government's unwillingness or inability to deal effectively with the question of power in the economy. The antitrust laws were based on the belief originally that power can be outlawed. This was revised in the 1920 U.S. Steel decision that outlawed the abuse of power. Size alone was no longer a sin, because the Supreme Court was compelled to face reality in place of the utopian dream of the classical economists.

The U.S. government has still not yet faced the fundamental issues vital to the prevention of the abuse of power in the economy. Power cannot be *outlawed,* as the evolution of capitalism and socialism should have demonstrated even to their most faithful followers. It can only be *controlled.*

How can power be controlled without interfering with those rights of the individual that do not conflict with the rights of others? To control power, it must be made accountable. To make it accountable, individuals must have the right to participate in the decision-making process that reflects power and commits those individuals to its will.

Classical economics, being built on a foundation in which power plays no role, has led many economists to assume that the rights of individuals are protected by "natural laws." This erroneous assumption has led them to the conclusion that the government should not intervene in the decision-making process of the economy. A more realistic look at how economic decisions are actually made would have indicated that power is very unevenly distributed and when left unchecked has led to inequity and exploitation.

Past experience with inequity and exploitation has been the driving force behind the evolution of democratic governments. Until we learn how to make power in both the private and the public sectors accountable to those it governs, the rights of individuals cannot be protected.

The Three Levels of Participation in the Economy

Traditional economists were able to develop economic theories without considering the use of power in economic decisions because economics can be conveniently divided into two categories. First is the purely mechanical process of maximizing resources (and the problems associated with that, such as unemployment and inflation). The second category is much more basic and sophisticated and has been virtually ignored by traditional economists. It involves the political, social, and psychological determinants and consequences of economic activity.

Economists generally concentrate on the first category, the simple supply and demand aspects of economics; the second category, the more complicated and crucial features of the economic decision-making process, are usually designated as externalities—recognized, but kept out of economic theory and policy.

What I am discussing here lies within the second category of economics—the political and social consequences of the decisions made in the powerful board rooms of the private sector, which have a profound impact on the quality of life and even survival. In the U.S. economy, the vast majority of people have little or no input in the critical areas. Since vital economic decisions by a *few* commit *all* people to the consequences they produce, many nations have begun to take steps to correct this flaw by reexamining the basic values and perceptions that form the foundation of economic theory and policy.

The concepts of freedom and democracy, two vitally important elements of individual and social behavior, were treated in the development of economic theory as though they existed in a vacuum. The eighteenth and nineteenth centuries produced utopian political philosophies of freedom that the classical economists emulated in their theories of the free market. The liberal trend in classical economics defined freedom as the ability of all individuals to pursue their own interests. Such a concept of freedom was consistent with the static assumptions made about the order of society at the time.

Actually, as humanity evolved through the Industrial Revolution, we proved to be far more innovative, untraditional, skeptical, and experimental than we would have had to be if society had fitted the pattern assumed by the classical economists. In fact, for society to have remained static, humanity would have had to be unaware of the economic opportunities that existed.

Although the pursuit of self-interest is an element of freedom, much more is required for freedom to produce equity than the concepts developed at a time when the world and its problems were much simpler. This is especially important to the political economist because an economic system should be not only efficient but also equitable. Persistent inequity or inefficiency is likely to destroy *any* social organization sooner or later.

The static perception of society entertained by the classical economists created a lack of realism in traditional economics that has persisted to this day. It has led economists to concentrate on market theories and price adjustments and to all but ignore the structural and social influences on the basic economic process. This concentration of "pure economics" has isolated the discipline from the other social sciences and has resulted in theories and policies that are not serving mankind as well as they should.

The heart of politics is the organization of power. The heart of economics is the optimization of production, distribution, and consumption. It is not possible to analyze realistically the economic process without making the use and organization of power an inherent part of it. Abstract market theories isolate the economic discipline from the real world.

Power exists in many forms. As I have said, it plays an important role in the decisions made in corporate board rooms, especially in the huge organizations of the global industrial and financial conglomerates. It is present in the organized labor movement. It plays a central role in the public sector. It is inherent (actively and potentially) in the military establishment and in such establishments as the Trilateral Commission and the Council on Foreign Relations.

To traditional economists the problem of power belongs to another discipline and is treated at best as an externality. They fail to realize that their own theories are based on a very specific concept of power—namely that in a free market, it is not significant. Even in theories of monopoly and oligopoly, power is analyzed only in regard to its impact on price and quantity of output. The question of quality and equity in regard to the social product and its impact on individuals and society is virtually ignored.

In traditional economics, as reflected in free-market theories, the role of government is well nigh excluded from the economy because the private sector is assumed to possess no power that needs to be controlled in the public interest by the public sector. The slogan "that government governs best which governs least" has deep roots in classical economics and in the conservative economics of today. It follows naturally from the belief that power plays no central role in economic decisions. By excluding power from the economic structure and consequently treating government as an externality, the use of which should be minimized, the whole economic structure was built on an unrealistic foundation.

The fact is that government has come to play a very important role in the economics of all industrialized countries. The reason for this steadily increasing role can be found in the evolution of market structure and the organization of power. As economic evolution changed the structure of the simple market and the static society, power began to play an important role in nearly every aspect of economic activity in the private sector. Inequality in the use and organization of power became the source of inequity and exploitation that created many of the haves and the have-nots of the Industrial Revolution.

The main political driving force of the have-nots in the western democracies has been the fight against exploitation and inequity. They have called upon government and nonpublic organizations to help them in their struggle. As political power began to be more widely distributed in this century, especially after World War I and during the Great Depression, those who benefitted from this began to press for a better distribution of income and a variety of other improvements in the quality of life.

The drive for greater equity gave rise to greater government intervention in such areas as income distribution, protection of the small firms from the arbitrary power of large firms, protection of workers from hazardous working conditions, social security, retirement benefits and health insurance, unemployment compensation, and assistance for the disadvantaged and the handicapped. Numerous western democracies became welfare states, with such countries as Sweden in the lead and the United States lagging.

With the expansion of power in the public and private sectors, with the expanding role of government, and with the growth of private corporations to a level where many employ between 100,000 and one million workers, the question arises what role does the individual play in the economic decision-making process or, more specifically, what power does the individual exercise? The belief that in a democracy the will of the people is the deciding factor in the decisions made by their representatives in the legislative chambers assumes that such decisions really are made in these legislative chambers. It has already been observed that many economic decisions with political and social consequences are made in the board rooms of the large multinational corporations and the powerful global financial institutions.

The most important consequences of the decisions made in corporate board rooms are their impacts on people as producers and consumers, and their influences on domestic and international relations. Their impact on international relations in particular is becoming increasingly critical as we invent ever deadlier weapons for "settling" international conflicts.

Recent history should leave no doubt, if doubt still exists, as to the political consequences of economic decisions made in the private sector. For example, in 1928, the "Seven Sisters" oil companies met in Scotland to tame competition and to bring order into an industry that provided vital energy to a developing world. They formed an unofficial cartel that owned most of the known crude oil or oil refineries in the Middle East, Canada, Venezuela, and United States. They operated without any significant challenge until 1960, when Libya broke the unwritten agreement and sold oil to refineries outside the system. In the meantime, they played an important role in the internal political affairs of the oil-producing countries, making certain that their interests were protected. The father of the last Shah of Iran owed his rise to the economic power of the oil companies. Hence, the political system of Iran became intrinsically a part of the economic system of the Seven Sisters.

U.S. public policy as expressed by several presidents regarded the Middle East oil-producing region as vital to U.S. interests. Yet the crucial relationship between the Middle East and the United States was created and controlled by the Seven Sisters. The democratic process did not enter into these decisions. Decisions were made in a few board rooms and committed the U.S. government to policies obliging it decades later to protect America's "vital interests" (the creation of which the vast majority of people had no part in or knowledge of).

The point here is not that there is necessarily anything evil about the decisions made in the board rooms of the large global corporations and financial institutions. It is only that the role the corporate and financial sectors play in foreign policy is outside the democratic political arena. U.S. foreign policy is to a large extent determined by the requirements of the national economy. This includes the country's need for resources and foreign markets. Of the forty most vital resources on which the U.S. economy depends, almost two-thirds come from beyond its borders, from all over the world. For U.S. corporations to thrive and grow, they must expand their sales and some of their operations beyond the national economy. They must buy, produce, and sell in the markets of the world.

Foreign policy that emanates from U.S. legislative chambers and the Oval Office now accepts as *given* the decisions made much earlier by the multinational corporations and their financial allies. Government participates in many important cases only after the crucial economic decisions have already been made by the corporate sector. By the time the chosen representatives of the people enter the stage of the international economic drama, the plot is well-advanced and it is too late to alter the course of events.

It does not follow from this that the road to freedom and democracy is better if the government leads and directs the economy. The Soviet Union has shown that the transfer of power to the government in the name of the people is not enough. Only four years after the Bolshevik Revolution, Lenin was already highly critical of the Soviet bureaucracy. By 1930, there were five million bureaucrats, and Leon Trotsky declared that the means of production may belong to the people but the people are ruled by the bureaucracy. Owning the means of production did not give the people control over their destiny. Freedom and democracy do not flourish in either capitalism or socialism when important decisions involving the entire nation are made without the participation of the vast majority of the people.

Participation in this connection does not mean that all people are directly involved in the development and execution of policy. That is clearly impossible. The term is used here in the Jeffersonian sense. People have access to accurate information that they use in electing and judging their representatives. It also means that the private corporate sector is made accountable in areas where decisions affect an entire community, the nation, or other parts of the world. (This is further discussed in chapters 14 and 15.)

To some extent, there is similarity between U.S. and Soviet politics. In neither systems do the people become involved in many of the more sophisticated economic decisions that all too frequently lead to such grave political and social consequences as war, imperialism, and alienation.

The fact that twenty million American stockholders own U.S. corporations does not mean that they make the decisions. Most chief executives and top management who control the large corporations own an insignificant amount of stock. The stockholders who give them the control are so widely dispersed, generally, that the control exercised by the board and by management is rarely challenged except by corporate raiders.

Eighteenth- and nineteenth-century concepts of freedom and democracy have been made obsolete by time. Whatever the definition of freedom, it must include the participation of the people in the major decisions affecting survival and the quality of life. Democracy is the political organization that provides the opportunity for participation.

In the public sector, freedom and democracy come into play at the ballot box. If people do not participate in this process, they are not making use of their political power. This political leverage is especially important in the social welfare issues of a nation. Voting rights alone are not enough for realistic participation. In a U.S. presidential election, barely 50 percent of those eligible to vote do so. In the Soviet Union, almost 100 percent vote in an election. It would be absurd to conclude from this, however, that there is twice as much participation on the political level in the Soviet Union as in the United States. Going through the motions of voting is not the same thing as genuine political participation, which requires that voters know the facts behind the issues in a pluralistically organized election.

What counts in political participation is the extent to which elected officials actually represent the voice of those who elect them in the political-decision-making process. Before the Great Depression in the 1930s American labor was largely unorganized, and those unions that existed possessed no political power as a result of laws designed to prevent the growth of union power. Consequently, labor had very few candidates who represented its interests in legislative chambers and the halls of Congress. Workers could vote, but usually only for people representing business, finance, property holders, and, in some states, farm interests. Before the 1930s, they possessed no effective vehicle for participation. The same was true of women, black Americans, and other minorities.

During the Great Depression and after World War II, democracy began to spread in the United States, and workers, women, and ethnic minorities began to participate more in the political-decision-making process. What brought this about was a redistribution of power through effective organization.

An increasingly important area for activity is the decision-making level of the private sector (discussed earlier in this section), which often has vital national and international political consequences that eventually commit the nation's resources and military power. In this area, wide participation is almost nonexistent in the United States, thus revealing a serious flaw in our system.

This flaw is located in the second category of the economic process (the political and social consequences of the corporate sector's decisions, as discussed at the start of this section), which is why it has been all but ignored. In the following pages, this category is analyzed to allow for the inclusion of human welfare in the economic process.

Rational Participation as a Prerequisite for a More Humane Society

We should remember that politics is the use and organization of power. The primary objective of power is the distribution of wealth and privilege and the protection of those who benefit from it. Power, as we have seen, is exercised in the decision-making process at various levels.

The United States has not one, but three political systems, (the economic market, the corporate political area, and the government) as explained in the preceding section. They constitute in essence three separate but interdependent political systems. In each of these areas, power is exercised differently, That is, the rate of participation varies, and the effect of this has an important impact on the outcome of the economic decision-making process. A fact of considerable importance in all three areas is that the organizational structure was designed for a far simpler world and must be changed if participation is to become a reality.

The least participation exists in the corporate political area. Even stockholders do not have much to say in the formulation of policy in the large corporations. The five U.S. oil companies that together with British Petroleum and Dutch Shell founded the Seven Sisters in Scotland in 1928 did not consult the stockholders, the government, or the population as a whole in this action. The same is true of American investors in the Third World and in many other enterprises that eventually have an impact on international political relations.

This is a matter of utmost importance, because this lack of participation in an area where important policies are made that have such tremendous impact on the lives of people represents a serious weakness in the traditional democratic process. *Power must be made accountable whether it is located in the public sector or the private sector; otherwise, people will be alienated instead of motivated.*

In the market sector of the economy, participation is more widespread, but it must be analyzed in terms of quality as well as quantity. In the U.S. economy, consumers have a tremendous variety of products to choose from. Their demand determines to a large extent the goods and services the economy produces. Many economists define this as a free-choice, free-market economy.

Since the purpose of participation is to avoid alienation and to produce a sane and harmonious society, the *quality* of participation is of vital significance. There are two essential questions in this respect so far as market demand is concerned: what are the needs of humanity and the environment, judged by the objective of a sane and harmonious society, and how is demand determined? (This has already been described in chapter 8.)

The present-day interpretation of demand is a complete reversal of earlier beliefs that had their origin in religion. It represents a transition from almost no freedom of the individual, in which life-styles and demand were determined to a considerable extent by the rules contained in religious gospel, to life-styles and demand determined, without rules, by the individual.

In the world of today (as explained in the second section of chapter 8), demand is actually determined in a far more sophisticated way. In most of the developed countries, advertising via mass media has to a large extent replaced religion and other influences as the shaper of culture and the initiator of demand.

In theory, advertising is intended to inform consumers about the products they purchase. In practice, business employs the mass media to influence consumer demand by using psychological techniques with the objective of increasing sales and profits. It does this today with the help of sophisticated advisors who specialize in tempting consumers to buy things they do not necessarily need, either for survival or for the good and harmonious life.

Demand in the U.S. economy is synchronized to a considerable extent with the needs of the producer in a private, oligopolistic market. The needs of the producer, if they are legitimate economic needs, are important to the success of the economy. This question has already been examined in chapters 6 and 8. Here we are concerned with the origins and goals of consumer demand.

Human beings are greatly influenced by the ideas and customs dominating their environment. In the U.S. economy, for business to do well, the ideas and customs that must dominate have to focus on materialism to the point of waste. Products are designed not to last, so that their replacements can keep production lines moving. Today emphasis is on the newer, the better, the different, the latest, and so on, using so fast a pace that products become obsolete and unwanted before they are paid for, frequently before they have even been used to any extent.

The point is that in contrast to earlier days (when only very few people possessed material comfort and luxuries) religion diverted the masses from the temptation of material things, so mass media techniques today are designed to arouse temptation that feeds consumer demand and leads to increased sales. This is in one sense a logical development in the transition from an agrarian society to a developed society. In the former society, most goods were scarce and available mainly to the rich. Today, in the U.S. economy, industries depend on mass demand to keep them operating at full capacity.

To repeat, there have historically been only two major influences on consumer demand: one based on customs and laws, either secular or religious (as during the feudal period), and one in which the market determines demand.,

In the first case, the customs and laws were presumably consistent with the needs of humanity. The masses of people did not participate to any great extent in the determination of demand.

In the second case, where demand is determined largely by market forces, it is presumed that individuals can judge their own needs and those of the environment without depending upon laws. The notion is that people, all acting individually so far as demand is concerned, will somehow manage to satisfy human and environmental needs in both the present and the future.

Although the individual has a greater feeling of freedom in the market economy, it by no means follows that this necessarily leads to the satisfaction of essential human and environmental needs. Neither system has succeeded in providing a combination of rules and individual freedom that will lead to such ends.

The champions of the corporate market economy claim that if there are no rules and laws, consumer demand will reflect a free society. Needless to say, such illusions should give way to reason and the development of a system in which culture and consumer demand effectively reflect genuine mass participation of consumers who are sufficiently informed to understand and respect human and environmental needs.

On the other hand, the government level of power in the United States is democratically organized, but participation is greatly limited by two conditions. Lack of knowledge and understanding of the facts underlying the important issues that determine the quality of life reduces the effective use of that power, which in a democracy should reside in the people. In addition, many of the important issues originate in the private sector, and the outcome is virtually determined by the time they reach the public sector, (as was explained earlier in this chapter).

The vital question to be answered in the development of a realistic foundation for a humanitarian society is how can freedom and democracy be made into meaningful concepts in a world that has changed so radically from the one that served as their cradle? The answer to this question lies in the creation of conditions that lend themselves to a workable system of democratic participation in the economy.

Democratic participation does not mean equal participation because the conditions necessary for equality exist neither in nature nor in the world created by humankind. Equality is not a prerequisite for mass participation in the decision-making process. What is required is that people have an opportunity to participate in the decisions shaping their lives—not equally, but fairly. People are alienated by the absence of fairness, not by the absence of equality! Again, participation, to be meaningful must exist at the two levels at which decisions are made—namely, the private sector (in which production, consumption, and distribution of income are determined) and the public sector (which is government).

Much of what needs to be done in achieving democratic participation will at first seem virtually impossible. This is to be expected if we judge the future by the past. The task before us, however, requires that we avoid being blinded by the limits of the past. Formerly we did not have at our disposal the tremendous advantages made possible by modern technology and growing experience.

Not only must we avoid relying of what was possible only in the past, but we must also resist the temptation to build new utopias. This requires following an interdisciplinary, goal-oriented approach and having the courage to allow the nineteenth-century utopian dream to pass into history.

14

Social Goals and the Economic Market in the Enlightened Society

Economics Redefined in Terms of Human Needs and Goals

The vital relationships between individual and society profoundly affect survival and the quality of life. We are the children of our hereditary past and our physical and social environments. The simple pleasure–pain criteria of utility theory is inadequate for dealing with human choice when long-range effects on the individual and the environment are involved because important characteristics have been woven into the fabric of society that cannot be changed at will.

When humanity is viewed holistically, a relevant approach to economics conflicts with the oversimplistic interpretation of human behavior in traditional economic theory.[1] The objective of economics is to make the most of available resources in terms of human needs and wants. Economists call this optimization, as was explained in chapters 3 and 9.

When the conditions of an optimal solution to the economic problem are identified in terms of goals, economics becomes relevant as a vehicle in satisfying the needs of humanity and the environment as a prerequisite for survival. It is vitally important that the policies influencing our supply and demand be designed to accomplish this. Only if we turn our backs on traditional economics in which the "free choice" of individuals is an end in itself, without becoming an authoritarian society in which the needs of the individual are ignored by the state, can this be accomplished.

The inability to develop a decision-making process that reflects a balance between the needs of the individual on the one hand and the needs of society and the environment on the other is a dilemma that faces most nations, including the United States and the Soviet Union. In the United States, the values and the culture are dominated by materialism and an individualism that regards society as parasitic. This is reflected in the general opposition to social planning except for the purpose of war or national military strategy.

In the Soviet Union, the state is regarded as the protector of the needs of the people and the environment, but the individual is expected to conform to the rules and the decisions made in regard to supply and demand without having adequately participated in them.

It is not too difficult to understand the thinking that produced both points of view. The philosophies teaching that individualism and free choice lead to the greatest good were produced in Britain by two historical developments: opposition to the arbitrary powers of church and state, and the development of entrepreneurial capitalism. The philosophy that led to the belief that government must guide the people to a moral and useful life originated in the opposition to the abuses of individualism and free choice that characterized Britain and the United States in the nineteenth century. Both of these philosophies reflect the nature of their origin—an ideological revolt against existing conditions perceived as unfair or undesirable. As a result, they oversimplify both the problem and the solution.

Optimization becomes functional only when it focuses on human, social and, environmental needs. In order to give this the highest priority as an economic goal, the decision-making process of the people must become the means to this end. Since the structure of the decision-making process is political, economic goals and optimization cannot be realized without the art of politics. An understanding of this fact once again alerts us to the need for an interdisciplinary approach to economics. The evolution of traditional economics in Britain and the United States all but ignored the political and social character of economics.[2]

Two of the most important political concepts are freedom and democracy. Both of these are vital components of the economic notion of optimization. Just as laissez-faire is an oversimplification based on obsolete and irrelevant assumptions, so democracy and freedom as defined by most nineteenth-century scholars fail to take into account the world that evolved from the Industrial Revolution and from subsequent changes produced by enormous advances in science and technology. Just as a satisfactory house cannot be built without the proper materials and tools, so economic optimization cannot be achieved without the right kind of political tools employed by industry and government in the use and allocation of resources and labor.

Democracy is still generally regarded as a system based on free elections and two or more political parties. This definition rests on a philosophy that perceives the decision-making process as being located in a legislative chamber occupied by people elected by those they represent. We have already seen in chapter 13 that this is far too limited a definition in a world in which vital decisions are made inside the organization that manages the economic process—the corporation. Such decisions, which have far-reaching consequences, involve the traditional democratic process only peripherally. In other words, democracy as it is practiced today does not lend itself to the establishment and execution of goals that will satisfy the needs of the people and the environment. It is futile and ironic to talk about economic optimization without considering political improvements designed to make both the private and public sectors more responsible and responsive to the will of the people.

The key question we must face is whether a modern economy can operate successfully without making the quality of life subordinate to the needs of the corporation or the state. Economic goals are necessary if the economic process of optimizing is to be more than an aimless effort with unpredictable consequences. Although capitalism became a very successful economic system so far as the production of goods and services is concerned, it accomplished this in spite of the classical theories on which it was built because it was able to pursue a more pragmatic course. As a result of the gap between the classical model and the more pragmatic experience, capitalism developed somewhat aimlessly so far as human and social goals are concerned.

There remains a great deal of work to be done by social scientists trained in economics before the transition can be made from the relatively static, single-point-of-reference analysis of today's economists to the really dynamic, multiple-point-of-reference analysis required for interpreting the economic realities of today. (See the first section of chapter 12.) Nevertheless, we are not beginning at zero. We have acquired some knowledge in regard to economic goals that can serve as a starting point. We have also acquired experience in regard to economic capabilities, experience that should help us in the setting of goals.

The task before us is to develop the concepts of freedom, democracy, and social responsibility in such a way that they help us to reach economic goals conducive to the survival and health of humanity. This is by no means a novel objective. The great religions and philosophies have had similar objectives but they were too often lost in the search for a utopia. It is time for more social scientists to face reality and help us in this endeavor.

Social Goals and the Critical Significance of Comprehensive Plans and Programs

In the eighteenth and nineteenth centuries, such writers as Adam Smith, John Stuart Mill, and Karl Marx understood the place of economics in total human development, and they were regarded as social scientists. Like John Stuart Mill,[3] the earlier political economists, as they were called, recognized the need for human goals, built on moral values, as a prerequisite for developing socially constructive policies.

The goals and values economists or any other social scientists adopt, explicitly or implicitly, determine their whole approach to problem solving—including the methodology of their research, their conclusions, and their policy recommendations. Twentieth-century traditional economics is oversimplified by the belief that economics is not a moral science (or art) and that social goals and values can be ignored, except as they pertain to the principle of quantitative optimization.

In the real world, the use of social goals is an indispensable necessity for objective research. Gunnar Myrdal, the Swedish Nobel laureate, believed that clearly stated social goals and human values purge research of distorting biases.[4]

Social goals are intended to improve the quality of life. One goal is to prevent problems that, if allowed to develop, would produce social "evils." Preparing young people through education and training for the jobs that are likely to be available when they enter the job market falls in that category of objectives because it reduces the likelihood of unemployment and underemployment. Other social goals are intended to eliminate social evils that already exist. Slums and extreme poverty are examples of that.

Another kind of social goal is intended to create a degree of fairness in a world in which power and wealth, when left without checks and balances, create privileges for some while alienating others. The creation of economic "safety nets" in housing, health services, and education is an example. Such social goals are achieved with the establishment of priorities and cannot be left to the workings of the market system.

There are many examples of the adoption of social goals in capitalist countries. Prince Otto von Bismarck, the conservative German chancellor of the late nineteenth century, helped to create the first social security program and the first national health system in the world. Thomas Jefferson helped to create the public school system in the United States. Several western countries shortly after World War II enacted full-employment legislation to guarantee their governments' participation in the prevention of unemployment. These priorities were established for a variety of purposes. But they have one thing in common: they were designed to improve the quality of life. This has contributed to a better image of the capitalist system by making it fairer than it would otherwise have been for those who lack power, position, and wealth.

Today in some countries, both capitalist and socialist, one or more of the following priorities have been established with full political commitment: affordable, decent[5] housing for all (in some countries rent is fixed at 6 percent of a family's income); free education based on merit (for those who lack aptitude for higher education, free training in the various trades); free health care (in some countries this includes preventive, ambulatory, and catastrophic treatment); free or inexpensive mass transportation (this is intended to give people mobility without furnishing expensive private transportation); and free recreation (this is based on the need for rest and rehabilitation to keep people in good health).

What the establishment of such priorities means, in the countries establishing them, is that the economy produces a few vital necessities for all people plus many more, but less vital, necessities and luxuries for those who can afford to pay the price. The necessities for which priorities have been established are paid for by a variety of taxes, since, of course, even vital necessities are not gifts of nature. The establishment of social goals and priorities involves a redistribution of income that can be accomplished successfully only in a full-employment economy that is productive and consequently not hindered by transfer payments to the unemployed and underemployed.

Social goals and priorities should not be chosen in an authoritarian way. To do so would deprive the people of the opportunity to participate in their selection. The urgency for social goals and priorities is clear. The level of inequities that will inevitably develop in any social system must not be allowed to reach a point at which it produces widespread alienation leading to political instability. In other words, a successful economic system must be able to achieve a certain level of fairness and equity.

The establishment of social goals and priorities is not an argument against private enterprise or the market economy. On the contrary, as Bismarck and Franklin Roosevelt instinctively knew, it strengthens both. A purist interpretation of the economic market, however, based on the traditional concept of the "economic man" whose decisions are always rational and whose only needs are economic needs, leaves no room for social goals and priorities. This is why traditional economists insist that value judgments have no place in economics.

The limitations of the market can be demonstrated with an example of shortages in a vital commodity at the same time that the market is in equilibrium according to traditional economic theory. The market for housing can be in equilibrium, in the traditional sense of that term, while it is unable to reach a considerable part of the population because the price of housing and land values are not within the reach of low- and moderate-income families. Those who cannot afford housing are not considered part of the market, and their plight has no effect on the concept of equilibrium.

However, in modern economic societies in which politically established priorities supplement a market economy, the question of incomes being too low has become a relevant economic issue. As a result, in the so-called welfare economies, shortages can exist while the market is in equilibrium. It is recognized that income distribution reflects factors other than productivity. Even under the best circumstances, a complex modern economy is bound to produce serious inequities. The public response can be to subsidize high-priority items such as housing, or it can be indifference.

One of the most difficult problems in carrying out public policy aimed at eliminating social inequities is the clear identification of social goals. At times, these are determined by means of a political process only to run into constraints too formidable to give way. As a result, the goals get lost in an array of projects that themselves may be related to the goals without ever actually culminating in them. The following example is a case in point.

City X contains a large slum section in which 30 percent of the city's inhabitants live. The average earnings in that section are only one-third of the average income received in the city as a whole. The crime rate is far above the city's average, and the city's welfare rolls are made up almost entirely of residents of the slum area. This situation is considered by the community and by the nation to be a serious social problem. The city government, therefore, decides to eliminate the slum. This means that certain steps have to be taken, and these can be looked upon as "intermediate public goods" intended to lead to the final social goal, the elimination of slums.

In order to achieve the final goal, the population of the slum area requires education, job training, work, and other programs dealing with problems of mental, physical, and emotional health. Finally, the slums need to be replaced with decent housing, consistent with productive living and good citizenship.

Unhappily, constraints associated with the adoption of the various required programs cannot be surmounted. They may be racial, political, economic, or social in origin, but they stand in the way. The only thing finally undertaken is a housing program. Old slums are replaced with new units, and the poor people move from the old to the new. What should be expected?

In the preceding example, the housing program, although on the surface desirable in itself, is not a final goal. It is a means to an end or an intermediate public good. Without the various other programs (intermediate public goods), the housing program will not by itself produce the final goals: greater productivity and opportunities for a better life plus the removal of not only the slums but also the poverty and social ills that produce them. Consequently, the slum conditions come back as fast as they are cleared.

Two of the most serious shortcomings of collective action programs are the naivete with which social goals are adopted and the scorn that public programs receive when they do not reach their objectives. Social goals must be based on political reality. Constraints must be analyzed and either removed or taken into account. It is unrealistic to assume that the accomplishments of social goals can be whatever the electorate wants them to be, unless it is also assumed that given social constraints, such as racism, can be removed. If collective action produces intermediate public goods that do not result in the elimination of the social problems for which they were intended the social benefits of the intermediate public goods are next to zero.

Assume that a social problem exists in the form of our previous example, namely neighborhood deterioration and its resulting consequences of low labor productivity submarginal incomes, and a high crime rate. Although housing deterioration is a symptom of this problem, the real social objectives are to raise the productivity of the community and to reduce the crime rate.

Although costs must be considered in the elimination of social problems, it is at least equally important to look at the environment in which these problems exist in order to determine whether proposed expenditures will result in their elimination. Not all causes of poverty and the resulting slums can be readily removed. There are social constraints that the ballot and the courts seem to be able to remove only slowly if at all. Nevertheless, there are some intermediate public goods that can be made available without delay. Education and job-training programs, health programs, housing-maintenance programs, labor-mobility programs, and others must be undertaken simultaneously with housing-renovation programs. Only with such a comprehensive approach will the social problem of slums be alleviated.

Such programs must be comprehensive to produce the desired results. The proper combination of the inputs is to some extent determined by particular circumstances, but costs must be considered.[6] The neglect of costs and economically sound input combinations is one of the worst features of some present social programs.

Low-income families are going to be freed from slum living only if their productivity and usefulness to society are increased. The present approach, which is usually limited to solving the housing problem for low-income families, is in no way geared to this objective. As a result, the social benefit of the present housing program is very low.

Whether or not government undertakes to eliminate a social problem depends upon the political priorities that have been established. A number of countries have succeeded in eliminating slums and the high social costs associated with them. There is no reason to believe that it cannot be done if the funds are made available and the proper organizational structure capable of dealing with such problems is established. It should be borne in mind that annual expenditures appropriated for the elimination of slums may turn out to be quite reasonable when they are viewed as discounted social costs (that is, when they are compared to the cost of the social problems produced by slums).

Just as preventive medicine may be the cheapest way to deal with health issues, preventive social action may be the least expensive way to deal with social problems. Obviously it is the way that involves the least human suffering. In countries where this has been recognized, the addition of vital social goals and social priorities to the market economy has made the economic system not only fairer and more equitable, but also more efficient.

The Advantage of Anticipating Problems and Planning for Their Prevention in a Market Economy

The word *planning* has been all but ignored in traditional micro-economic theory. This is strange in the light of the considerable volume of planning exercised in the private sector of the economy, especially in the large corporations, where investments can be enormous and time lags until a product reaches completion can be five years or longer.

Planning should be viewed in the light of what it really is. At its best, it is a cooperative effort, democratically organized, combining goals, policies, and procedures in a way that is likely to improve the human condition. It is unrealistic to assume that this objective can be reached by leaving it to chance or to a market that responds only to prices.

Planning is not always, of course, a democratically organized, cooperative effort. This is true in the private sector as well as the public sector. In considering the role of planning, it is important to distinguish between arbitrary decisions and decisions reached through democratic procedures.

Planning is as much a part of a successful capitalist system as it is of a socialist system. The resistance to planning, so far as the public sector is concerned, is that it is regarded as a substitute for a market economy. So far as the private sector is concerned, traditional economic theory by and large ignores it.

In fact, both the public and the private sectors engage in a considerable amount of planning. We have seen that large corporations must plan for the availability of important resources as well as markets for their products. Without such planning, they could not risk the large investments necessary for their operations.

So far as the public sector is concerned, the U.S. government is currently responsible for about 25 percent of total spending in the

U.S. economy. This involves a considerable amount of planning by the White House (through the Office of Management and Budget), Congress, and numerous departments and agencies. The question is no longer whether planning must play a role in a modern capitalist economy such as the U.S. economy. That has already been answered unmistakably in the affirmative. But rather, the question is *what* roles should planning play in the *private* sector and in the *public* sector in view of past failure of much planning in the public sector because of haphazard, half-hearted, perhaps deliberately inept efforts (as in certain environmental agencies). If the private corporation were as weakly committed to planning as the public sector and employed people as inexperienced in planning and as uncommitted to it as some hired by the various levels of government, the economy would be far less productive.

Planning is in fact a vital part of a modern private-enterprise market economy, and it is no less vital in the public sector of a modern democracy. The belief that planning is one side of the coin of a socialist economy—the other side being public ownership of the means of production—illustrates the ignorance that exists in regard to a modern capitalist economy. Those who believe that do not realize that modern economies, whether socialist or capitalist, have similar problems and may have to employ similar procedures to deal with them. *How* they employ such procedures may explain the true difference between the two systems.

Authoritarian planning is not limited to authoritarian socialist economies. In the old days of Henry Ford, planning in the Ford Motor Company was centrally organized without the participation of management below the level of Mr. Ford and one or two of his closest associates. The same was true of Sewell Avery at Montgomery Ward and in numerous other cases. Today a number of well-managed corporations execute their long-range plans with the participation of every level of management and labor.

The same distinctions in planning exist within governments. In such nonsocialist countries as Sweden and Denmark, there is considerable democratic planning, as there is in socialist France. There are also considerable differences in approach to planning among the Eastern European socialist nations. In all cases, however, planning involves goals. It requires an accurate analysis of the structural complexities, a selection of the appropriate intermediate social goods, a realistic appraisal of social constraints or obstacles, and, finally, a long-range commitment of resources. An example will illustrate this point.

Monetary policy designed to combat inflation (a recognized social problem) has, let us assume, fallen short of its social goal—a stable, noninflationary economy. To obtain desirable results, monetary policy has to be combined and correlated with all other economic policies and with the market sector of the economy. It must also be based on a realistic appraisal of the structure of the economy to avoid the substitution of new social problems for the one against which it is directed. Simply to restrict the money supply (create tight money) as a weapon against inflation is an example of poorly planned monetary policy because it lacks the prerequisites for achieving desirable social goals.

The best-organized financial markets that show superior strength during periods of tight money are those trading in the financial instruments of the federal government and the large national and multinational corporations. By contrast, the weakest financial markets during such periods are those financing housing and the public services of state and local government. As a result of such institutional factors, monetary constraints have had the effect of shifting the flow of loanable funds from such politically high-priority necessities as housing, health care, education, transportation, and public services in general to such lower priorities as a second or third car, television sets, and stereo equipment.

The traditional economist will answer : "If this is the will of the market, so be it." That is no longer a good enough answer. The financial market structure is such that it favors luxuries over necessities for the reasons indicated in the above paragraph. In addition, the necessities that the market does not supply are in part at least provided by the government through the establishment of high political priorities. Demand is no longer limited to the market. The government has become the middleman in converting *need* into *effective demand*. This is the way the government alleviates social problems it has been unable or unwilling to prevent. It is clear, however, that to create an effective demand for necessities through transfer payments *after* the market has done its job is to invite more inflation. This is an example of poor planning.

Since monetary constraints are imposed when the nation is already suffering from inflation, the vacuum filled by the government becomes an inflationary gap. This inflationary gap is caused by the failure of the private market to allocate resources in line with high-priority necessities and the ability of the people to use the government for supplementing the market in providing such necessities.

The question of transfer payments arising from the low incomes generated by underemployment is another example. It is likely that if productivity does not keep pace with technology, transfer payments will continue to increase. Productivity of labor is not merely the ratio between capital and labor. It depends on many things. It is affected by attitudes, the quality of capital, the quality of technology, the quality of education and training, financial resources, political and business organization, and opportunity, as well as other important factors. Inflation is a serious symptom of our economic problems; underemployment and unemployment are two of its major causes.[7] The failure to do something constructive about underemployment is another example of poor planning.

The belief that economic growth is built solely on adequate investment and that this in turn depends solely on the level of profits and profit expectations is much too simplistic a point of view in an economy characterized by multinational corporations, political democracy, and high technology. "Adequate" profits do not necessarily lead to domestic investment. The market does not automatically allocate "adequate" profits into human-capital development correlated with productive employment opportunities. Underemployment is a far more complex social problem than can be explained with capital/labor ratios.

The market cannot correlate political evolution with economic capabilities in a democracy. The inability of the market to do this should not be regarded casually. In the absence of intelligent planning, the gap between political evolution and economic capabilities can become a major factor in chronic inflation and other serious problems.

Rapid technological advances and the gradual exhaustion of natural resources, brought about by the simultaneous occurrence of scientific and economic development and a world population explosion, have a profound impact on the market structure of the U.S. and other economies. Scientific and technological discoveries occur at a much faster pace today than even a few decades ago. At the same time, the impact of a world population explosion, combined with rapid advances in industrialization, has created serious environmental problems as well as shortages of high-priority resources—problems governments have been called upon to take steps to solve. Long before the energy crisis that came to the surface in 1973 with OPEC's quadrupling of crude oil prices, the U.S. government knew that such resources were limited. Indeed, when OPEC was created in Bagdad in 1960, the United States should have made plans immediately, to prevent the waste of this scarce resource made artificially cheap by neocolonial policies. Our policies resulted in the Western nations becoming dependent on the Middle East, and this dependence led to political actions that have made the Middle East one of the critical trouble spots of the world.

The alternative was found *after* the crisis surfaced. The demand for oil was reduced considerably by a more efficient use of this scarce resource, and an active search for new oil wells resulted in development of the considerable Alaskan, North Sea, and Mexican supplies, while alternative energy sources (such as nuclear, thermal, and solar) were also explored. This action is an example of planning *after* a problem surfaces. The costs and hardships were much greater than if the planning had been done before the energy crisis did its damage.

The important point is that critical shortages cannot be avoided and the environment cannot be adequately protected without a commitment to relevant social goals and an intelligent method of *timely* anticipation and planning. Many economic problems will remain unsolved until this is fully understood and appreciated. This is not likely to happen, however, until a way is found to make the application of planning democratic and humane.

The Role of Information in a Democratic Society

All life on earth is subject to the laws of nature. We know that individuals, groups, and even species that cannot adapt within the available time limits perish. Social institutions, too, must adapt to changes in the environment or perish.

In a system in which social institutions and human decisions determine the inputs and outputs of the economic process, adaptation depends to a considerable extent on the efficiency of the information apparatus. The knowledge needed includes both economic and noneconomnic factors, for all of these are essential in the process of adaptation.

In traditional economic theory, there is only a single source of information from which the economy, via the market system, takes its cue for adaptation to change. This single source is the information received from the price mechanism. On the basis of this extremely limited system of information, the traditional economists developed the concept of the optimum, or efficient, economy.

An information system may be simple or complex, depending on the simplicity or complexity of the social unit it serves. In any case, it is composed of three parts: types of information, use of information, and information response.

In a simple animal society such as an ant farm, all three parts are comparatively small. All information is geared to survival and procreation, and it is passed from generation to generation. Scout ants play the role of information gatherers, and responses are automatic.

In very primitive human societies, the information system is also very simple. The highest priority is given to survival and procreation, and a rigid culture and scout system make up the information mechanism. Human beings, however, have psychological needs, which in primitive cultures lead to witchcraft and supernaturalism.

As human societies develop, they become much more complex, until human and environmental needs involve the whole spectrum of the arts, the sciences, and technology. This development is generated by and commensurate with the physical and social development of humanity. The types of information required to meet the needs of modern men and women involve all areas of human knowledge and experience.

If survival and the quality of life do not matter, then such complex information is not required. Individuals need then only be guided by their own pleasure and pain indexes to assure optimum pleasure. Or, if this seems absurd, then it can be assumed, as John Stuart Mill did, that each individual's pleasure and pain index includes the higher aspirations of a just society.

To apply this principle to the laissez-faire theory, the assumption has to be made that people somehow possess the altruism and the information to make rational decisions in regard to their own individual needs as well as the needs of society and the environment. The classical economists made this assumption and were able to lay to rest any concern about the complexities of society and the information system. They confined themselves to the magic price mechanism of the self-adjusting market.

The types of information needed in a modern society are vast and intricate. The information apparatus must be able to supply pertinent data relevant to the individual and everything that makes up the environment. Such information is divided into the various disciplines making up human knowledge. Fortunately, this data can be handled by modern computer technology.

The price mechanism was a single point of reference in classical economics just as planet earth was a single point of reference in Newtonian physics. We have seen that the operations of an economic system involve many centers of information or points of reference, of which the price mechanism is only one.

What are the important sources of information that will provide the data we must have in order to satisfy individual and social needs conducive to sane living? An example will illustrate the kind of data that must be known and considered in addition to the price generated by market supply and demand.

The conditions under which people live have impact on their health and on their ability to enjoy life and to contribute to the well-being of others. We spend a good part of our lives as producers of goods and services—what economists call the supply side of the market. Traditional economists have concentrated on *what* we produce and have paid almost no attention to *how* we produce and work. The *how*, as we have seen, has an important impact not only on the quality of life but also on productivity, a major concern of economists.

To deal with this problem effectively, we must draw upon the information available in all the areas of human knowledge concerning the well-being of individuals and society. This is no longer difficult in the age of computer information. The important point in this connection is that the information should neither come from above in an authoritarian manner, nor be limited to sources dependent upon the people who control production in the private sector (through the media, which cannot survive without advertising). A better way to deal with the problem of information vital to democracy in the political sense and optimization in the economic sense will have to be adopted if democracy and optimization are to be more than mere slogans.

Just as we have highly advanced observatories to study the structure of the universe, so we need "observatories" to check the accuracy, adequacy, and objectivity of the information received from all parts of this country and the world. At present, the news media themselves attempt to do this, but there are serious shortcomings. The mass media derive income from advertisers, which can be inimical to an objective presentation and interpretation of information; also the media are not adequately prepared to examine the accuracy of so-called facts from the wire services, the government, and other sources. Without that, an information system becomes an often-innocent ally of propaganda.

There is, of course, investigative reporting. This has produced excellent results, and should be continued, providing the standards employed are high so as not to victimize people and issues in order to sell news.

The news media should be the *first* source of news, consistent with the principle of the freedom of the press in a democratic society. There should, however, be another layer to guarantee accuracy, adequacy, and objectivity in the information system.

The following is a case in point. In the fall of 1986, President Reagan addressed the United States on television. In his talk, he pointed out that defense expenditures between 1961 and 1981 had fallen sharply as a percentage of the federal budget and that social expenditures, including social security, had risen significantly in that period. He failed to say that in 1961, social security expenditures were not included in the federal budget, but social security revenues were. This was changed in 1967, so that in 1981 both social security expenditures and revenues were part of the federal budget.

A moment's reflection will show that the president's assertion was incorrect because he did not allow for the change in statistical measurements between the two years he chose for his comparison.

Actually, if that had been taken into consideration, as it must be for statistical accuracy, it would have shown that defense expenditures and social expenditures remained almost unchanged as percentages of the federal budget.

This error was not reported by the media. Indeed, for weeks, much of the media were quoting the president and lamenting the neglect of the military and the overly generous increase in social expenditures. If we judge the accuracy of information by all the errors allowed to pass unapprehended by the media, the quality of our information system must be seriously questioned. The impact of this failure on the quality of democracy is obvious.

The information system could be greatly improved if "information observatories" could be established to serve as the guardians of accuracy, adequacy, and objectivity in the media. These could be established in a number of our leading universities. With the aid of modern computers, they could store an almost infinite amount of raw data that could be programmed to produce needed information almost instantly. If errors were made by the electronic or print news media, they could be almost instantly corrected by the information observatories before the reader or listeners formed opinions based on the misinformation received.

Even if the sources of information are adequate, objective, and easily available, information must be used in such a way that the response to it is conducive to solving problems. Since decisions involve disagreements generated by conflicting views and interests problems can be solved and balance achieved only through a system of well-organized compromises based on accurate information.

Compromise is a vital social strategy for achieving human objectives and balance. The utilitarian price system and much of the utopian philosophies of the past three centuries have detracted from the essential role of compromise. It has made compromise seem like something less than the ideal, less than the optimum. Once the utopian approach to life is laid to rest with other fairy tales, it becomes clear that in the real world, conflict is normal and compromise is essential to problem solving. This is a fundamental condition in all human relationships. However, to deal with conflict, (previously discussed at the start of chapter 6), we must have adequate knowledge derived from a democratic-pluralistic information system.

An economic system that does not make conflict the basis of its problem-solving process cannot deal effectively with the needs of humanity and the environment. The classical economists avoided getting involved in the human drama by ruling out the dynamics of time and value judgments. As a result, compromises had to enter the economic process through the back door, which proved highly unsatisfactory. Conflict and compromise must become an integral and acceptable part of the economic process and, in time, an integral part of economic methodology. An essential requirement for that is the development of an adequate information system capable of providing responses leading to successful adaptation to change.

15
A Pragmatic Approach to a
More Humane Economy

A Rational Approach to Goals and Means

The reader has seen that highly unrealistic assumptions about people and society have created serious inconsistencies between our values and our way of life. As a result, many problems have arisen that could have been avoided if our policies had been based on more accurate observations and assumptions.

The ability to change in a timely and rational manner is of critical importance in a world in which the key to survival is adaptability. We, however, are animals of habit, and change does not come easily. If we become more realistic about ourselves, we will certainly acquire a better understanding of the world around us and resist needed change with less blind obstinacy.

Life links every individual to both the past and the future. Preexistence is the time in which our heredity and environment evolved. Postexistence is the passage into history and eternity of the dimension we have added through our progeny and our works. Thus, each human being becomes a part of the future to a greater or lesser extent, and each generation has a significant impact on the activities of following generations. Its values and goals—derived in part from past experience—serve as a catalyst in the evolution of culture. When we oppose necessary adjustments, we create problems not only for ourselves and our contemporaries, but also for those who inherit the world after we are gone. In a society dedicated to improving the human condition, social responsibility on the part of *all* individuals and groups, including corporations, is of utmost importance.

The means we choose for reaching our goals must be selected with care, for they, like the goals, have an impact on survival and the quality of life. A better understanding of vital human needs—and an environment favorable to these needs—becomes a paramount condition for reaching our *major* goal of improving the quality of life.

Economists and other social scientists have failed to realize that by adopting a segmented approach to the social sciences, they have put obstacles in the way of gaining a better insight into our problems. They have concentrated on optimization without paying enough attention to the other factors vital to improving the human condition (the fundamental goal of economics). They have professed that "more is better" without adequately considering how "more" is obtained or what impact "more" and the methods used to obtain it have on the quality of life. This and the overemphasis on self-interest have made economics an ally of extreme materialism and excessive self-indulgence.

We have seen that to satisfy the needs of the corporate economy we have allowed self-gratification to take the place of rational living. Self-gratification has led to a consumption pattern of instant pleasure that has spread into every aspect of our lives.

The employment of rational means for achieving the higher goals of life is a matter of values and education. At present, our culture, which is the source of both, reflects to a great extent extreme materialism, which has its origins in an economic philosophy of self-indulgence.

The task before us is to encourage a culture consistent with the values required for improving the human condition. At the same time, the corporate economy must learn to produce efficiently and profitably without making the needs of the consumer and the environment subordinate to its own ambitions.

A realistic approach to encouraging such a culture and system of values requires that we concentrate in the present on what is *possible*, and that we plan the future with an eye on what *ought to be*. This balance between the present and the future combines materialism and idealism.

Based on historical evidence, both the concept of laissez-faire and Marx's prediction of the state withering away are unrealistic in the present and foreseeable future. Neither is a basic human end but rather the means to such ends. The classical economists assumed that a state without any power over the economy would lead to the greatest good for the greatest number or, in the words of Alfred Marshall, an improved human condition—a basic goal. Marx saw the capitalist state as contributing to the workers' exploitation and believed that when communism was achieved, the power of the state would wither away. The Marxist goal was a better life through communism, which was Marx's means to the end (as discussed at the start of chapter 3).

Both the classical economists and Marx were opposed to the power of the state because they saw the worsening of the human condition when the state became a ruthless wielder of political power. Since power cannot be abolished in human society, but only controlled, the means to be searched for is not laissez-faire or the communist state withering away, but rather an economic society that lends itself to controlled power in both the public sector and the private sector (as covered in the second section of chapter 6). This is, of course, not a new idea. But at this stage of political evolution, neither balance between materialism and idealism nor an enlightened balance in the use of power has been achieved.

Balance in both cases can be reached only through a rational choice of goals and means. At present, we do not seem to have even a clear conception of which is which. There is a danger in that! If the means to an end, such as laissez-faire, is looked upon as an important goal, it becomes a matter of principle to defend it and not to deviate from it. In a world in which conditions change constantly and knowledge is imperfect, the rigidities resulting from such a confusion of goals and means can lead to disaster.

If the basic goal of our economic society is to satisfy the important biological, psychological, and social needs of the people, then the economy has to be so organized that it will achieve that goal. The first task is to choose a standard of measure by which its progress in terms of its goals can be judged. The present standard by which economic progress is judged—the size of Gross National Product and the rates of inflation and unemployment—is far too narrow a concept with which to measure improvement in the human condition.[1] The choice of indicators used for measuring the human condition should reflect the degree of success in meeting the important needs of the people as well as the requirements of a healthy environment. They should also measure failure in meeting these needs, which produces such problems as unemployment, inflation, crime, pollution, and overpopulation.

Table 15–1 is an example of the kind of indicators that may be used in measuring the human condition. The first index will serve as a base year for future annual indexes as well as an indicator of how the quality of life is perceived in that year.

The value given to each indicator in the base year will be only approximately accurate. Nevertheless, the results will be satisfactory, since the purpose of the index is to measure improvements in the human condition. This requires already well-known techniques employed for measuring changes occurring from year to year.

The indicators are very nearly determined, at least implicitly, as soon as basic goals are selected. If, for example, the basic goals are survival, improving the human condition, and peaceful coexistence with other nations, the basic indicators for measuring success in reaching these goals cannot merely be the size of the GNP, unemployment, and inflation. It is more likely that it must include such indicators as those selected in Table 15–1. The selection of indicators should involve the ablest minds in the various areas of social and physical sciences.

It is possible that not all indicators are equally important in arriving at an index that reflects the human condition. In that case, weights can be attached to each indicator, and the end result will be a weighted average of all indicators.

There should be at least four indexes measuring the human condition that, when used concurrently, would make the resulting information more relativistic and less absolute or arbitrary. All four indexes would have relevance in a world in which many problems are created by international as well as national policies and actions.

One index should be constructed from a sample made up of the nation's business, political, professional, and academic leaders and those who advise them. They should reflect a broad spectrum of the public sector and the private sector. They should be asked to give their own perceptions of the human condition to be used in the construction of the various indicators.

Another index should be made from a sample reflecting a broad cross-section of the population. This would give two perceptions of the human condition: one from the people who play an important role in the decision-making process and its execution, and the other from the population as a whole.

In a world in which national boundaries have lost much of their economic significance and political decisions have important international consequences, it is desirable that perceptions of the human condition reflect not only how a nation sees itself but also how it is seen by others. A number of countries should be selected for this purpose (objectively, if the result is to have meaning) and each country should construct two indexes modeled after the ones in the country to which the index applies. These indexes would serve an important purpose: they would show a nation how its human condition is perceived outside its national boundaries. This could provide very important information in the diplomatic solution to national conflicts.

A Rational Approach to the Market Economy

What is the role of the market in an economy committed to improving the human condition? Aristotle's "golden mean" that too much or too little of anything causes problems, applies to this question. How can there be too little or too much of a market? If the market is relied on to perform functions for which it is not suited, so that the result does not improve the human condition or fails to achieve other specific goals, it is "used" poorly or too much. For example, if the scope of the market is international, but political decisions are based on economic theories applicable to national markets, the market will perform badly. If the problems are structural in nature, a reliance on market forces alone will not solve them. These are irrational uses of the market because the desired goals will not be reached.

U.S. policies of the mid-1980s are an example of an irrational

Table 15–1

Base-Year Index (First of an Annual Series of Indexes)

Indicators of the Human Condition	Your Perception of the Human Condition				Relative Importance of Indicators (Statistical Weights)		
	Very Poor 1	Poor 2	Fair 3	Very Good 4	Lowest 1	Middle 2	Highest 3
Living condition							
Bottom third of population							
Middle third							
Top third							
Health care (quality and affordability)							
Bottom third of population							
Middle third							
Top third							
Pre-College education (quality and affordability)							
Bottom third of population							
Middle third							
Top third							
Higher education (quality and affordability)							
Bottom third of population							
Middle third							
Top third							
Housing (availability, quality, and affordability)							
Bottom third of population							

Middle third

Top third

Cultural and recreational facilities

Bottom third of population

Middle third

Top third

The inflation problem

The unemployment problem

The underemployment problem (families employed but needing assistance)

The motivation of workers

The standard of living of retired people

Adults and children on welfare (Percentage of Population)

Quality and affordability of nursery schools for working mothers

Drug addiction, alcoholism, and violent crime problems

The quality of the physical environment, (air, water, infrastructure)

Civil liberties

Law enforcement and justice

The level of political participation

reliance on market forces for correcting critical balance of trade deficits resulting largely from nonmarket structural developments. These developments include very high federal budget and trade deficits financed in large part with foreign savings; the use of highly skilled or specialized human and physical resources for military purposes at the expense of technological advance in the nonmilitary sector; an unprecedented rate of consumption on credit; the use of credit for corporate takeovers at the expense of growth investment; and the misuse of credit made available to the Third World at unreasonable terms, which has become an obstacle to economic development and a deterrent to the growth of new markets in the developing nations. New markets are badly needed by the developed nations including the United States if the full benefits of high technology are to be realized.

The U.S. government's failure to deal effectively with these problems and its decision to use changes in interest rates and exchange rates for alleviating them form a clear example of an excessive or irrational reliance on market forces.[2]

On the other hand, if an economy does not rely on the market for those things for which it is suited, and as a result fails to improve the human condition or fails to reach specific goals, the market is "used" too little. The Soviet Union's efforts to make greater use of market forces as a means of improving its economic efficiency and ultimately the human condition are a timely recognition that the market is an indispensable part of economic efficiency and the quality of life. To repeat, if the market is used for functions for which it is designed, it is used rationally. If it is not used at all, if its uses are too limited, or if it is used for functions for which it is not designed, it is used irrationally.

A rational economic market is, first of all, a market that helps to reach the most basic goal of an economy—to improve the human condition. To do this, it performs functions that are within its capabilities.

The functions for which a market is designed in the modern world include, first, its role as a sounding board for the voice of the people. Without a market, the people are left out of the economic process. The better the market functions (that is, the more democratically it is organized) the more it reflects the real needs of the people and the environment.

The key word is price. If some people cannot pay for the goods and services required for satisfying their vital needs, if the problem is income distribution, unemployment, under-employment, poverty, or a social ill, the market cannot be the source of the solution. It is not designed to solve such problems.

Another major function of the market is to produce goods and services efficiently, as a step toward improving the human condition and abolishing poverty. This is accomplished through rational competition.

What is rational competition? If our goals are "to survive and to improve the quality of life," then the methods we use to achieve these goals, if they are rational, must help us to do so. Competition, if it is rational, will serve as a means to that end.

The classical economists based their theories of capitalism on rational competition. Two hundred years later, competition is still used by economists as the central factor in the market system; but they misuse the term. There are large areas of *irrational* competition in our market economy. The growth of economic power and the dominance of technocratic values in our culture have corrupted the meaning of competition.

In the process of irrational competition, the victors in the struggle for power dominate the market in their own interest. Survival and human values are subordinated to greed and the growing insecurity that comes from irrational competition.

Nations also become victims of irrational competition. The rational competition inherent in free trade is replaced with an irrational competition for control over markets and resources. The cooperation inherent in the competition of free trade is replaced with a unilateral struggle for power embellished by alliances that increase the insecurity of all. This has always led to war rather than improving the human condition.

Rational competition (as discussed in the second section of chapter 11) is fortunately not an empty dream. If it were, survival would probably be impossible. It is, in fact, an attainable objective in the evolution and humanization of the economic process. It becomes unrooted when exposed to a society subject to irrational competition or irrational cooperation, both of which prevent the reaching of goals.

Rational competition is not based on power, but on achievement. In the laissez-faire model, power does not exist. In the market of the real world, power *does* exist, and rational competition is impossible unless the misuse of power is prevented. There is no way to control the misuse of power except by rules that are democratically established and executed.

The application of rules or regulations to control the misuse of power has a long and varied history. The relationships between people are controlled in civilized societies by rules called laws. In the economic sphere, rules or regulations should not take the place of markets, because markets are the voice of the people. Markets, however, should be implemented by rational rules so that the voice of some people does not silence the voice of others.

The market is uniquely suited for the following functions:

1. To provide a sounding board for consumers,

2. To provide a sounding board for producers,

3. To allocate efficiently scarce resources through rational competition in a market that is not dominated by power.

4. To eliminate national boundaries as economic obstacles through trade based on rational competition.

The market is ill suited for these functions:

1. To provide the necessary goods and services for people with inadequate incomes,

2. To eliminate slums and other social ills already in existence,

3. To prevent slums and other social ills from developing,

4. To match the future demand for labor with the future supply of labor in a world characterized by rapid change and leaps in science and technology,

5. To protect and preserve the environment,

6. To correct or prevent structural unemployment, underemployment, and inflation,

7. To alleviate other structural problems.

These are problems that can be prevented or corrected only through intelligent and democratic planning. The psychological opposition to planning in U.S. politics comes from the belief that only the market can restore health and normalcy to the economy. Once the market is viewed rationally, the opposition to planning will give way to a more realistic attitude toward a modern economy.

Planning, too, can be rational or irrational. The attempt to deal with poverty by creating a system of welfare that reduces incentives to work and leaves the problems that created the poverty unsolved, is an example of irrational planning. To subsidize farmers for not growing their products when advances in agricultural technology increase the supply of farm products is another example of irrational planning in a world in which one half of the people do not have enough food.

The opposition to birth control and the half-hearted attempts to deal with it are a third example of irrational planning in a world torn apart by population explosions. The replacement of slum housing, while the factors causing slums are left untouched, is yet another example of irrational planning.

There are many examples of *rational* planning that have resulted in the improvement of the human condition. The creation of the Tennessee Valley Authority in the 1930s brought cheap energy to a large area of the nation and contributed significantly to its economic development.

The planning that enabled us to leave the planet Earth and its gravity has greatly expanded our knowledge of the universe and has created tremendous potential for improving the human condition. So has the planning that led to the discovery of nuclear energy, provided we do not allow it to destroy us before we reap its benefits.

The planning that was inspired by the Great Depression (which resulted in the establishment of the Federal Housing Administration and the Federal Home Loan Bank System in the United States in the 1930s) has helped to increase private home ownership from 15 percent to over 50 percent. Conditions change, and the need for these agencies has also changed, but this does not end the need for planning so decent housing will be available for all people.

On the international level, the European Payments Union (EPU), which came into existence in 1950, is an excellent example of planning for international cooperation. The EPU consisted of fifteen European nations whose ideologies varied from the moderate left to the moderate right. Yet in the four years (1950–54) during which it facilitated European trade and payments, none of the nations used its veto power to reject any of the more than three hundred recommendations made by the EPU to its parent organization, the Organization for European Economic Cooperation (OEEC). *All* recommendations were accepted by the member nations, who saw their own interests benefit from international cooperation. The policies and recommendations of the EPU were designed to plan for the prevention of problems and the solution of those that already existed.

The EPU lasted only four years, falling victim to the Cold War and the creation of NATO and the Warsaw Pact. During its life, it served as a model for what can be accomplished through wise cooperation and planning.

The person who managed the OEEC for nearly ten years, Robert Marjolin, its secretary general, in a letter to this author dated February 3, 1954 threw much light on the subject of rational planning and cooperation.

> I think that the truth of the matter is that, behind all their disagreements, the member countries of the [OEEC] have a good many things in common. In particular, they have a strong common interest in maintaining the system of payments which has been established under the Union, and the system of trade liberalization which has been based upon it. They all recognize that, until something better can be produced, they must hang on to what they have for fear of finding themselves in a worse position. It is this basic fact which has enabled us so far to achieve decisions despite the rule of unanimity.

Mr. Marjolin's comments point to the need for rational planning and cooperation together with a rational use of the market. The OEEC member nations could not have gotten the benefits from multilateral trade that were essential to their recovery from World War II without the planning and cooperation inherent in the EPU and the OEEC. Their ability to recognize this enabled them to put together a program of rational planning and cooperation on the international level.

The way the United Nations operates in dealing with the problems of its members is an example of irrational planning and cooperation. Superpower politics between the United States and the Soviet Union is based on the principle of unilateral advantages. Their policies have not, since the end of World War II, reflected cooperative planning for improving the human condition. Yet, they are the leading and indispensable members of the United Nations. Without their cooperation, an international body is greatly handicapped in improving the relationships between nations. The declaration by both superpowers that they are committed to improving the human condition is made irrational by their adoption of unilateral (as opposed to cooperative) means. Thus the United Nations is less effective than it was designed to be.

There are many more examples of rational and irrational planning and cooperation. Most people want peace and an opportunity to live their lives in a world committed to improving the human condition. The means for doing this exist, but they must be employed rationally.

The surge of international organizations that came into existence at the end of World War II was a valiant effort to come to grips with the problem of international power and authority. As in most cases, initial efforts rarely succeed, but they light the way. The world may be very close to bringing the struggle for power and authority to a rational conclusion. Opposition to social planning in the United States should be reexamined. Planning is already an important part of the public sector. But most of it is done after the problems caused by the lack of *timely* planning have reached troublesome proportions. The question is not "to plan or not to plan," but *when* and *how* to plan.

A Rational Approach to Freedom, Power, and Authority

Freedom and power must be subject to rules in a society in which improving the human condition and abolishing poverty are the main *economic* goals; fairness in human relations, the main *political* goal; the ability to live a relatively secure and useful life, the main *psychological* goal; and peaceful coexistence, the main *social* goal. This is not an arbitrary selection of goals. They can be found in the major religions and in the writings of the great philosophers.

Rules define the relationships between people. They may involve property, the exchange of goods and services, national interests, the environment, birth, death and countless other matters. But they always involve people—people who are knowledgeable and people who are uninformed, people who enjoy good health and people who do not, people who command privileges and people who do not. There is no equality, and rules are intended to make life as fair as possible within the framework of unavoidable inequalities.

Rules establish the pattern of authority. Whether freedom and power are exercised in a manner conducive to reaching the great goals of life depends on whether the system of authority is rational or irrational (as discussed in the second section of chapter 10). When either freedom or power is exercised without limits or within limits that are too broad or too narrow for reaching any or all of the great and vital goals of life, then the system of rules and authority is irrational.

When workers have no recourse to arbitration in a controversy with an employer, the power of the employer is too great and the freedom of the workers is inadequate. When workers are represented by a large labor union that is able to coerce a small employer to accede to its demands or go out of business, the power of the labor union is excessive and the freedom of the employer is inadequate.

Power and freedom are used between employers and workers in a way that strangles motivation and productivity when an employer (the management in the corporate economy) wants to introduce new methods of operations that will increase output with the use of fewer workers. This is an example of a classical dilemma. The employer's position and the workers' position, seemingly rational to each, reflect a polemic dichotomy. Actually, neither the employer's nor the workers' position is rational. If the employer succeeds with a plan to increase output and productivity, the workers who become dispensable will certainly not regard this as an improvement in the human condition or as an effort to abolish poverty.

On the other hand, if the workers succeed in frustrating the employer's efforts to introduce more efficient methods, then they will stand in the way of making the economy more efficient, which will make it more difficult to abolish poverty.

The solution to the dilemma requires new alternatives. Three possible alternatives are an increase in the demand for the product in question, an increase in demand for other products in existing industries, or the development of new products and new industries. All three alternatives require a growing economy. Since the modern world is becoming increasingly interdependent, economic growth within a nation should not be planned at the expense of economic growth in other nations or the result will be economic warfare.

When the word *rational* is applied to the market, to competition, to cooperation, to authority, to freedom, and to power, these concepts acquire a new meaning, one that is logical in terms of stated goals and means. To achieve goals that are intended to improve the human condition and not merely the lives of those who enjoy power, wealth, or privilege, involvement becomes a vital link between desired goals and the achievement of such goals.

For a person to become involved there must be opportunity and motivation.[3] Without involvement, in a world in which insecurity and problems are common, people become aloof or even alienated from the goals and means that shape their lives. Without involvement, the essence of democracy is lost.

In the real world, involvement is very difficult. The problem is that people must be *motivated* to become involved. Political philosophers have pointed out that people must *believe* that they will personally benefit from becoming involved. That is why people who possess wealth generally have a greater interest in the affairs that affect them than people who are poor, especially those who see no light at the end of the tunnel.

To improve the human condition, the involvement of people is vital. The belief that a few at the top will lead the people to their goals is an illusion. A few at the top must play a major role in the human drama, but a way has to be found to make them responsive and accountable to the rank and file. Both the public sector and the private sector are involved in satisfying the needs of the people and the environment. In both sectors, decisions are made that are of a political nature (as discussed in the third section of chapter 13).

In the private sector, a decision to make a process more efficient, which is a technical economic problem, has an impact on people that affects their well-being in a way that can only be understood if it is exposed to an *interdisciplinary analysis*. The loss of a job not only affects income (an economic variable), but also a person's self-esteem (a psychological variable), and a person's family life (a sociological variable). The political variable (the decision-making process that sets in motion all the other variables) ought to arouse the interests of the people whose lives it affects, for if it doesn't, the benefits from democracy are lost, and these are as significant in the private sector as they are in the public sector.

A political decision in the public sector to reduce unemployment or to protect the environment from pollution does not merely have economic consequences; it affects the total lives of people. It is naive to suggest, as some economists of the Chicago School do, that economics and politics must not be intermingled. The fact is, they *cannot* be separated—either in the public sector or in the private sector!

Once this fact is realized, it follows that a way must be found to involve people, in varying degrees, in the decisions that determine the course of their lives. There is no other way that authority can be made rational, because it is the only way in which it can be made *responsible* and *accountable*. This is a necessary condition for the means to lead to desired goals.

People will not be motivated to become involved if the information necessary for understanding the issues is too complicated or too difficult to obtain. They will not become involved if they do not see themselves benefit from their involvement.

Without meaningful democratic involvement, the rational use of freedom and power is most unlikely. In today's world, that is the root of many problems. Such concepts as freedom, democracy, and an open society are becoming mere slogans, and people are becoming skeptical and cynical. Many are willing to leave their destiny in the hands of leaders who appeal solely to their emotions. They want to believe them because that gives them hope. There is and always has been danger in that!

The problem of involvement in the corporate sector is less complex but more strongly resisted. For one thing, the arguments for democracy and involvement in the public sector have been expounded by philosophers and statespeople since the days of Plato and Pericles. There has been no similar intellectual development applying to the politics of the private sector, which in its present form is barely a century old.

Involvement does not mean *direct* democracy; it merely means that the people become a part of the decision-making process by being correctly informed about the issues and by having their voices reflected in the decisions that personally affect them. This is not the case now. Democracy, therefore, although it exists in our laws, is not yet fully reflected in our lives.

We are, however, closer to achieving *rational* democracy, authority, freedom, competition, and cooperation than we have been in the past. The mechanism for getting information to the people in a way that is clear and comprehensible has been invented. It is the computerized electronic information system. Even the idea of such a mechanism was extremely remote only a century ago. Today the mechanism exists and its benefits are within our reach.

How this mechanism is to be used to accomplish the task of making information simple and understandable on all issues on which decisions are being made, and at the same time keep this information objective, is something that must still be worked out.[4] It is by no means an impossible task. In fact, private foundations may want to address themselves to this problem. The important point here is that the information system must be pluralistic to reflect the political system, and it should not be influenced by powerful pressure groups in the public or private sectors.

In a world of challenge and response, subject to continuous change, the need for adaptability is obvious. Even if an effective information system is developed, the information will not automatically lead to timely adaptability. Yet this is a vital element in improving the human condition. What are the factors that will facilitate timely adaptability? An interdisciplinary, holistic, rational analysis of the political economy by the best minds of our time, broadly trained in the related fields of political science, philosophy, sociology, psychology, and economics, may hopefully shed some light on this question.

Humanity as the Nucleus of a Society Dedicated to Improving the Human Condition

Alfred Marshall expressed the views shared by many of the classical economists when he wrote that the goal of economics is to improve the human condition and to abolish poverty. To implement this goal, humanity has to be put at the center, or the nucleus, of the political economy.

The political economy was defined in the nineteenth century as the interrelationship between economics and politics. Marshall took this a step further. In his view economics, "relates the economic aspect and conditions of man to his political, social and private life."[5]

Political economy, in the context of this book, is as broad as Marshall's perception of economics without sacrificing the integrity of the original definition. It is defined here as the relationship between the economic processes and the political decisions and social conditions that set them in motion.

Humanity as the nucleus of the political economy receives its information from its inner world and from the external world. The inner (or internal) world functions through various parts of the mind. The external world consists of past experience or heredity plus present experience or environment. All the parts of the internal and external worlds combine to produce the decisions and conditions that drive the economy.

The combining of all the parts into the whole makes the holistic system's approach desirable in the study of political economy. The parts of the whole fit into the various subdisciplines such as economics, politics, sociology, and psychology. Figures 15–1 and 15–2 show the relationship of the parts to the whole.

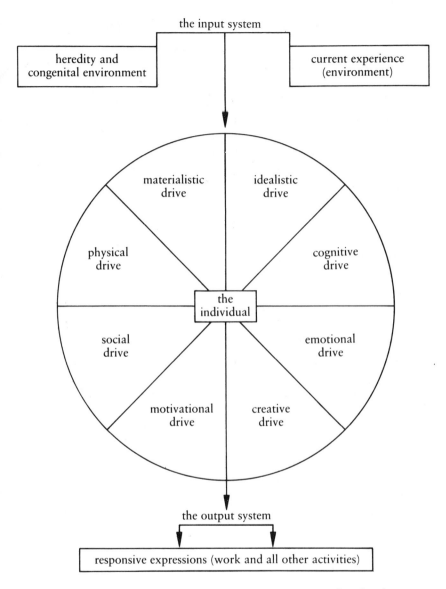

Note: The word *drive* is used to indicate responsive expression rather than latency. The so-called drives must be satisfied for humanity to develop an efficient output system.

Figure 15–1. *The Human Input-Output System as the Nucleus of the Political Economy*

Figure 15–1 shows the relationship of humanity's inner world to the external world. They have an impact on one another and together produce the human responses that result in all activity, including work. All current and past experiences affect all parts of the mind in varying degrees in different individuals.[6]

The quality of heredity and environment determines the quality of the mind, which in turn determines the quality of human response and expression. This includes work and all other activities.

To the economist, productivity is an essential measure of the quality of work. A major factor in productivity is the ratio between capital, technology, and labor. This ratio is, however, too limited to explain productivity in a modern political economy.

In the holistic sense, the quality of work or productivity is determined by everything that affects the quality of the worker.[7] Since productivity is at the heart of the optimization process of economics, all the social and psychological sciences should become involved in the input-output analysis of the political economy. They should be a part of the total system, not isolated from each other.

The Japanese economy and to some extent several European economies are cases in point. Their attempts at a holistic systems approach to the economy have had a significant effect on their own economic development as well as on the world economy. Indeed, the Japanese see the economic process as a total system that integrates the functions of management, labor, and government to a considerable degree.

The failure of the United States to face this issue realistically is a reflection of its segmented approach to the economic process. This is one of the reasons why the United States is losing ground in the international economy, suffering incredibly large trade deficits in recent years.

Each nation should seek its own systems approach. It should reflect its own experience, past and present, and its own conditions. Most important, it should employ rational means, because this is the only way to improve the human condition.

The quality of work or productivity is subject to all the internal and external influences shown in Figures 15–1 and 15–2, as well as others that may be added. If productivity is generally low in a firm, industry, or even an entire region or nation, the problem must be accurately evaluated before it can be corrected. This is a complex process, but there are no shortcuts. The Soviet Union is faced with such a problem, and, according to reports from Moscow, they are giving this the highest priority in their national agenda. The United States, too, faces a productivity problem that goes far beyond traditional economic explanations.

Problems of low productivity may be the result of lack of motivation or alienation. If that is the case, a solution should be found through changes in the environment. Allowing people to become more involved in the planning of their work or in the social activities related to their work may help them to identify better with their jobs and their company.

The problem may be due to irrational authority between management and its employees. This can be corrected by discovering an acceptable ratio between authority and freedom. Each party must feel that it is being treated fairly by the other.

Productivity may be too low for other reasons. In Figure 15–2, many of the possible external influences on productivity are shown. After the problem is identified, a decision has to be made whether it can be corrected by a more rational use of market forces, whether planning is required, or both.

If the problem is a breakdown of international trade as a result of market impediments such as tariffs and exchange controls and no other cause can be identified, the problem is clearly a market phenomenon that should be corrected. Usually such problems are deeper than that. They may involve a restructuring of the labor force that failed to keep pace with the swift advances in modern science and technology.

If the problem lies in a decline in the world demand for the products of traditional industries, the solution probably lies in the development of new high technology industries, if that is feasible. Such industries have the advantage of high value added, which encourages higher real wages.

An efficient market is always a desirable ally in the effort to improve the human condition. It must, however, have the benefit of intelligent social planning if it is to operate smoothly and rationally.

For example, the preparation of a labor pool able to meet the

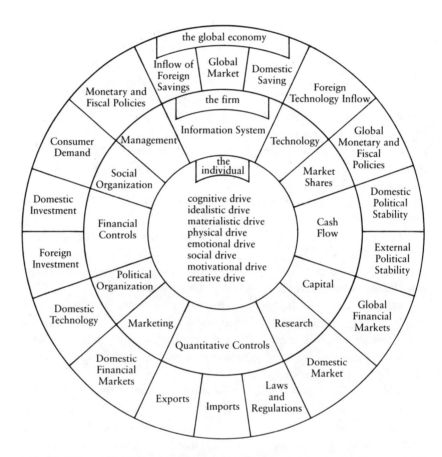

Note: This is a conceptual model. It is not intended to serve as a functional model because the list of inputs is representative rather than complete. The design of this diagram should not be interpreted to give any specific significance to the particular location of the variables in each category.

Figure 15–2. *The Holistic Input-Output System of the Political Economy*

challenge of a swiftly changing world cannot be left to market forces alone. The market should be implemented by an effective method of anticipation and planning. The market will send out signals, which should be interpreted and used for making and implementing plans that will prepare people for job opportunities when they reach the job market.

The problems in the Third World countries surely require the use of the market as well as rational planning so that scarce resources will be used both efficiently and wisely. Actually, some combination of rational markets and rational democratic planning is a technique that applies to all economies committed to improving the human condition. (See chapter 11 for a discussion of the roles of the market and planning in a modern economy.)

It is obvious that the dilemma of a modern economy can be extremely complex and difficult. The simple methods employed in classical and neoclassical economics—*automatic* market equilibrium and an *intradisciplinary* (meaning within each discipline) analysis of the input-output process of an economy—are inadequate for a realistic analysis of a modern political economy.

The classical concept of a spontaneous, automatic equilibrium depends on all the variables in the economic system responding to prices and to *nothing else* that might disturb their course in the "magnetic field" (the price mechanism) around an imaginary point of equilibrium. In the real world, many of the needs of humanity and the environment do not respond to prices at all, or at best incidentally. (See chapters 10–12.)

Balance can be achieved without such dubious assumptions. To achieve it, however, requires that the *means* (markets, planning, competition, authority, and others) to the goals we seek be rational. We must use our intelligence to discover this rational means, complex though it may be. If the world is too complex for automatic market equilibrium and humanity is too simple-minded for a rational system of balance to be feasible, then we are doomed to live in chaos.

A less cynical and more constructive view might be that since humanity was clever enough to discover the technology for studying the mysteries of the universe and the genetic riddle that programs our lives, we can probably discover the mystery of balance—if not all at once, then step by step. Our great leaps in science and technology give us reason to be optimistic. Perhaps we can now make a great leap in political economy.

We must bridge the great gap between the past (which was dominated by an emotional search for utopias) and the future (which, if it is to improve the human condition, must have the benefit of rational relationships between the means and goals). The technology for a satisfactory information system and for identifying the variables constituting the holistic input-output system of a political economy already exists. This technology is the computer and the interdisciplinary systems approach to the study of the individual and society.

The steps that remain to be taken in the future are:

1. The adoption of a holistic system approach for the political economy putting humanity in the center of the system.

2. The adoption of a pluralistic information system that is actually able to transmit significant information to all people, so that they will be able to make rational choices on the personal and political levels.

3. The adoption of meaningful definitions of freedom, liberty, democracy, authority, competition, cooperation, and so on that are more relevant to the conditions of the Nuclear Age and Space Age.

4. The adoption of the holistic input-output approach to the political economy that replaces the concept of automatic equilibrium with planned balance as a tool for preventing problems and solving them.

5. The adoption of a system of rational participation in the public and private sectors that will replace alienation with motivation, increasing economic efficiency and improving the human condition.

6. The discovery of a realistic method to make power in the private sector accountable, without transferring it to the public sector, so that the private sector will function in a socially responsible manner.

7. The development of a new approach to the political economy that will replace competition between mangement, labor, and government with rational cooperation as a means of improving the human condition.

8. The adoption of a rational method for measuring improvements in the human condition.

9. The discovery of a method of rational cooperation between the market economy and social planning as a means of improving the human condition.

10. The adoption of a holistic, dynamic, relativistic approach to economic development. This will help to lay to rest the fantasy that systems can be transferred from one nation to another.

These are realistic, obtainable objectives. They do not require radical structural changes in either the political or economic sectors of the U.S. economy or any of the economies in which economic and political development are making substantial progress. It is not unreasonable to assume that in the first part of the twenty-first century, all or most of the changes outlined here will be in place. This is not another utopian prediction because these changes are normal evolutionary developments that have already begun to have an impact in various regions of the world.

In summary, what is needed for a "more humane society"? First of all, we must elevate humanity to the center of the economic process from our present position as merely an economic input. We must exchange social Darwinism, which favors those able to acquire power, for a system dedicated to improving the human condition by making democracy, freedom, and authority rational and fair. We must replace the belief in the decline and fall of civilizations with the willingness and determination to adjust to evolutionary changes through the adoption of policies based on a dynamic, realistic, and relativistic perception of life instead of obsolete ideologies of the past.

Above all, we must build a sense of optimism about the future of humanity which is obviously a moral prerequisite for having children and grandchildren today.

Notes

CHAPTER 2

1. Keynes, John Maynard, *The General Theory of Employment, Interest and Money.* Harcourt, Brace, New York, 1947, p. 383.
2. Galbraith, John Kenneth, *The Age of Uncertainty.* Houghton Mifflin, Boston, 1977, p. 11.
3. Ibid., p. 11.
4. Smith, Adam, *The Wealth of Nations.* The Modern Library, New York, 1937, p. 625.
5. Ricardo, David, *The Principles of Political Economy and Taxation.* E.P. Dutton, New York, and J.M. Dant & Sons, London, 1943. Chapters 5, 6.
6. Mitchell, Wesley C., *Types of Economic Theory,* edited by Joseph Dorfman, 2 vols. Augustus M. Kelley, New York, 1967. Vol. 1, chapters 3, 4.
7. Ibid., vol. 1, p. 423. Original source: *The Edinburgh Review.*
8. Durant, Will and Ariel, *The Story of Civilization,* Part X, "Rousseau and Revolution" Simon and Schuster, New York, 1967, p. 937.
9. Milton Friedman is a leader of the Chicago School of economics, which regards the government as the obstacle to a free market.

CHAPTER 3

1. Robert Owen (1771–1858) was one of the best-known British social reformers of the nineteenth century. See Owen, Robert, *A New View of Society.* Longmans, London, 1817, pp. 19, 66.
2. Mitchell, Wesley C. *Types of Economic Theory.* Vol. 1, p. 423. Original source: *The Edinburgh Review.*

3. Friedman, Milton, *Capitalism and Freedom*. University of Chicago Press, Chicago, 1962, p. 9.
4. Marx, Karl and Friedrich, Engels, *The Communist Manifesto*. Russell and Russell, New York, 1963. p. 29.

CHAPTER 4

1. The short run is a special concept in traditional economics referring to a relatively short period in which market adjustments take place. Excessive profits become normal during such an adjustment.
2. Kindleberger, Charles, *American Business Abroad*. Yale University Press, New Haven, Conn., 1969, p. 179.
3. An oligopolistic industry is composed of a few large firms that generally do not engage in destructive price competition. The steel, copper, and nickel industries are examples.
4. For a more exhaustive discussion of this issue, see Galbraith, John K., *The New Industrial State*. Houghton Mifflin, Boston, 1967.
5. Max Weber (1868–1920) was a German sociologist and political economist. See his *Protestant Ethic and the Spirit of Capitalism*, Scribners, New York, 1958.
6. Friedman, *Capitalism and Freedom*, p. 9.
7. Galbraith, *The New Industrial State*, p. 87.
8. Ibid., p. 88.
9. A craft union is an organization of craftspeople with specific skills (such as master carpenters) in contrast to the industrial union, which organizes all workers of a particular industry, such as the United Auto Workers (U.A.W.).
10. See note 9.

CHAPTER 5

1. For a specific reference see chapter 3, note 3.
2. See the final section of chapter 3.
3. See the first section of chapter 3.
4. See the first section of chapter 4.
5. The reason why the present U.S. arms buildup has not resulted in a serious inflation is explained in the first section of chapter 5.
6. A subsistence wage as defined by Ricardo is a wage high enough to permit a worker to take care of himself and his dependents without public assistance.

7. Such societies provide a safety net for people who live at or below poverty level.

8. See the third section of chapter 6. The concept of the productivity of labor is useful as an explanation of the limits of real wages, but it is improperly used as an explanation of underemployment or specific wages.

9. These deficits transfer income from all taxpayers, including those with relatively moderate incomes, to the owners of the bonds and bills that make up the national debt.

10. The monetarists are chiefly the followers of Milton Friedman and other so-called conservative economists.

CHAPTER 6

1. David Ricardo was the first classical economist to analyze the factors of production, land, labor, and capital in the context of economic development. See chapter 2, note 5.

2. Professor John Kenneth Galbraith has described this in his *American Capitalism—The Concept of Countervailing Power*. Houghton Mifflin, Boston, 1952. I am indebted to him for his astute analysis of the U.S. corporation.

CHAPTER 7

1. See Locke, John, *Treatises on Government*, London, 1888; also his *Essay Concerning Human Understanding*, London, 1887. Locke (1632–1704) was a leading English philosopher of his time.

2. Marshall, Alfred, *Principles of Economics*, 8th ed. Macmillan, London, 1946, pp. 58–59.

3. Ibid., p. 137.

4. Ibid., p. 59.

5. There are some stirrings in that direction, but they have not found their way into the mainstream of economic theory. See, for example, the work of James Tobin and William Norhaus on net economic welfare. "Is Growth Obsolete," *Fiftieth Anniversary Colloquium*, Columbia University Press, New York, 1972.

6. See the third section of chapter 6.

7. In classical economics, economic rent was also considered a part of the national income. It is largely a forgotten concept in modern economics because it is concealed by other names that are all lumped

together as profits. To the classical economist, it was a term that explained the part of income above what was necessary to keep the economic process moving. In agriculture, for example, the classical economist regarded the necessary part of income as subsistence wages and a fair return on capital. The land that was just good enough to earn that was called marginal land. Land *better* than that earned economic rent.

CHAPTER 9

1. Smith, Adam, *The Wealth of Nations,* pp. 421, 423.
2. Fromm, Erich, *The Sane Society.* Rinehart, New York, 1955, p. 37.
3. For a more exhaustive discussion of these changes see Galbraith, John Kenneth, *The New Industrial State.*

CHAPTER 10

1. Fromm, Erich, *The Sane Society,* chapter 3.
2. Ibid., pp. 95–101.
3. Marx conceded this when he pointed out that capitalism had to precede socialism. In countries where economic development is initiated with socialism, as in the Soviet Union and China, capital is also generated through the exploitation of the worker. In both cases, it can be argued that ultimately the benefits of economic development will reach most, if not all, people. See Marx, *Communist Manifesto.* See also chapter 3, note 4.
4. Nietzsche, Friedrich, "Beyond Good and Evil," in *The Basic Writings of Nietzsche.* Modern Library, New York, 1968.
5. Sartre, Jean Paul, *The Wall,* 1939; and *Nausea,* 1938.
6. Simon, Herbert A., *Organization.* Wiley, New York, 1958.
7. Toffler, Alvin, *Future Shock* and *The Third Wave.* Bantam, New York, 1970 and 1980, respectively.

CHAPTER 11

1. The word *traditional* refers to the main body of modern neoclassical economists, including the so-called monetarists.
2. Keynes, *The General Theory of Employment, Income and Money,* book IV.

CHAPTER 12

1. If they move at different rates of motion, special assumptions need to be made to get them all to the point of equilibrium at the same time. This is mathematically feasible, but a most unlikely solution in the real world.
2. If the economy is not standing still, assumptions must be made about its movements and the movement of all economic variables that lead to equilibrium. Such assumptions can be made mathematically but not empirically, especially if changes in technology, for example, occur frequently and are great in scope.
3. As stated previously, this (equilibrium) is possible mathematically with a process of stepwise adjustments with a multiple of variants out of phase. It is impossible empirically when the out-of-phase dimensions are large and frequent, as they are in the modern world.

CHAPTER 14

1. The word *holistic* means emphasizing the organic or functional relation between parts and their whole—in this case between the biological, psychological, and sociological aspects of a person and the total person.
2. These theories also influenced economic development in certain other countries, such as South Korea and Taiwan.
3. Mill, John Stuart, *Principles of Political Economy*. P.F. Collier and Son, New York, 1900.
4. Myrdal, Gunnar, *Objectivity in Social Research*. Pantheon Books, New York, 1969.
5. The word *decent* is used here in the same sense as it is used in laws such as the U.S. housing acts of the 1960s.
6. The various intermediate social goods must be carefully selected and executed to result rise in the desired social goals.
7. Unemployment causes budget deficits to increase by about $40 billion for each 1 percent in unemployment. Ordinarily such large deficits are inflationary.

CHAPTER 15

1. Professor James Tobin and others have somewhat widened the concept of economic progress by the use of a new measure, "the new welfare product." See chapter 7, note 5.

2. Interest rates and exchange rates can be used effectively when the problems are of a pure supply-and-demand nature and the market can be expected to solve problems, but not when the problems are of a structural character.

3. This is the heart of post-World War II French existentialism. See the final section of chapter 10.

4. See the final section of chapter 14 for suggestions.

5. Marshall, Alfred, *Principles of Economics*. Macmillan, London, 1946, p. 43 (originally published in 1890).

6. This concept has been developed in a variety of forms by psychologists and behavioral scientists such as Sigmund Freud, Eric Fromm, and John Broadus Watson.

7. The word *worker* is intended to include everyone active in the internal operations of a firm.

Index

About the Author

K urt Flexner, born in Vienna, Austria, in 1916, came to the United States at the age of twelve. He received his initial professional education in engineering, which enabled him to earn a livelihood during the Great Depression. His real interest was in economics and political science, however, and he earned his undergraduate degree at Johns Hopkins University and a Ph. D. in economics at Columbia University.

Flexner's professional life has extended over academia, the financial industry, and government. He taught at New York University for thirteen years and Memphis State University for nineteen years; for seven years he served as deputy manager of the American Bankers Association (ABA) and spent nearly three years as chief financial institutions advisor in South Korea for the U.S. Agency for International Development. While at the ABA he directed a plan for improving the mortgage market, which eventually became "Ginny Mae," and while in Korea he helped to create the Korean Housing Bank and was instrumental in modernizing the Korean Banking system.

Retired from full-time academic life, Flexner continues to manage the Economic Club of Memphis, of which he is the cofounder, writes a newspaper column, and lectures in an intergenerational seminar at Bard College not far from Rhinebeck, New York, where he lives with his wife.